What reviewers are saying about *The Pro Book*...

"If you are serious about becoming a top flight player, *The Pro Book* definitely belongs in your arsenal. Highly recommended."
Tom Shaw - *Pool & Billiard Magazine*

"*The Pro Book* ranks among the best. For those who aspire to succeed at the highest level, it is a steal at any price."
John Cash - *The National Billiard News*

"*The Pro Book* is recommended if you are dead serious about improving your game. If you really are ready...you will not be disappointed."
Bob Campbell - *All About Pool*

"This 'complete training manual' can be your foundation to find the highest level you can play to. The last part is worth the price alone."
Paul Thornley - *News & Cues*

"*The Pro Book* is a complete program for the developing player and you won't be disappointed when you buy it. It is my all time favorite."
The Monk - *teacher & columnist*

This book is dedicated to my father,
Robert Henry Henning
1922-1996

THE PRO BOOK

Maximizing Competitive Performance for Pool Players

BOB HENNING

Bebob Publishing, Livonia, MI

THE PRO BOOK

Maximizing Competitive Performance for Pool Players

By Bob Henning

Bebob Publishing
P. O. Box 530411
Livonia, MI 48153

All rights reserved. No part of this book may be reproduced or transmitted in any form or by any means, electronic or mechanical, including photocopying, recording, or by any information storage and retrieval system without written permission from the author, except for the inclusion of brief quotations in a review.

Copyright © 1997 by Bob Henning

Eighth Printing 2013

Printed in the United States of America

International Standard Book Number: 1-887956-23-9

**cover design by John Church
table graphics by John Church
original cover photo by Kathleen Henning
derivative cover photo illustration by John Church**

Table of Contents

INTRODUCTION 1

SECTION I   **THE PHYSICAL GAME**

CHAPTER 1   **Fundamentals** 5

    The Power of Distinction 6
    The Principles of Effortless Function 6
        Simplicity 6
        Gravity 7
        Alignment 8
        Rhythm 10

CHAPTER 2   **Execution** 13

    Agreement 13
        Physical Agreement 13
        How to Recognize It 15
    Reference Training 16
        The Power of Naming 17
        Knowing Your Percentages 17
    The Pro Book Reference Series 18
    Position Shots 18
        Targets 19
        Rails 19
        Windows 20
        Left and Right-Hand Shots 20
        Extended Shots 20

PRO BOOK

Boundary Shots	21
Training Guidelines	21
Understanding Shot Graphics	22
The Pro Book Reference Shots	23
Safeties	**39**
The Pro Book Reference Safeties	41
Kicks	**57**
The Pro Book Reference Kicks	58
Kick Safeties	**70**
The Pro Book Reference Kick Safeties	71
Banks	**79**
The Pro Book Reference Banks	80
Drills	**88**
The Pro Book Reference Drills	89

CHAPTER 3 — Equipment — 93

The Truth About Equipment	**93**
Playing Conditions	**94**
Inspecting the Table Bed	94
Assessing the Cloth	95
Knowing the Rails	96
Understanding Pocket Strategy	96
Playing With Balls	97
The Effect of Humidity	99
Set-Ups and Sabotage	99
The Power of Rules	**100**

CHAPTER 4 — Conditioning — 101

Exercise	**102**
Needs and Benefits	102
Stretching	103
Aerobic vs. Anaerobic	104
A Physical Training Program	104
What about Lifting Weights?	106
Relaxation	**107**
The Importance of Breathing	107
Breathing Exercises	108
Relaxation Recognition	110
Relaxation Exercises	110

CONTENTS

Diet & Nutrition **114**
    Nutrition and Performance 114
    Are You an Athlete? 114
    A Competitor's Diet 115
    The Pre-Game Meal 119
    Special Needs for Pool Players 120
    Taking Supplements 120
    Performance Boosters 121

SECTION II   THE MENTAL GAME

CHAPTER 1   Mental Training **127**

The Unstoppable You **128**
Mental Conversation **128**
Disappearing Mental Obstacles **130**
Affirmations **131**
    The Power of Affirmations 131
    A List of the Best 132
    Using Affirmations 135
Making a Tape **136**
    Subliminal Messages 137
    A Pre-Competition Tape 138

CHAPTER 2   Concentration **139**

    Getting the Distinctions 139
    The Secrets of Focus 140
    The Shot Sequence 140
    Roving Focus 142

CHAPTER 3   Rituals & Routines **145**

Rituals **145**
    Preparatory Rituals 146
    Transition Rituals 146
    Recovery Rituals 147
Routines **147**
    The Table Evaluation Routine 148
    The Pre-Shot Routine 152

PRO BOOK

CHAPTER 4   **Game Styles** **157**

    The Shotmaker 157
    The Defensive Player 158
    The Percentage Player 158
    Playing Against a Different Style 159
    Playing Against a Similar Style 160

CHAPTER 5   **Match Dynamics** **163**

In The Box **164**
Match Roles **165**
    Don't Know Him / You are Favored 166
    Don't Know Him / He is Favored 167
    Don't Know Him / Evenly Matched 167
    Played Before / You Won 168
    Played Before / He Won 168
    Never Played / You are Favored 169
    Never Played / He is Favored 170
    Never Played / Evenly Matched 170

CHAPTER 6   **Momentum** **171**

Momentum as Energy **171**
Momentum and Confidence **173**
Momentum and the NOW **174**
Defining Match Momentum **175**
The Dynamics of Momentum **175**
Controlling Momentum **176**
    None Established / How to Take It 177
    He Has It / How to Take It 177
    You Have It / How to Keep It 178
    You Have It / How to Lose It 179
Special Situations **180**
    He Makes a Critical Mistake 180
    He Makes a Great Play 180
    You Make a Critical Mistake 181
    You Make a Great Play 181

CONTENTS

SECTION III THE EMOTIONAL GAME

CHAPTER 1 **Motivation** **185**

    Passion 186
    Commitment 187
    Attitude 188

CHAPTER 2 **Goals** **189**

  The Nature of Reality **189**
  They Can Start or Stop You **190**
  Guidelines for Successful Goals **190**
  Visualizing the Future **191**
    Ten Year Future 192
    Five Year Future 193
    Three Year Future 194
    One Year Future 195
    Six Month Future 196
    Three Month Future 197
  Creating Powerful Goals **198**
    Ten Year Goal 199
    Five Year Goal 200
    Three Year Goal 201
    One Year Goal 202
    Six Month Goal 203
    Three Month Goal 204
  Event Goals **205**
    Result Goals 205
    Performance Goals 205
  Key Points to Using Goals **206**

CHAPTER 3 **Peak Performance** **207**

  Scouting Your Best Game **208**
  The Elements of Peak Performance **210**
  Emotional Arousal **212**
  Energy **213**
  Accessing Your Best Game **214**

Using Images.. 214
Managing Cycles 215
Creating a Vision Statement...................................... 215

SECTION IV — PUTTING IT TOGETHER

CHAPTER 1 — Letting Go — 219

Using Your Brain 219
    The Left Brain 220
    The Right Brain 220
The Obstacles to Letting Go 221
    Fear... 222
    Ignorance 222
Training vs. Performance 223

CHAPTER 2 — The Training Program — 225

Examples 227
The 30 Day Program.. 229

CHAPTER 3 — Game Plans — 259

Match Planning.. 260
    The Pre-Match Plan... 260
    The Competition Plan.. 261
Match Review 262
The Pro Book Game Plans 262
    Example Event.. 263
    Event #1.. 268
    Event #2.. 273
    Event #3.. 278
    Event #4.. 283

CHAPTER 4 — A Final Note — 289

Introduction

"If there is a book you really want to read but it hasn't been written yet, then you must write it."

—Toni Morrison

When I became serious about pool in 1987, I looked everywhere for the resources to assist my quest for world-class play. I was happy to find several books, tapes, and instructors willing to share knowledge and technique. Most of these experts said pool was 75 to 90 % mental, but when I looked for material to assist me in that area, I could not find it. I was forced into the literature of other sports to discover the latest developments in sports psychology, mental training, and competition dynamics.

I tried everything that looked advantageous. Most of the time I felt like Tristan Jones, the famous and colorful sailor. He set a world record once by sailing a small sailboat in the highest altitude lake in South America, Lake Titicaca. The Peruvian authorities refused to let him return with his boat down the Andes to the coast, so he went out the other way—through the uncharted Amazon backwaters—the Mato Grosso. I have this vivid image of Tristan pulling his little boat up a shallow tongue of water while his native companion beat the water with a paddle to keep the piranha away. Tortured by hordes of mosquitoes, he would sometimes drag the boat for two or three

THE PRO BOOK

days up a prospective channel before it came to a dead end and he had to haul it back.

I have not reached the ocean yet as Tristan finally did, but I can smell the salt. I've gone from an average ball banger with little competitive experience to a seasoned competitor. I have won tournament matches from national and world-class players and cashed in professional events.

Nothing ever stands still or stays the same, and that includes your pool game. You either progress to a higher level or you regress to a lower. You are either expanding or contracting, as a great sage once said.

The purpose of the *Pro Book* is to maximize your competitive performance. It contains breakthrough material on the physical game, the mental game, the emotional game. It is designed for players who want to *get professional* with their training efforts. If you read it, you will get a lot, if you *work* it, you will get a lot more. Good luck and good shootin'!

Bob Henning

Note: I greatly celebrate the participation and contribution of women in pool. I have chosen to use masculine pronouns, however, while referring to both genders, to facilitate smooth reading and avoid awkward phrasing.

THE PHYSICAL GAME

THE PRO BOOK

Note Page

* Write down what would you like to get from this book.

Fundamentals

"Form ever follows function."

—Louis Henri Sullivan

There are four different areas in the physical game that demand to be managed if a player is to fulfill his potential. They are *fundamentals, execution, equipment,* and *physical conditioning*. The first area a beginner needs to contend with is the *fundamentals: stance, grip, bridge, aim,* and *stroke*. It is also an endless area of study for intermediate and advanced players who want to refine their competitive games.

If your fundamentals are more dependable than your opponent's, you are likely to win in the long run. You will be able to play under a variety of conditions with a high level of consistency. You will intimidate your opponent because you will be hard to break. If you don't have well-trained fundamentals, you will not hold up under pressure.

The *Pro Book* is not designed for beginners. It assumes that you understand the basic fundamentals and have spent time fine-tuning them. For a list of books and tapes that address the basics with photographs and definitions, look at the end of this book.

The Power of Distinction

One of the greatest trainers of all time once said that *"power lives in the ability to make distinctions."* What this means is that mastery of any discipline, sport, art, or field is dependent on the ability to recognize fine lines between things that are the same and things that are different. The deeper your understanding of a subject, the finer are your distinctions.

For example, if a person had never been exposed to snow, he would not *know* snow. If he was eventually exposed to it, he would come to know it simply as *snow*. If he moved to a cold climate and lived there for a year, his greater experience would allow him to see finer distinctions such as slush, powder, good-packing, and icy. If he traveled to the Arctic and lived with the Eskimos, he would come to recognize over 30 different names for *snow*, just like they do.

In pool, powerful and dependable fundamentals come from having done the work to accumulate a vast knowledge of distinction—a great understanding of what works and what doesn't. Fundamentals work best if they conform with certain basic principles and knowing those principles can help you organize your study of fundamentals.

The Principles of Effortless Function

Simplicity

In scientific thought, the *simple* always overrules the complex. For instance, even though we can make a mathematical explanation that proves the sun revolves around the earth, you won't get any great minds to agree with you. Why? Because the mathematical explanation of the earth revolving around the sun is about a thousand times less complicated.

FUNDAMENTALS

This concept of simplicity applies to engineering, invention, and all other fields of knowledge and application. The simplest machine that will do the work is the most efficient—the less moving parts, the better.

How does this apply to the fundamentals of pool? Let's take a look at your stance as an example. The most efficient stance for you, for any particular shot, is the stance which is the simplest to successfully execute that shot. Your most efficient stance is decided by the make-up of your body. It is determined by your bone structure, cartilage, and musculature.

A simple stance is free of extraneous twists and turns. It is the natural fall of your body when it is lined up on the shot. Your most simple and dependable stance is unique and specific to you, not contrived to answer requirements set by someone else. *You* are senior to the stance, not the other way around.

In practice, look at your fundamentals from this point of view and start cleaning out the junk that makes them complicated. There is power in simplicity.

☞ **Simplicity is the key to efficiency.**

Gravity

All pool playing takes place in reality, so the laws of the physical universe take precedence. The most important and least unforgiving of all laws is the *law of gravity*. All things must fall <u>DOWN</u>, and this includes all parts of your body and your equipment.

The principle of gravity relates directly to simplicity. If any parts are *not falling down*, then something is holding them up against the force of gravity. In the example of stance, your body and all its parts are held together (and up) by the natural binding force of your tissue—joints, ligaments, etc. Anything *held up* in addition to that is held with muscle tension.

Ever wonder why you play so good in practice, but it falls apart under the heat of competition? If your stance contains unnecessary muscular tension, you are asking those muscles to remain at a consistent level of contraction despite the presence of different types and quantities of hormones and chemicals.

As soon as there is an increase in pressure, there is an increase in adrenaline, and tiny muscles start working differently than they did when you were practicing. You cannot count on the consistency of muscle tension. You can, however, count on gravity—it is always the same.

Commit some of your practice time to examining all your fundamentals from the point of view of gravity. Get your stance and stroke consistent with those demands. Feel the pull of gravity in your grip and in your bridge. Focus on feeling the weight of your cue stick.

   ⚑ **Gravity is the key to balance and stability.**

Alignment

Alignment is the key to consistency. It is associated with the word *line* and the concept of *lining up*. When we use the term alignment in pool that is what we mean—the proper lining up of things which need to be lined up. As it relates to fundamentals, this concept builds on the principles of simplicity and gravity.

The Alignment Line

The alignment line includes the shoulder, the upper arm, the elbow, the lower arm, the grip hand, the head, the eyes, the cue, the cue ball hit, and the cue ball line. All of these variables need to be on a single straight line. Other points, such as the cue ball center, the object ball hit, and other body points, are also lined up, but sometimes on parallel lines.

FUNDAMENTALS

The finer you make the alignment line and the more consistently and accurately you line up the parts, the better you will play. *Consistency* is your goal. Make sure your eyes are always in the exact same alignment with all other parts so that you develop a dependable catalogue of sight pictures.

Strive to make finer and finer observations about all aspects of alignment. For example, don't be satisfied just knowing where your hand is relative to your cue. Discover exactly on which finger pads the weight of the cue rests.

Planes

An important part of alignment is the understanding of planes. Just as the cue ball can be understood in terms of the horizontal and the vertical axis, alignment can be understood in terms of horizontal and vertical *planes*.

There is a plane that is exactly parallel to the surface of the table and extends in all directions without limit. This is the *horizontal plane*. In practice, it is valuable to visualize this as a sheet of glass to understand how different variables align to it. The horizontal axis of the cue stick runs consistent with this *sheet of glass*. No wavers, dips, or rises exist in the proper alignment of the stroke if the cue stick remains locked into this plane. This same plane extends from the cue ball aim point and through the cue ball and is always parallel to the horizontal axis of the cue ball. A line drawn between your two eyes is always in the same place relative to this plane.

The *vertical plane* runs perpendicular to the horizontal plane—at exact right angles. This plane corresponds to the *alignment line* and extends up and down without limit. It passes through the slate of the table and forms angles of exactly 90 degrees. Everything that lines up on the *alignment line* will be on this vertical plane. If you sight with a dominant eye, that eye is on this plane. If you sight with both eyes, this plane is always in the same place between your two eyes. This vertical plane also runs right through the cue ball at the cue ball aim point and is either parallel to, or consistent with, the vertical

THE PRO BOOK

axis of the cue ball. Visualize this plane, in practice, as a sheet of transparent, perfectly smooth glass.

Make sure you know how all of your fundamentals line up relative to both of these planes. They are the planes that rule pocket billiards.

> ⚑ **Alignment is the key to consistency.**

Rhythm

Rhythm is the foundation of freedom. It is the key to personal style and optimum performance. First, you have to know *what* to do, then what you *can* do, and then *how* to allow yourself the freedom to do it. There is no possibility of *dead stroke* without rhythm.

In the movie "Cool Runnings," the Jamaican bobsled team struggled for a good performance. Even though three of the four team members could run the 100 meters in under 10 seconds, they could not get off to a fast start. At the starting line, they counted down in German, just like all the other teams.

They ended up in last place after a terrible run where they barely managed to get in, and stay in, the sled. John Candy, playing their coach, stormed in on them later that night. "You have to find a way to stay loose out there," he said, "and I can't help you. You have to find it on your own."

Sanka, the team comic, found the answer. "We can't do this being who we are not," he said, "we can only be the best that we are, and the best that we are is Jamaican." They showed up on the hill the next day *walking and talking Jamaican*. They slapped hands and did the timing count like a reggae song. They had a great start, cutting over two seconds off their time and moving into eighth place.

The point of this story is that your rhythm will determine how well you utilize the fundamentals you train. Your rhythm, more than anything else, is a function and expression of

FUNDAMENTALS

yourself. Don't try to copy someone else's rhythm and **never, ever** surrender your own.

When you have the proper rhythm, your mind will give your body the freedom to do what it needs to do. You will experience a high level of confidence and effortlessness. When you are playing in your own rhythm, your fundamentals will fall into place naturally. With the proper rhythm, you will *stay loose* out there. Learn your natural inner rhythm and bring it to your game. If you are not absolutely positive that you have found yours, keep experimenting. Keep looking for it.

⚑ **Rhythm is the key to "dead stroke."**

THE PRO BOOK

<u>Note Page</u>

* Analyze your fundamentals in terms of the basic principles.

Execution

"Much effort, much prosperity."

—Euripides

Agreement

The theory of *agreement,* which applies to both the physical and mental realms, is a powerful training concept. When all parts of your mind are in agreement with a proposed action, you have *mental agreement* and your mind is free to turn control over to your body. When all parts of your *body* are in agreement, you have physical agreement and are free to execute with confidence. When you consistently attain *agreement* in both realms, you are in *dead stroke.*

Physical Agreement

Think of what composes your physical presence when you are on a shot. This includes your body, of course, but it also includes wherever your body connects to the physical universe. Your bridge hand is on the table and your feet are on the floor. You are connected to your cue through your hands, and the weight and heft of your cue are translated to the other parts of your body. You are also connected to the outside physical world through your senses: sight, hearing, touch, smell, and taste.

Psychologists say that each individual uses *one* primary sense more than the others. Most people, when they concentrate, use predominately *that* sense. You may be primarily visual, like most pool players, and therefore sometimes distracted by what you hear. You may be concentrated on a shot visually and kinesthetically, but your ears are listening to conversations, music, or other sounds around the room. If your ears are in agreement with what you are doing, you should only hear the cue tip contacting the cue ball, the cue ball rolling on the cloth, the click of contact, and the ball dropping into the pocket.

If your senses, feet, and hands agree on a specific outcome, you are likely to achieve it. But what about the thousands of muscles, bones, joints, and nerves that connect your feet to your hands, eyes, and ears?

Imagine you are down on a shot. Imagine that you are a great country of individuals, organized into different muscles, nerves, bones, and organs. Imagine each individual doing exactly what is appropriate to deliver a successful shot. Pretty awesome, yes? Now imagine a country of individuals where there is widespread contention rather than agreement. Picture people in the streets yelling and screaming. Picture riots and demonstrations. This is what is going on inside your physical body when you do not have physical agreement.

The key to *physical agreement* is education and training. Your body, as a complete entity, has to be trained to recognize when it is in agreement and when it is not. When a physical position or a specific shot is required that the body is not familiar with, it is difficult to achieve agreement. It is always easier to agree when you understand and feel comfortable.

If you have played seriously for several years, you have accumulated a vast body of physical knowledge about the game and about yourself as a physical entity. You may think of *agreement* as simply having confidence. When you miss a shot

EXECUTION

you should have made, you may see it in terms of something being off, i.e. your head moved, you jumped up, etc. All of these recognizable errors stem from a condition of not having attained *agreement* before executing the shot. Train yourself to recognize *physical agreement*. In practice, put your attention through your body and learn to recognize when this agreement is present and when it is missing.

Be in agreement with the physical universe. Respond to the messages you receive. For example, if you become aware that your shoelace is loose, tie it! Not at the end of the rack, but *when* you receive the mental message. The physical universe doesn't need to make reservations, it tells you what is needed in the moment. If you choose to ignore it, then you receive the consequences.

Chalk your cue when you become aware of it. Powder your hand when you feel stickiness. Handle any physical distraction that requires energy to ignore, and that includes sharking by your opponent and others. If you have to use energy to resist being distracted, then you are *already distracted*. Nip those situations in the bud. Handle them with the same matter-of-fact attitude and demeanor you use to chalk your cue stick.

How to Recognize It

So how can you tell when you are in *physical agreement*? It's easy once you discover it. When you are in *physical agreement,* you experience your preliminary strokes as being *super easy*. In other words, there is zero resistance in your practice strokes because everything is working together for a common purpose. There are no dissenting or contrary muscles. There is balance and harmony.

Remember: SUPER EASY>>>>SUPER EASY>>>>SUPER EASY>>>>SUPER EASY>>>>SUPER EASY>>>>SUPER EASY!

THE PRO BOOK

Reference Training

There are two different ways to gain mastery of a performance art. The first way is to engage yourself in the art and keep doing it day after day, month after month, and year after year. If you keep doing it long enough, you will accumulate a vast background of experience that you can call upon while performing.

The second way to gain mastery is called *reference training*. In this method you learn the basic forms inherent in the art, train until you can execute each one flawlessly, and then learn how to adapt and connect them to create a performance. This way of learning is superior to the first.

In figure skating, for example, skaters learn maneuvers like the spread eagle, the camel spin, the axle, and many more. When they skate a routine, they string these maneuvers together in creative ways. The same concept applies to musicians who learn chords, scales, keys, and rhythms. All musical performances are made up of these components.

Although pool players have been talking about different shots and moves since the beginning of the game, the concept of reference training in pool is relatively new. One of the first people to think in terms of standardization was Ray Martin in his book *The 99 Critical Shots of Pool,* first published in 1972. This book is a collection of shots, many of them applicable to the game of Straight Pool.

The greatest breakthrough in reference training for pool players, however, came from Bert Kinister in his video *The 60 Minute Workout for Eight Ball and Nine Ball,* which was introduced around 1991. In this revolutionary tape, Bert broke basic position play into a number of standard shots that a player could learn and use as reference shots in competition. This video had an enormous impact on the skill level of developing players. A whole population of pool players elevated their games in dramatic fashion. Bert, an advanced level BCA

EXECUTION

instructor, continues to offer some of the most advanced training and coaching material available in pool.

The Power of Naming

When you name something it becomes an entity exclusive of itself and separate from all other things. This process of naming is related to the process of distinction we looked at in Chapter One.

The power of naming dates back to the beginning of time and mankind has always associated the act of naming with mastery and authority. In the Bible, Adam was granted dominion over and the right to name all living things. When you name something, based on your knowledge of it, you put yourself in a position of authority.

When you can consistently execute a reference shot **and** know it by name, you have that same authority and mastery. You can call it forth in your mind by name and get an instantaneous and perfect mental picture. Your muscles recognize it and know how to produce it.

Knowing Your Percentage

You have probably heard the old saying *"knowledge is power."* Knowing your percentage to successfully execute any reference shot is also power. You can gain this knowledge by charting the results of your practice sessions. Charting your percentages *periodically* allows you to track your progress and to compute an average.

The simple act of putting attention on your percentages in practice puts pressure on you similar to the pressure you face in competition. You probably will not perform as well when you are charting your results as you do when you are not. The act of measuring brings an *observer* into the practice session in the form of your own mind. Your best performance when charting

THE PRO BOOK

with this *observer* is a good indication of how well you can play under pressure. Measuring brings reality to your estimation of your ability.

Charting will also increase your understanding of other players. Assessing percentages is a type of focus and the more you exercise it, the more efficient it becomes. The more accurately you can assess the proficiency of others, the better you can formulate your strategy to win.

The Pro Book Reference Series

The Pro Book Reference Series is designed for training purposes. It breaks the game of pool down into basic tools that can be used to respond to any table situation. There are sections for position shots, safeties, kicks, kick safeties, and banks. There is an additional section on drills. Each reference shot is named and laid out on a table graphic complete with cue ball hit, notes, and a chart for recording your performance.

The purpose of this system is to make your practice time more effective, your memory more efficient, and your execution more dependable. If you train with *The Pro Book Reference Series,* your understanding of the table and your ability to play will be greatly impacted.

Position Shots

There are 16 standard position shots in *The Pro Book Reference Series* and each one is named by number, such as Shot #1, Shot #7, and Shot #15. They apply to all pool games, especially Eight Ball and Nine Ball. These 16 reference shots cover the practical offensive possibilities in pool today, with the

EXECUTION

exception of specialty games such as One Pocket and Banks. All other position shots can be viewed as variations.

The secret of pool is in the cue ball and your ability to put it where you want it. This, in turn, is limited by your understanding of the table and the *real* limitations of specific shots. The actual cueing of the cue ball is important only as it relates to cue ball position.

Targets

A shot can be defined by its *targets*. The target of the object ball is one of six pockets and the target of the cue ball is a point within a specific position zone. The most strategic of these zones is the *center* of the table. It commands more of the playing field than any other zone and also designates the *no scratch* line. If the cue ball comes directly through the center of the table, you will never scratch. Most of the position shots in *The Pro Book Reference Series* have the cue ball traveling to or through the center of the table.

Rails

Shots can also be defined by which *rails*, if any, are contacted by the cue ball after it strikes the object ball. For an object ball going into a specific pocket, there are a limited number of rail combinations that can be used to take the cue ball to a specific position zone.

For instance, let's suppose you want to shoot an object ball into the far corner pocket and bring the cue ball to the center of the table. Depending on the location of the object ball and the cue ball, there are only a *specific* number of no rail, one rail, two rail, and three rail ways to accomplish this.

THE PRO BOOK

Windows

Each shot defined by pocket, cue ball target, and rail sequence has a specific *window of workability*. If you move the both CB and OB far enough to the left you will reach a point where the CB target cannot be made. The same will happen if you move the shot line far enough to the right. The shot can only be successfully executed within its boundaries.

For every shot with a window of workability, *The Pro Book Reference Shot* is in the middle of that window. This allows for equal extrapolation both left and right.

Left And Right-Hand Shots

Shots can also be defined as either *left-hand or right-hand*. Imagine standing in front of a side pocket and looking at the playing field. Shots going into the far left corner are left-hand shots. Shots going into the far side pocket with the cue ball traveling to the left are also left-hand shots. Shots going into the far right corner or the far side pocket with the cue ball going to the right are all right-hand shots.

All shots are included in these four categories. The shots going into the near corners and side are actually the same shots viewed from the other long rail. For consistency and convenience, all of *The Pro Book Reference Shots* are pictured as left-hand shots.

Extended Shots

Some standard shots have a category of secondary reference shots that are called *extended shots*. These are the same as the root shot except that the cue ball travel is extended to a more distant, standard position target. Extended shots are named with the abbreviation "x" such as in Shot 5x, Shot 6x, and Shot 9x.

EXECUTION

Boundary Shots

An important type of secondary reference shot is called a *boundary shot*. This is a shot that defines either the left or right side of the *window of workability* of a standard shot. When you *know* a reference shot and its boundary shots, you know the *whole* shot. You can extrapolate anywhere within the window.

The left boundary of a left-hand shot is always named with an "a" such as Shot 5a, Shot 8a, and Shot 12a. The right boundary of a left-hand shot is named with a "b" such as Shot 5b, Shot 8b, and Shot 12b.

On the *Pro Book* table graphics, a boundary shot is represented with a dotted line and has the same targets and rail sequence as the root shot. To practice, set an object ball at the end of the dotted line closest to the pocket and the cue ball at the other end.

Training Guidelines

The most important concept is to *learn each shot as a separate entity*. Each reference shot must have its own discreet place in your memory and be independently known. Learn the standard 16 first, and then their extended variations. When you know these well, move on to the boundary shots and their extended variations. When you know all the secondary shots, you will have 68 reference shots at your command and that's just the left-hand shots. Master the right-hand shots and you will have 130 standardized shots at your disposal, all keyed in your memory by the *basic sweet sixteen*.

Some are easy and others are more advanced. Don't be concerned if some seem difficult, just keep working on them. Focus on learning to set them up and recognize them first. All of the balls are positioned on or in the diamond squares at increments of 1/4 diamond to make this easy. If you have a pool table, mark your reference shots on the cloth with pencil marks or removable stickers so you can set them up exactly over and over. Write the name of each shot on a 3" X 5" card, fold the

THE PRO BOOK

bottom to create a stand, and set it on the table when you are practicing that shot. Do this until you can create a perfect mental picture of the shot on command.

Next, focus on the line the cue ball takes after the object ball is pocketed. Practice until you can bring the cue ball exactly along that line on a consistent basis. Once you can do that, focus on the speed of the shot until you can leave the cue ball inside a five-inch circle for standard shots and an ten-inch circle for long or extended shots. Don't be concerned about how long the learning process takes. If you train on a regular basis, you will eventually gain this level of proficiency.

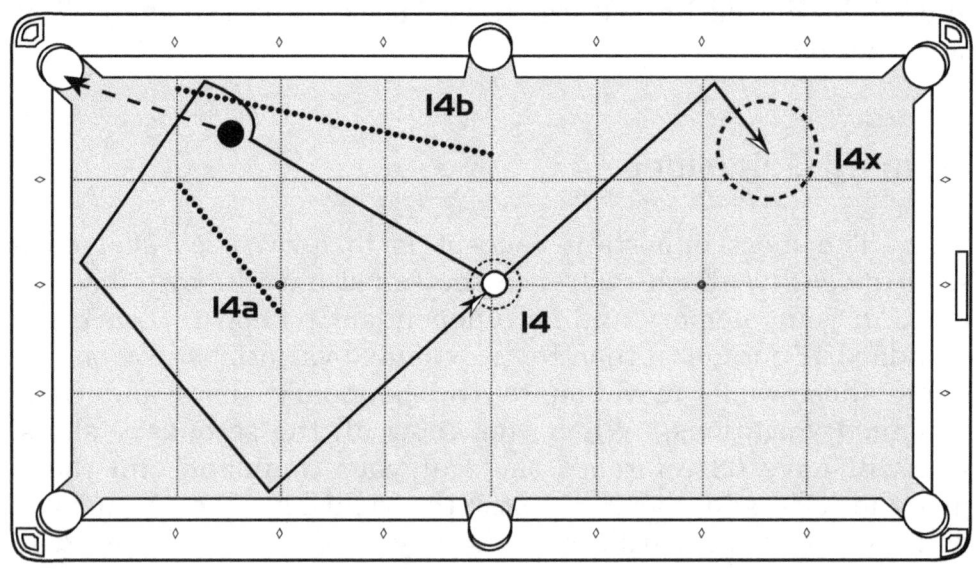

○	Starting Cue Ball Position	- - - - -	Intended OB Path
⊙	Final Cue Ball Position	··········	Boundary Shot Line
●	Target Object Ball	————	Intended CB Path
○	Obstructing Object Ball(s)		
(⸱⸱⸱)	5 inch Target	(⸱⸱⸱⸱⸱)	10 inch Target

EXECUTION

The Pro Book Reference Series — Shot #1

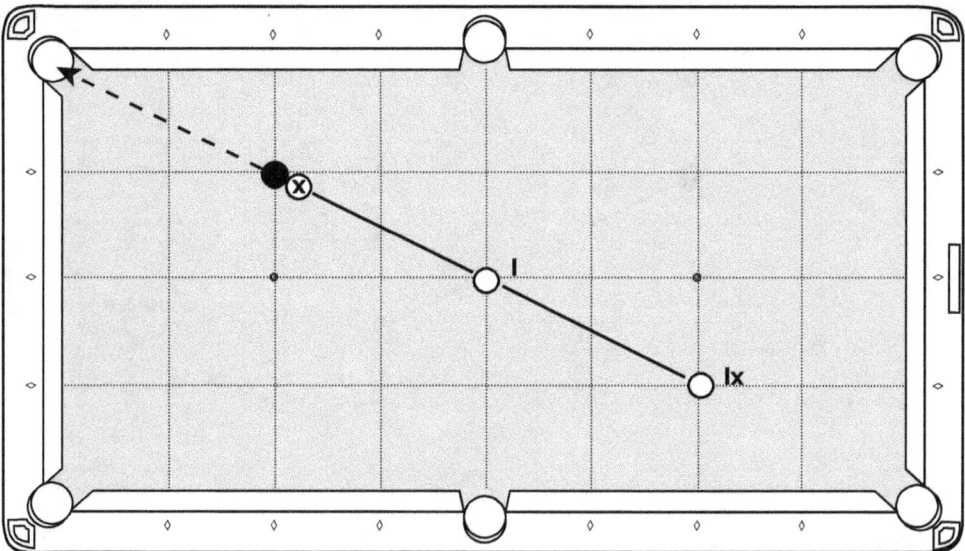

Notes:

Place the CB at the center of the table and the OB as shown. Shoot the OB into the corner and stop the CB at contact. Do not float the CB more than 1/2 ball to the left or right. When you can do this 90% of the time, practice stopping the CB 2 or 3" past and 2 or 3" before the OB. When you can do that regularly, place the CB at 1x and do the same.

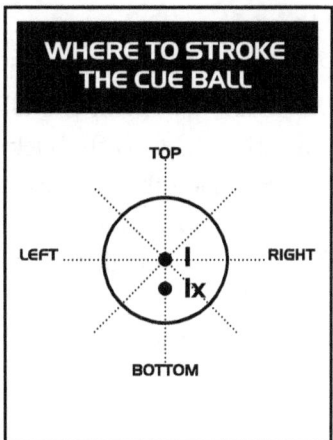

WHERE TO STROKE THE CUE BALL

DATE	SHOT	%	DATE	SHOT	%	DATE	SHOT	%

THE PRO BOOK

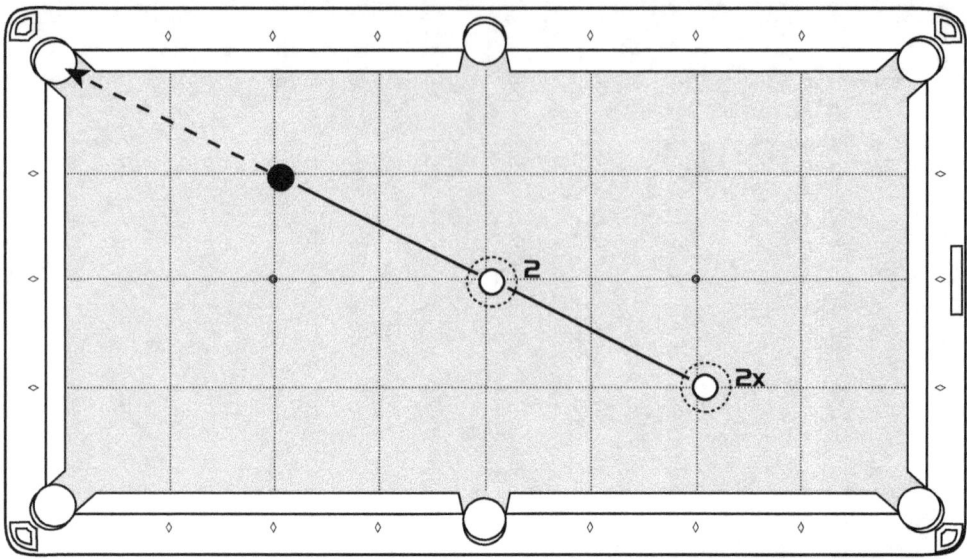

Notes:

Place the CB at the center of the table and the OB as shown. Shoot the OB into the corner and draw the CB directly back to a 5" target at the center of the table. When you can do this 85% of the time, start practicing the extended shot by drawing the CB all the way back to the position marked 2x. Always learn the shot by name first, line second, and speed third.

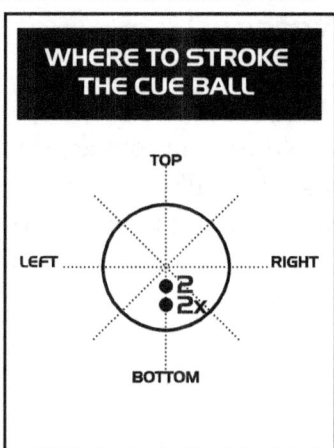

DATE	SHOT	%	DATE	SHOT	%	DATE	SHOT	%

EXECUTION

The Pro Book Reference Series — Shot #3

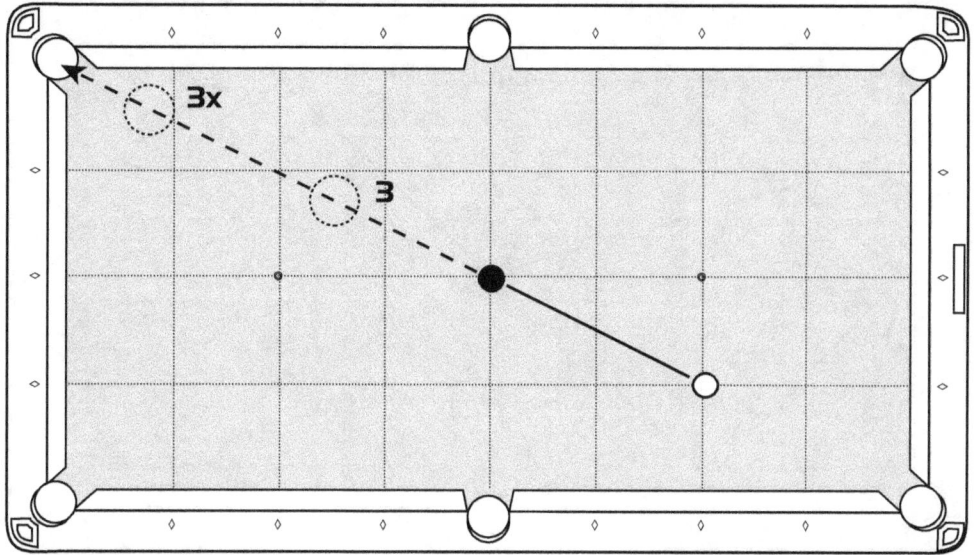

Notes:

Place the OB at the center of the table and the CB as shown. Sink the OB into the corner and roll the CB to a 5" target as pictured. When you can make this 16 out of 20 tries, (80%), include Shot 3x in your routine and practice rolling the CB to the target marked 3x. Learn each shot independently and by name first, line second, and speed last.

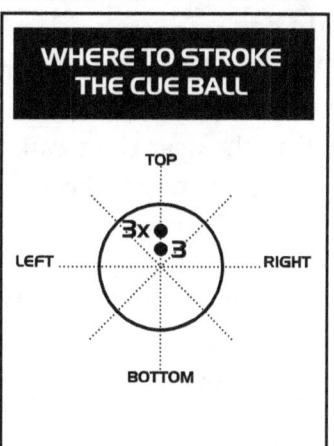

WHERE TO STROKE THE CUE BALL

DATE	SHOT	%	DATE	SHOT	%	DATE	SHOT	%

THE PRO BOOK

The Pro Book Reference Series — Shot #4

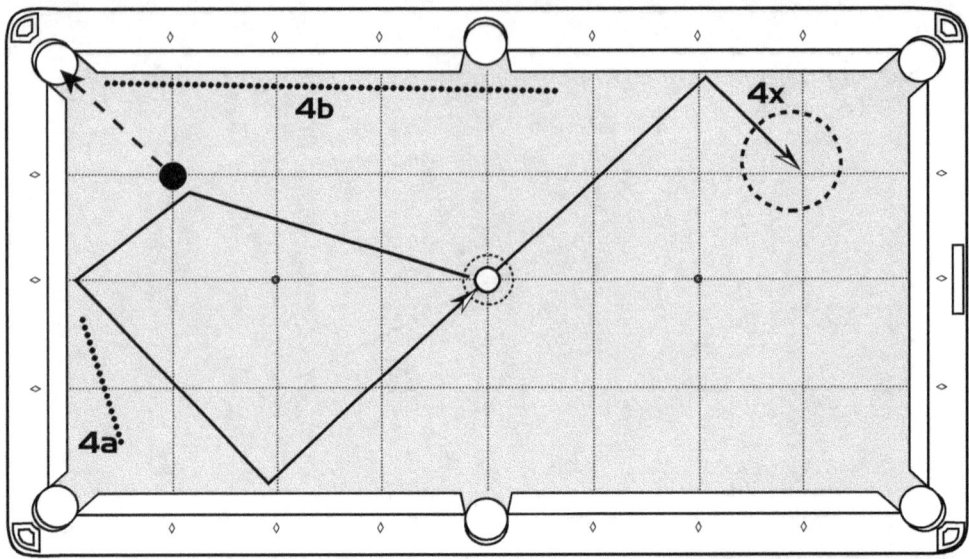

Notes:

Place the CB at the center of the table and the OB as shown. After striking the OB, send the CB to the near short rail, the far long rail, and back to a 5" target at center table. When you can do this 75% of the time, start practicing Shot 4x to a 10" target as shown. When you can do this 70% of the time, include the boundary shots 4a and 4b and their extensions 4ax and 4bx in your practice routine.

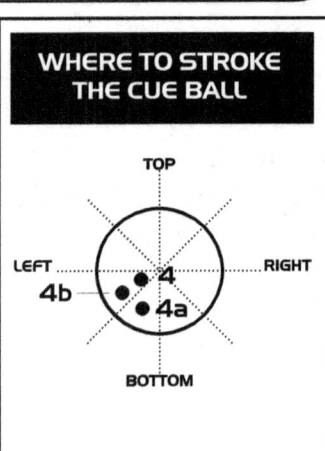

DATE	SHOT	%	DATE	SHOT	%	DATE	SHOT	%

EXECUTION

The Pro Book Reference Series — Shot #5

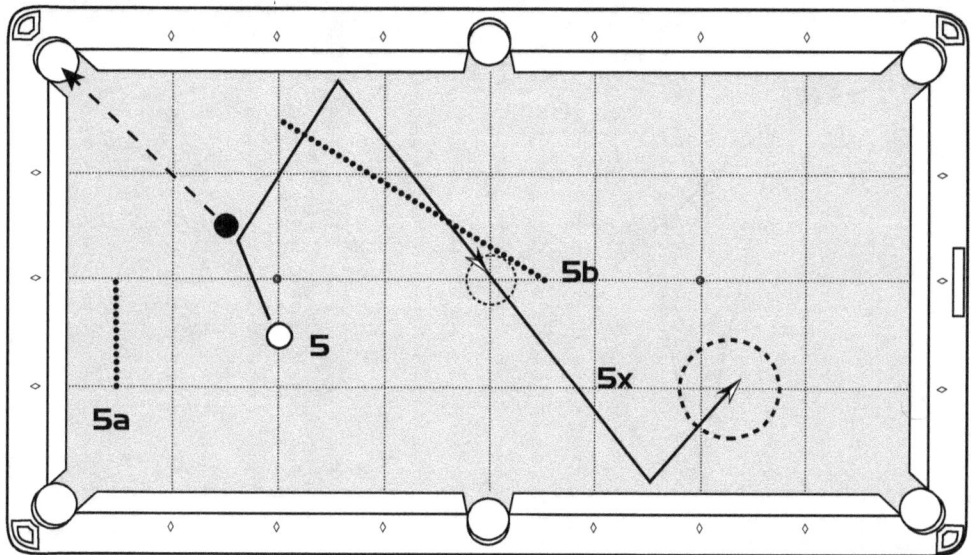

Notes:

Place the CB and OB as shown. Shoot the OB into the corner and take the CB to the near long rail and out to a 5" target at center table. When you can do this 75% of the time, practice the extension shot 5x to a 10" target as shown. Next, include the boundary shots 5a and 5b and their extensions. Learn the name of each shot first, the line second, and the speed last.

(Shot 5b and the CB strike points are slightly changed from the first three printings the of PB.)

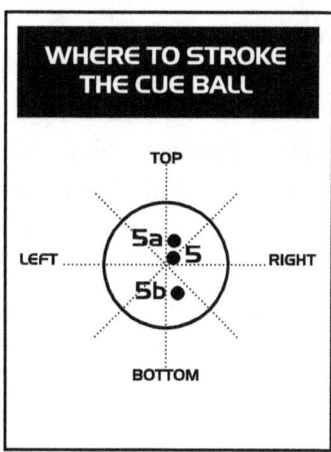

WHERE TO STROKE THE CUE BALL

DATE	SHOT	%	DATE	SHOT	%	DATE	SHOT	%

THE PRO BOOK

The Pro Book Reference Series — Shot #6

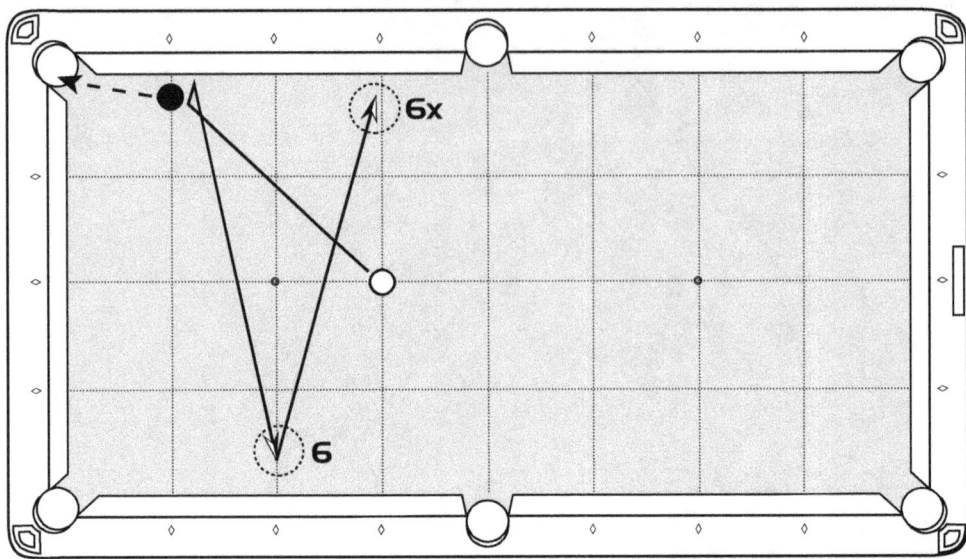

Notes:

Position the CB and OB as shown. Shoot the OB into the corner and bring the CB to a 5" target as shown. Practice doing this without hitting the second long rail. When you can accomplish this 75% of the time, include Shot 6x in your training. Practice this shot without hitting the third rail with the CB. Learn to recognize each shot as an independent entity.

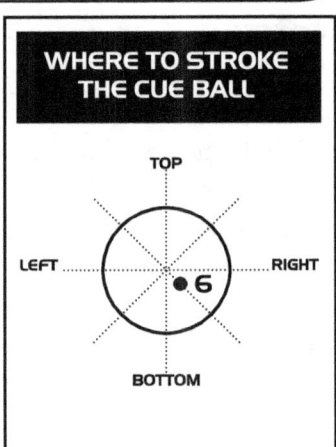

WHERE TO STROKE THE CUE BALL

DATE	SHOT	%	DATE	SHOT	%	DATE	SHOT	%

EXECUTION

The Pro Book Reference Series — Shot #7

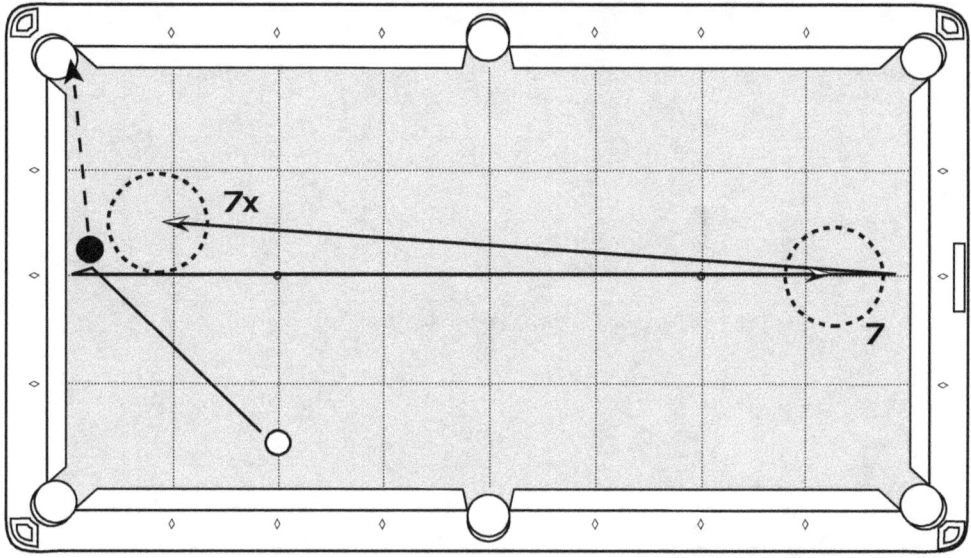

Notes:

If you have to get from the short rail and you cannot go diagonally through the center of the table, Shot 7 becomes crucial. Shoot to a 10" target without hitting the second rail. When you can score 70%, start working on Shot 7x, the extended version. Shoot Shot 7 without contacting the last short rail. Make sure to learn each shot as a separate entity.

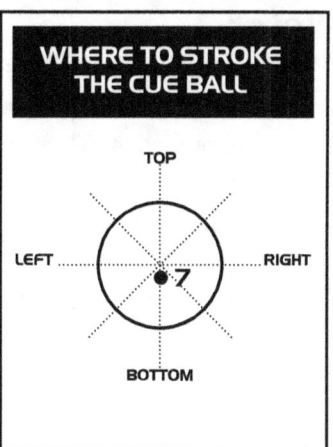

WHERE TO STROKE THE CUE BALL

DATE	SHOT	%	DATE	SHOT	%	DATE	SHOT	%

THE PRO BOOK

The Pro Book Reference Series — Shot #8

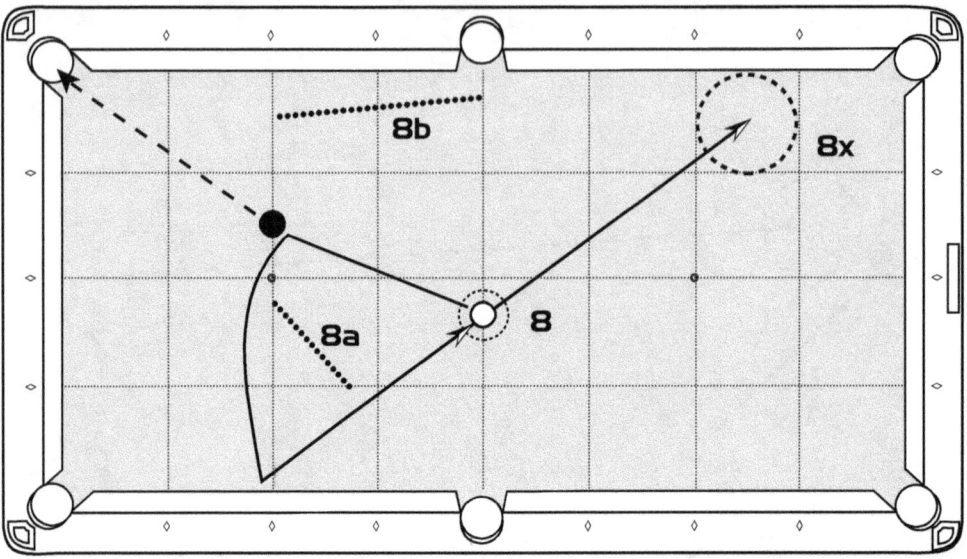

Notes:

Position the CB and OB as shown. Shoot the OB into the corner and draw the CB to the far long rail and out to a 5" target near center table. When you can do this 70% of the time, start working on Shot 8x which extends the CB travel to a 10" target. Shoot without hitting the second long rail. Then practice the boundary shots 8a and 8b and their extensions.

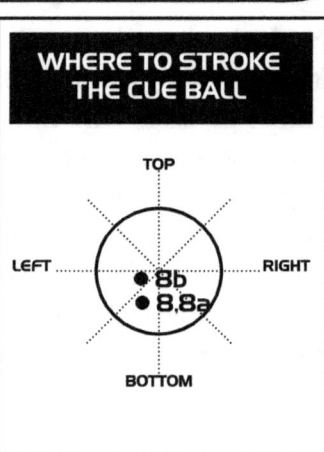

WHERE TO STROKE THE CUE BALL

DATE	SHOT	%	DATE	SHOT	%	DATE	SHOT	%

EXECUTION

The Pro Book Reference Series — Shot #9

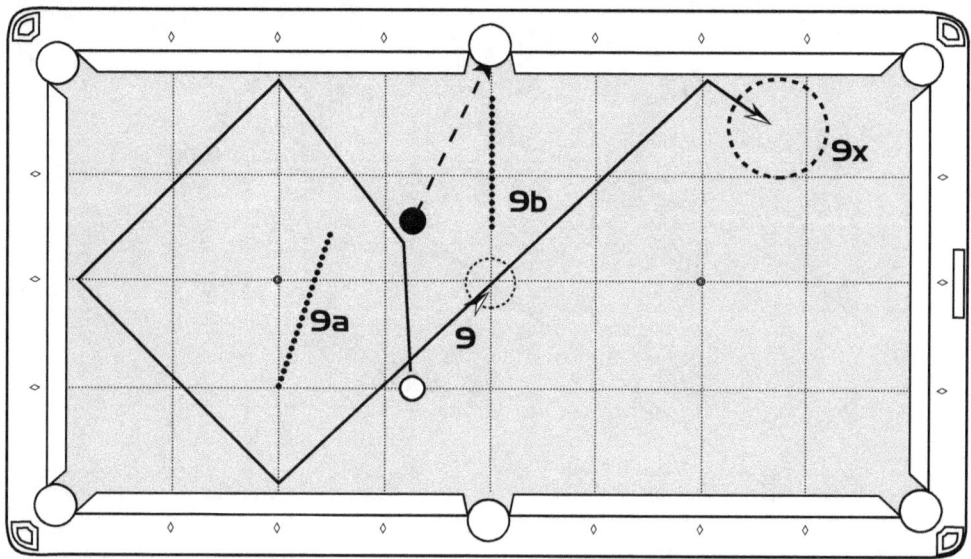

Notes:

Position the CB and OB as shown. Shoot the OB into the side and send the CB to the near long rail, the short rail, the far long rail and to the target at the center of the table. When you can consistently score 75%, start working on Shot 9x and send the CB to the 10" target. When you can do this 70% of the time, work on Shots 9a and 9b and their extensions.

(The CB strike points are slightly changed from the first three printings of the PB.)

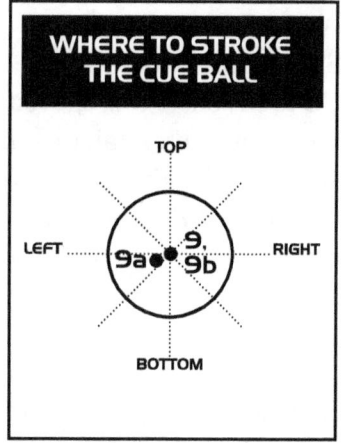

WHERE TO STROKE THE CUE BALL

DATE	SHOT	%	DATE	SHOT	%	DATE	SHOT	%

THE PRO BOOK

The Pro Book Reference Series — Shot #10

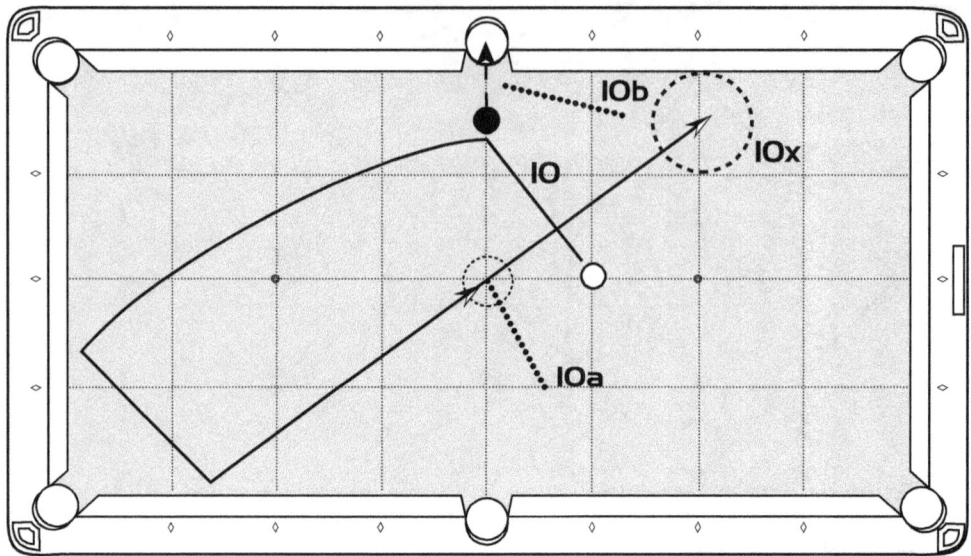

Notes:

Shoot the OB into the side pocket and bring the CB to the short rail, the long rail, and out to a 5" target at center table. When you can do this 70%, practice the extension shot to a 10" target as shown. When you can do that successfully, practice Shot 10a and 10b and the associated extensions.

(The first three printings of the PB did not have a boundary Shot 10b)

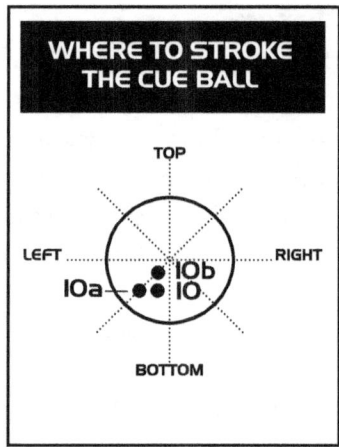

DATE	SHOT	%	DATE	SHOT	%	DATE	SHOT	%

EXECUTION

The Pro Book Reference Series — Shot #11

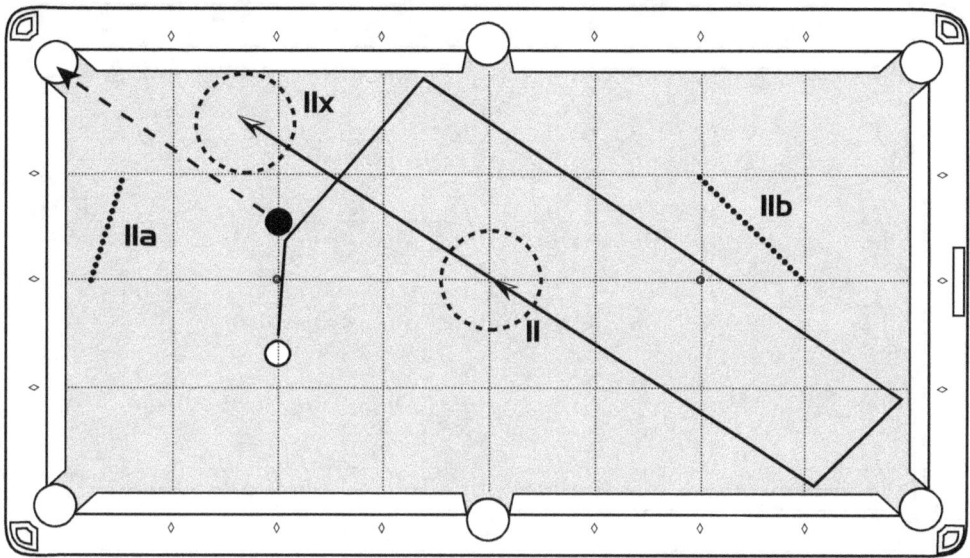

Notes:

This is an important recovery shot. Place the balls as pictured and shoot the OB into the corner and send the CB to the first long rail, the far short rail, the second long rail and to a 10" target at center table. When you can do this 70%, work on the extension shot. Learn the boundary shots and their extensions last. Learn each shot as a distinct entity.

(The CB strike points are slightly different from the first three printings of the PB.)

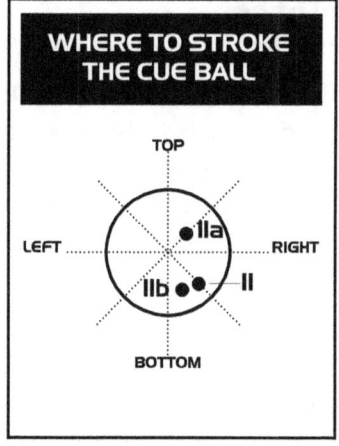

DATE	SHOT	%	DATE	SHOT	%	DATE	SHOT	%

THE PRO BOOK

The Pro Book Reference Series — Shot #12

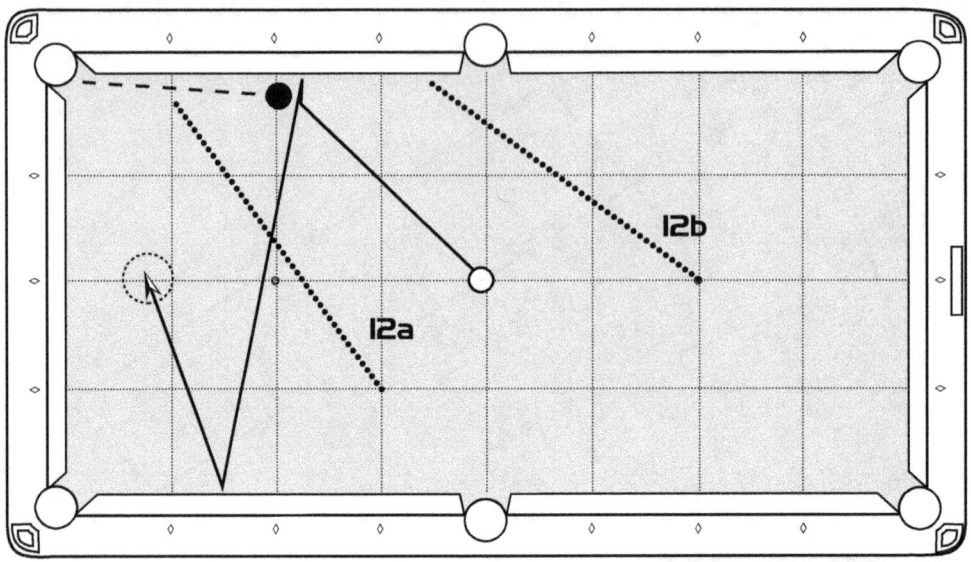

Notes:

Place the CB in the center of the table and the OB as shown. Shoot the OB into the corner and send the CB to the near long rail, the far long rail, and to a 5" target as pictured. When you can do this 70% of the time, work on the boundary shots, 12a and 12b. Learn the shots by name first, line second, and speed last. Learn each one as a distinct shot.

(Shot 12a and the CB strike points are slightly changed from the first three printings of the PB.)

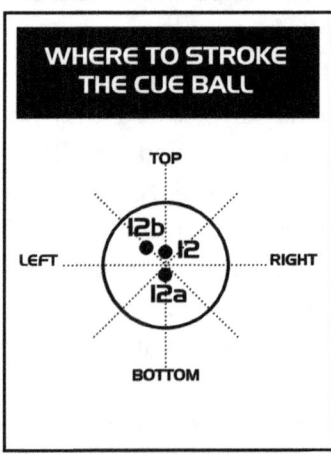

WHERE TO STROKE THE CUE BALL

DATE	SHOT	%	DATE	SHOT	%	DATE	SHOT	%

EXECUTION

The Pro Book Reference Series — Shot #13

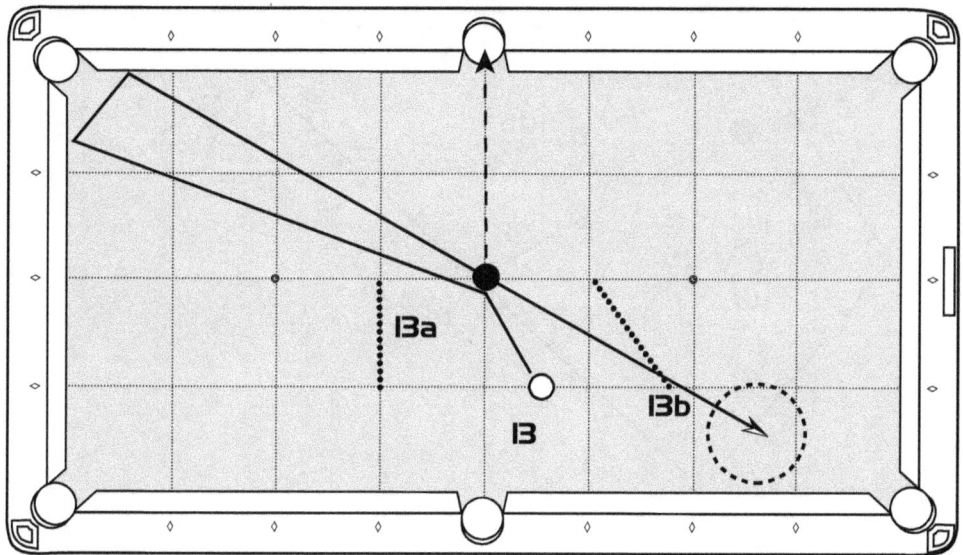

Notes:

This is a recovery shot. You will not use it very often in competition, but when you need it, you will be glad to have it. Place the balls as shown and shoot to send the CB to the short rail, the near side rail, and through the vicinity of center table to the 10" target shown. Learn to recognize the boundaries of this shot by practicing Shot 13a and Shot 13b.

(The CB strike point for 13a is slightly different than in the first three printings of the PB.)

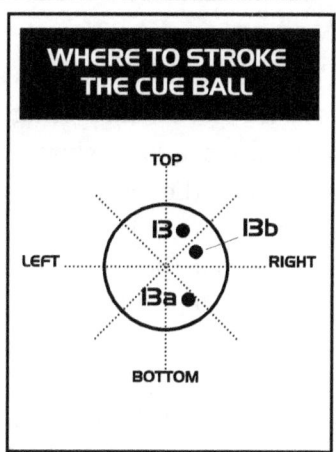

WHERE TO STROKE THE CUE BALL

DATE	SHOT	%	DATE	SHOT	%	DATE	SHOT	%

THE PRO BOOK

The Pro Book Reference Series — Shot #14

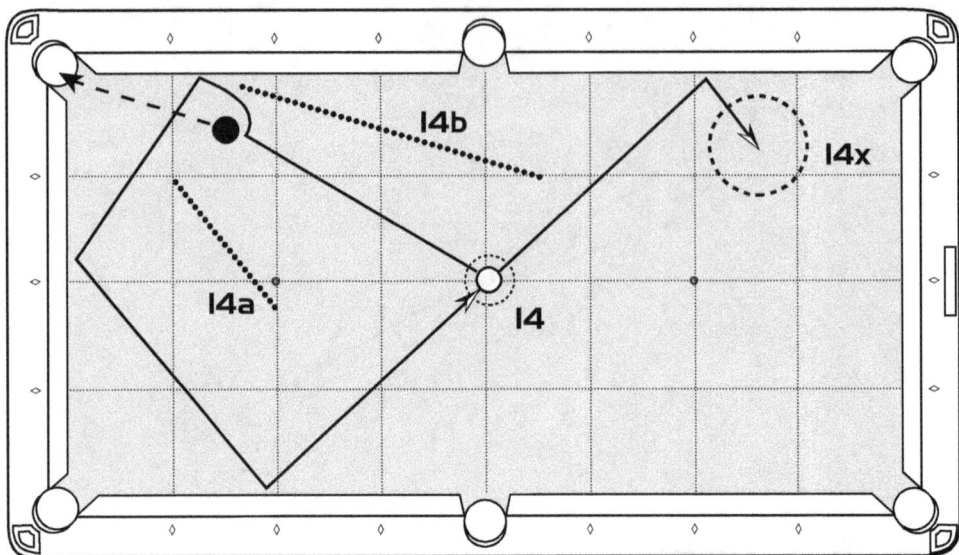

Notes:

Position the OB and CB as shown. Shoot the OB into the pocket and bring the CB to the near long rail, the near short rail, the far long rail, and out to the center of the table. When you can do this 75% of the time, learn Shot 14x. When you can put the CB on a 10" target, learn Shot 14a and Shot 14b and then their extensions. Learn each shot independently.

(Shot 14b and the CB strike points are slightly changed from the first three printings of the PB.)

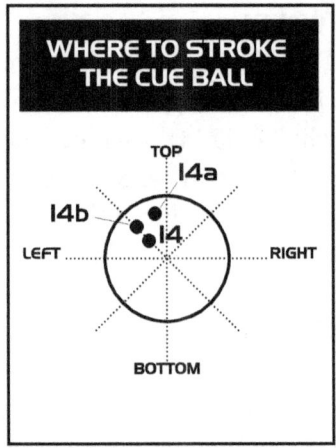

WHERE TO STROKE THE CUE BALL

DATE	SHOT	%	DATE	SHOT	%	DATE	SHOT	%

EXECUTION

The Pro Book Reference Series — Shot #15

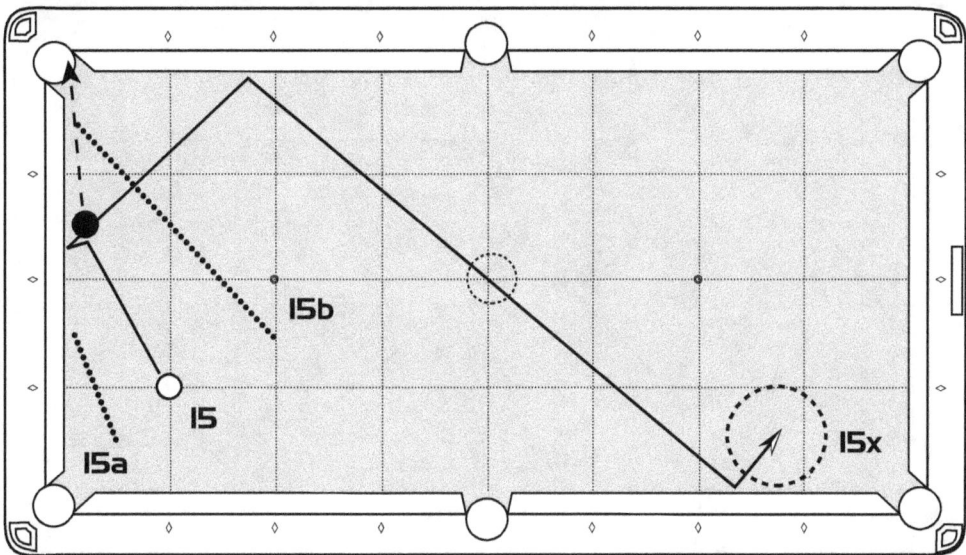

Notes:

Place the CB and OB as shown. Shoot the OB into the corner and send the CB to the near short rail, the near long rail, and out to a 5" target in the center of the table. When you can do this 75% of the time, start working on Shot 15x. When you can put the CB into a 10" target 70% of the time, include the boundary shots 15a and 15b and then their extensions.

(The CB strike points are slightly changed from the first three printings of the PB.)

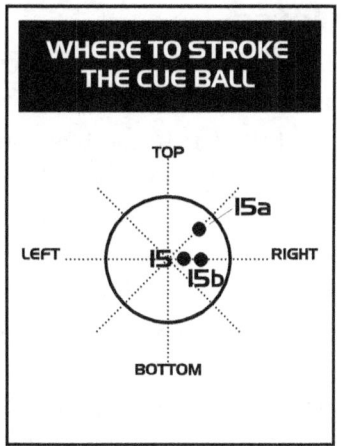

WHERE TO STROKE THE CUE BALL

DATE	SHOT	%	DATE	SHOT	%	DATE	SHOT	%

THE PRO BOOK

The Pro Book Reference Series — Shot #16

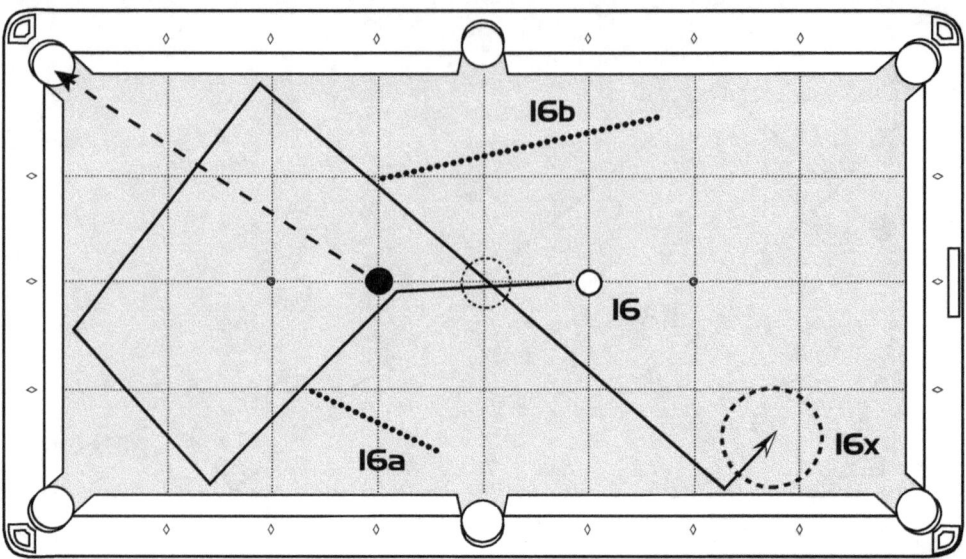

Notes:

This is an important recovery shot. Place the balls as shown and shoot the OB into the corner. Send the CB to the first long rail, the short rail, the second long rail and out to the center of the table. When you can do this 65% of the time, start working on the extended shot 16x. When you can put the CB into a 10" target, move on to the boundary shots and their extensions.

(The CB strike points are slightly changed from the first three printings of the PB.)

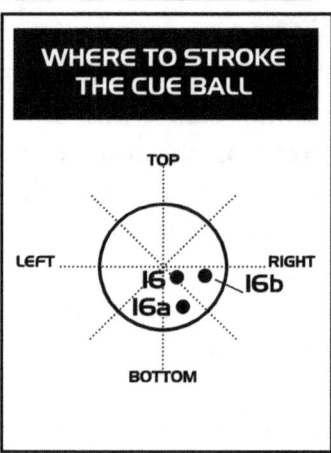

DATE	SHOT	%	DATE	SHOT	%	DATE	SHOT	%

EXECUTION

Safeties

The objective of playing a *safety* is to turn the table over to your opponent, but to *retain control*. The most desired outcome is to get the table back after his inning with your position significantly enhanced, hopefully with *ball in hand*.

The *cue ball trap* is the most aggressive of safeties because it is definitive and low risk. In this safety, you move an object ball, and park the cue ball behind existing balls. In the best scenarios, you don't have to move the cue ball at all, you simply stop it. Whenever you can limit the number of balls you have to control and the distance you have to move them, you minimize your risk. In addition, a *trap safety* leaves the cue ball close to obstructing balls which increases the chance of a bad hit by your opponent.

The objective of a *distance safety* is to leave distance between the cue ball and the active object ball. You take advantage of available obstructing balls, but that is a secondary objective to achieving distance. The best *distance safeties* leave the object ball on one short rail and the cue ball on the other.

The objective of a *hook safety* is to move both cue ball and object ball so that they are hidden from each other by obstructing balls. You are moving both balls, so the risk factor is higher than with the *trap*. In addition, if you leave a *window*, where your opponent can see the object ball, you may not have the distance or strategic positioning to fall back on as you do in a *distance safety*. If you can successfully leave the cue ball and object ball separated by obstructions, however, you have a powerful situation.

The Pro Book Reference Series contains a total of 16 reference safeties. Except for specialty games, all other safeties can be viewed as variations of these. Remember to learn each

THE PRO BOOK

one by name first, line second, and speed last. A few principles which apply to defensive strategy are:

1. When in doubt, do something simple.

2. If possible, always put distance between the cue ball and the object ball.

3. If possible, send the object ball into an area of other balls to increase the chance of a bad hit.

4. Concentrate on *one* ball, either the cue ball or an object ball.

5. Hide the cue ball in a way that eliminates kicking possibilities.

6. If there are clusters on the table, try to move the object ball into position to break them.

7. Go ahead and try for a low percentage shot if the outcome will leave a safety if you miss.

EXECUTION

The Pro Book Reference Series — Safety #1

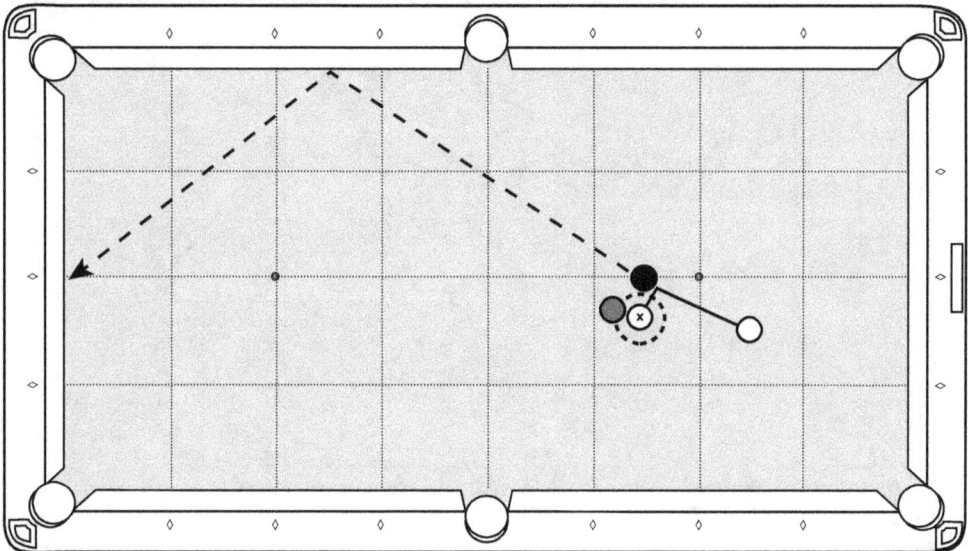

Notes:

This cue ball trap can occur anywhere on the table. It is the most common safety and can be devastating to your opponent. In some cases you can stop the CB in its tracks. Other times you may need to move it a couple of inches one way or the other. Practice sending the OB to a rail and freezing the CB to the blocking ball. Vary the CB starting position so that different hits are required. Practice them all.

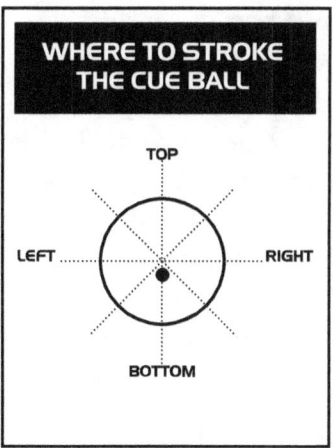

DATE	RATIO	%	DATE	RATIO	%	DATE	RATIO	%

THE PRO BOOK

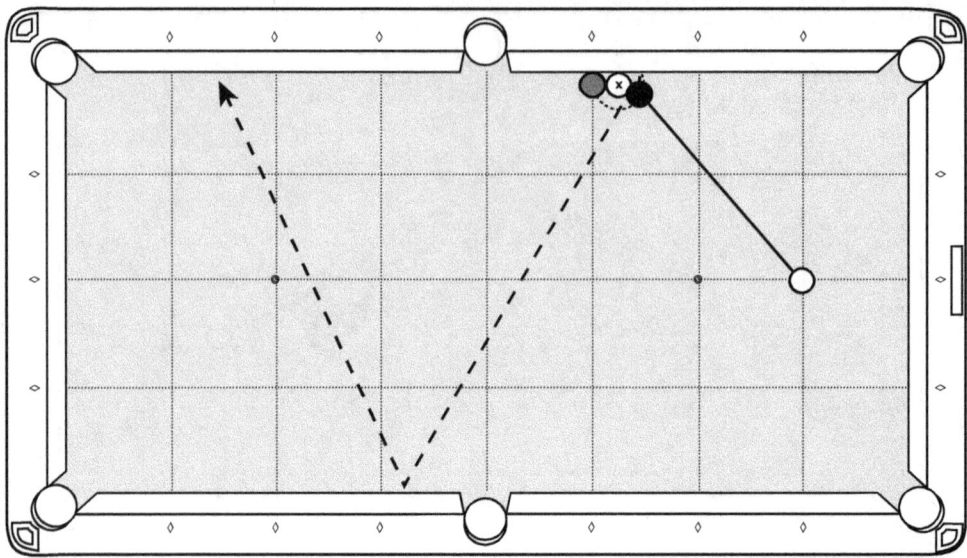

Notes:

Move this trap safety to different locations on the long rail and practice to discover how and when it can be made. The key to this safety is controlling the CB and keeping it behind the obstructing ball. A possible danger lies in accidently banking the OB once in the side or twice in the corner. Learn to recognise the angle and clearance necessary to avoid hitting the obstructing ball with the OB.

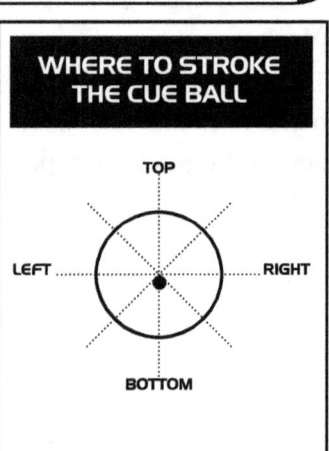

DATE	RATIO	%	DATE	RATIO	%	DATE	RATIO	%

EXECUTION

The Pro Book Reference Series — Safety #3

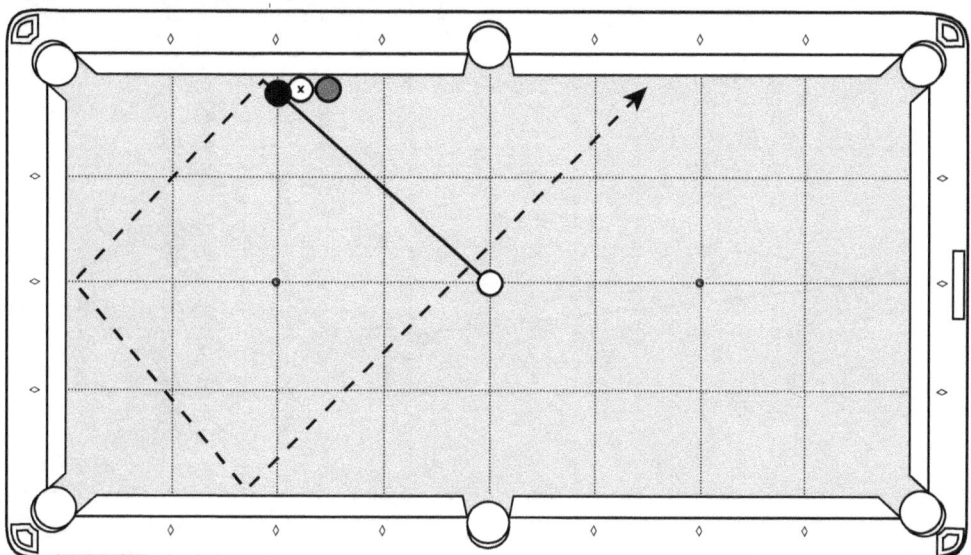

Notes:

This is a very low risk safety with a high probability of getting ball in hand from your opponent. The one crucial item is to stop the CB behind the blocking ball and freeze it if possible. Use the rails to send the OB down table, but keep it away from the corner pocket to minimize the opportunity for a lucky kick. Practice this safety at different places on the rail.

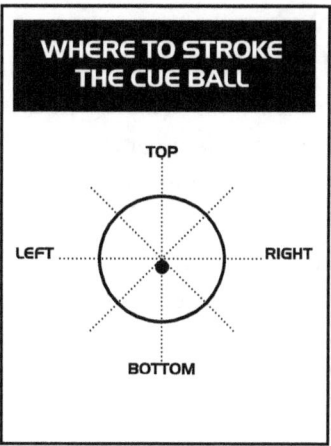

WHERE TO STROKE THE CUE BALL

DATE	RATIO	%	DATE	RATIO	%	DATE	RATIO	%

THE PRO BOOK

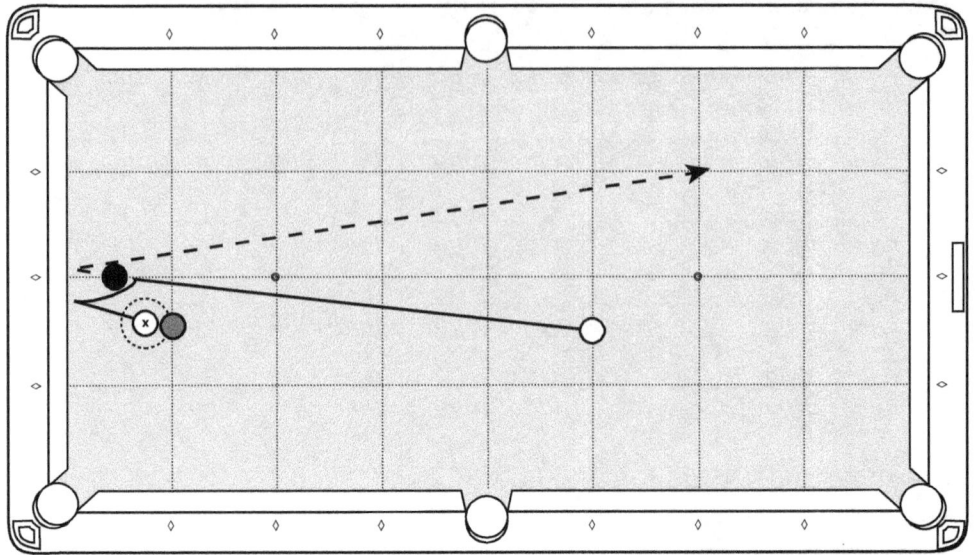

Notes:

This cue ball trap is an important safety that comes up frequently and in different variations. It demands a certain feel and it is more difficult to execute than it looks. If you roll out past the obstructing ball you will leave your opponent a shot. First, confirm that you will avoid banking the OB into the side or corner pocket. Then focus solely on placing the CB behind the obstructing ball.

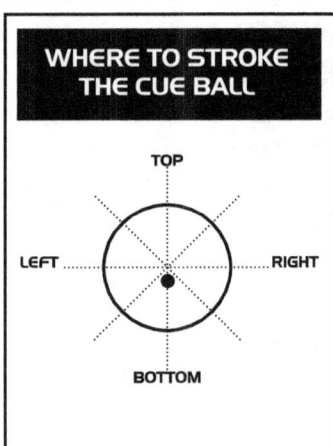

DATE	RATIO	%	DATE	RATIO	%	DATE	RATIO	%

EXECUTION

The Pro Book Reference Series — Safety #5

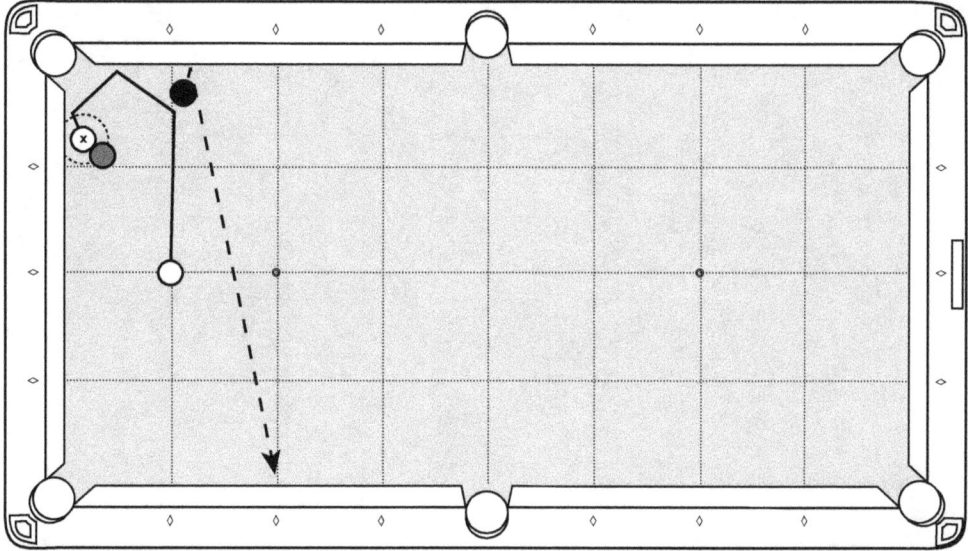

Notes:

Set this safety up as shown. Hit it with full inside english and about a half-ball hit. You can hit it firmer than you expect because the english will kill the CB off the rail. The main objective is to freeze the CB behind the obstructing ball. The second objective is to park the OB near the second rail. When you work on this safety, set the balls up in slightly different positions to learn the limitations.

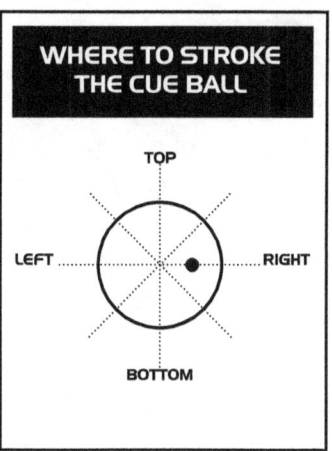

WHERE TO STROKE THE CUE BALL

DATE	RATIO	%	DATE	RATIO	%	DATE	RATIO	%

THE PRO BOOK

The Pro Book Reference Series — Safety #6

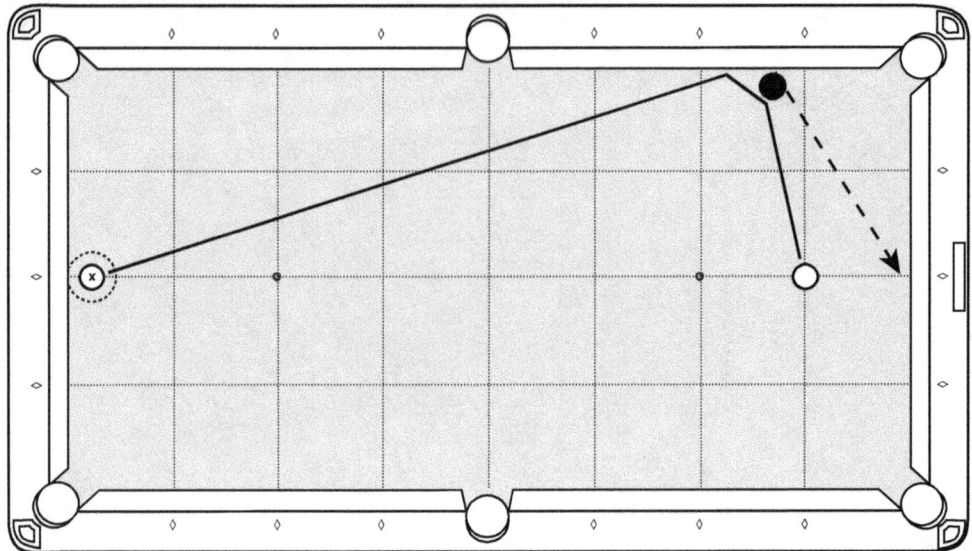

Notes:

This distance safety comes up frequently and is often a good alternative to the tough bank. Take advantage of obstructing balls on the table, but keep your focus on getting the maximum distance between the CB and the OB. It is best to freeze the CB to one rail and the OB slightly off the other. If you leave the OB on a rail and the CB off, your opponent may have a spin shot.

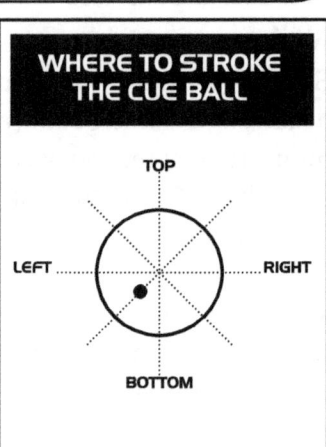

WHERE TO STROKE THE CUE BALL

DATE	RATIO	%	DATE	RATIO	%	DATE	RATIO	%

EXECUTION

The Pro Book Reference Series — Safety #7

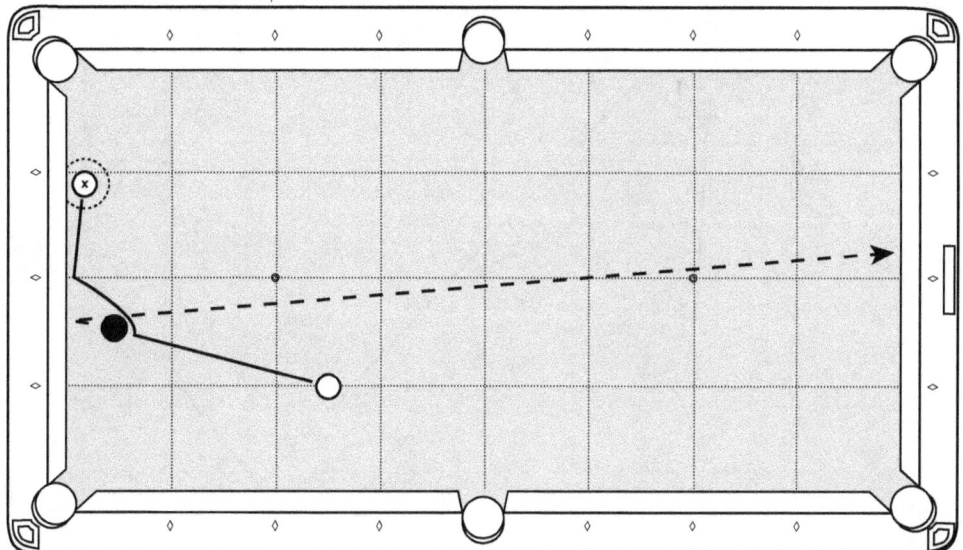

Notes:

The focus on this distance safety is on OB placement. Make sure to put it close to and near the middle of the rail. The CB is hard to control and good placement on the OB will protect you. When you practice, move both balls up and down the short rail and aquaint yourself with the particularities of this shot. Sometimes it is better to stun the CB to the long rail and use english to take it to the short rail.

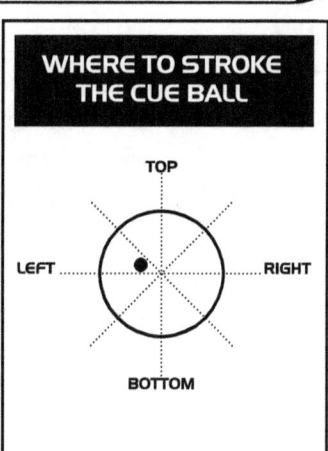

WHERE TO STROKE THE CUE BALL

DATE	RATIO	%	DATE	RATIO	%	DATE	RATIO	%

THE PRO BOOK

The Pro Book Reference Series — Safety #8

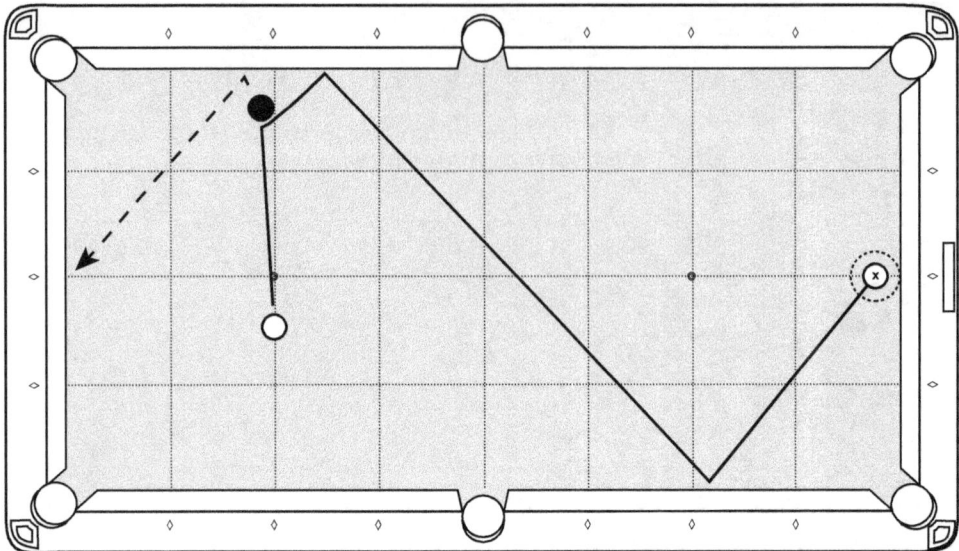

Notes:

This safety requires the use of the second long rail to get the CB to the end rail. The key focus in this shot is sticking the CB right on the rail. This eliminates the ability of your opponent to draw or to use english and greatly reduces his options. Set this safety up in different positions to learn its limitations. Pick rail targets for the CB and be sure not to scratch in the corner.

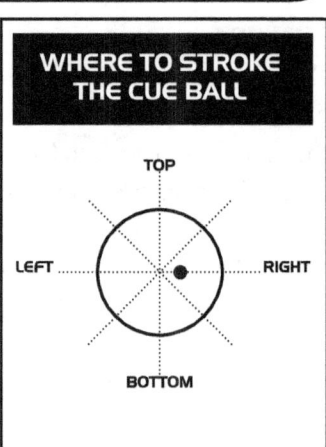

DATE	RATIO	%	DATE	RATIO	%	DATE	RATIO	%

EXECUTION

The Pro Book Reference Series — Safety #9

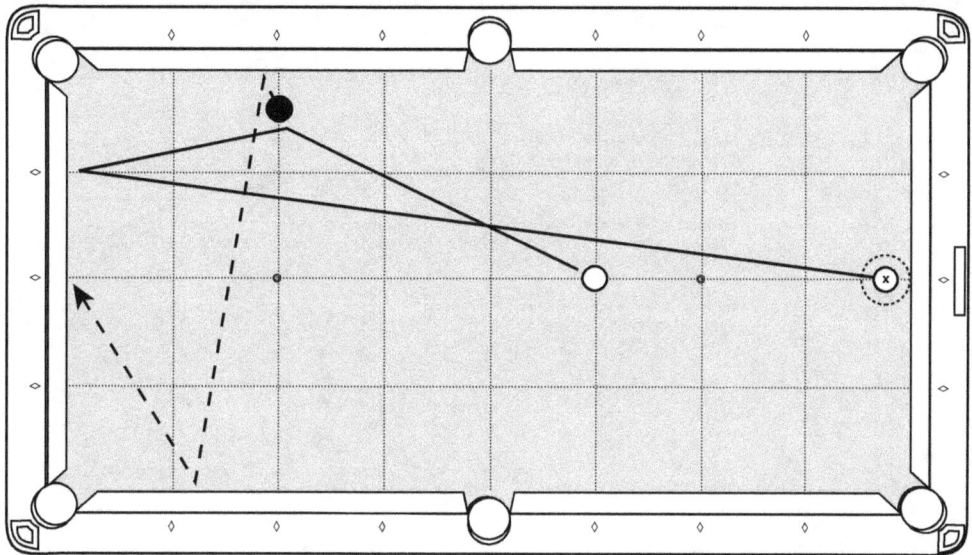

Notes:

This distance safety can get you out of some tough situations. The pictured layout requires a 1/2 ball hit with the CB cued just below center. When you can do this successfully, practice with the OB at different starting points along the rail and with the CB approaching from different angles. Knowing the hit and when the balls will kiss is essential to mastering this safety.

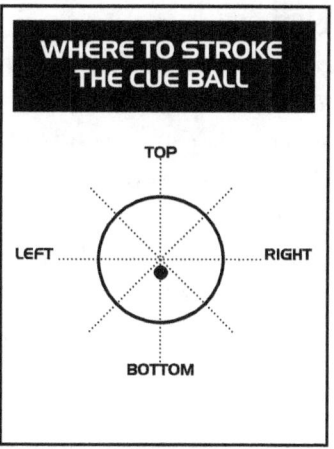

DATE	RATIO	%	DATE	RATIO	%	DATE	RATIO	%

THE PRO BOOK

The Pro Book Reference Series — Safety #10

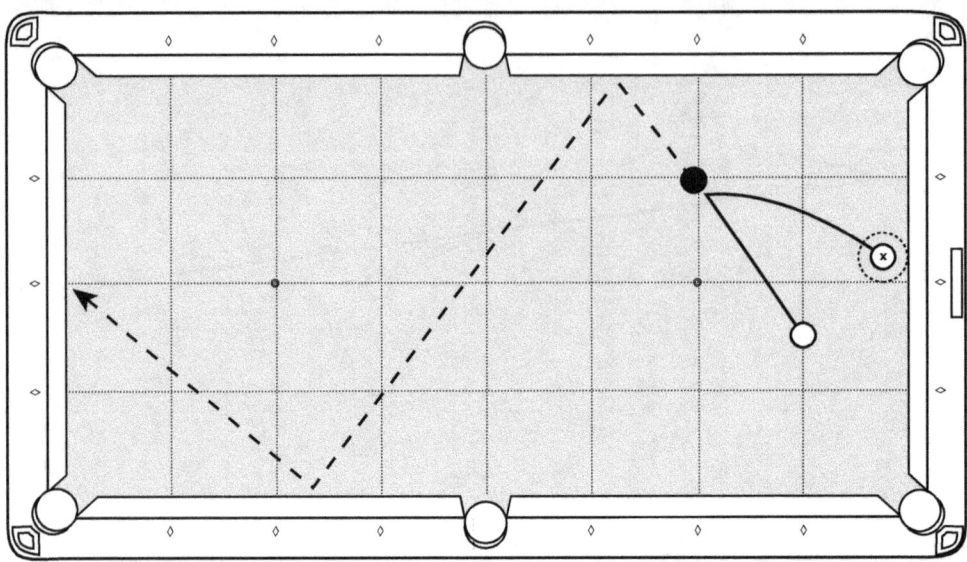

Notes:

Sometimes this distance safety is a game saver. Your first objective is to place the OB on the short rail. Your second is to leave the CB tough. Practice it thoroughly and you will have confidence in your ability to put the CB on one end rail and the OB on the other. The key is to hit the OB with slightly less than a full ball hit. Your first rail target is the 3rd diamond.

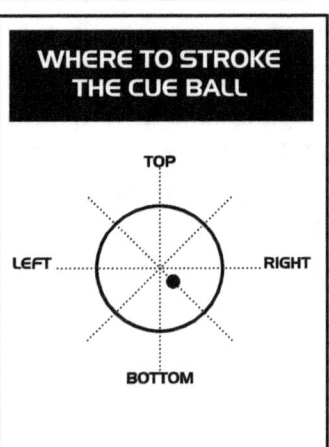

DATE	RATIO	%	DATE	RATIO	%	DATE	RATIO	%

EXECUTION

The Pro Book Reference Series — Safety #11

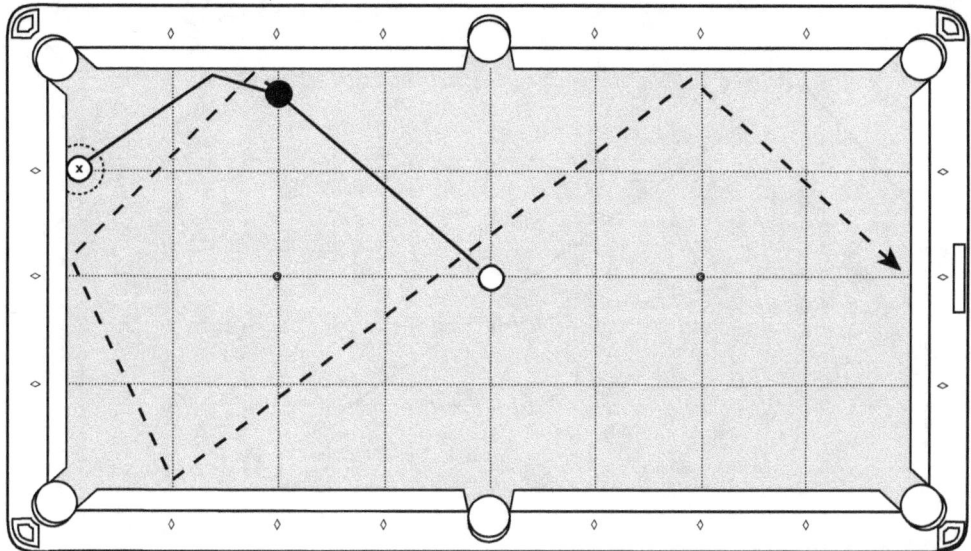

Notes:

This distance safety is executed with a full hit and just enough follow to take the CB to the short rail. It takes a firm hit to send the OB four rails, so be careful not to overpower the CB and scratch in the corner. Once you master this safety, move the OB up and down the long rail to practice different variations. This shot has a wide range where it can be employed successfully.

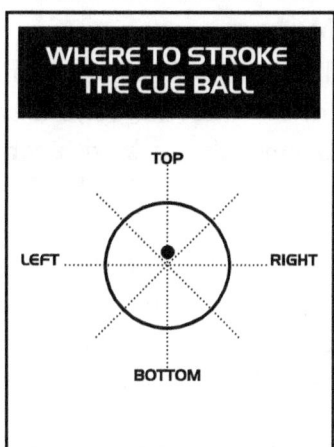

WHERE TO STROKE THE CUE BALL

DATE	RATIO	%	DATE	RATIO	%	DATE	RATIO	%

THE PRO BOOK

The Pro Book Reference Series — Safety #12

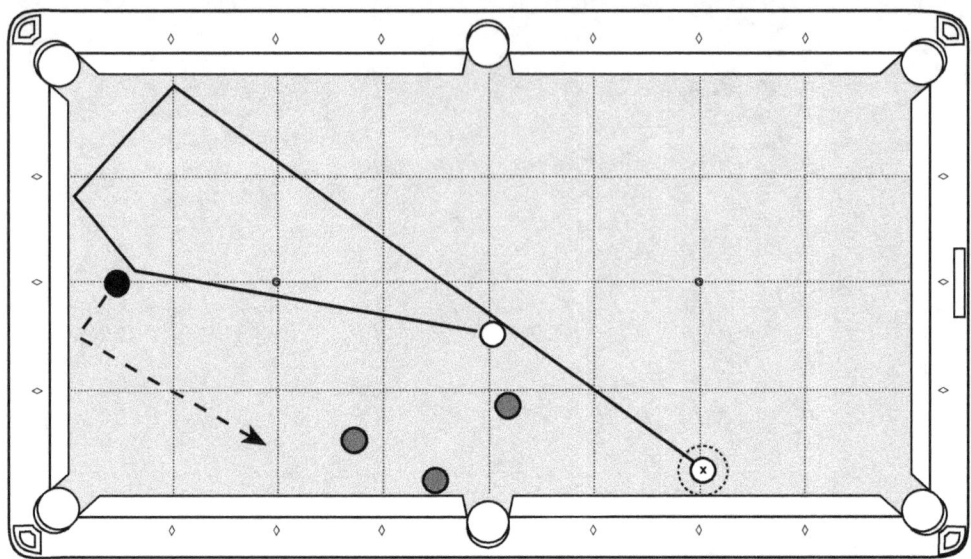

Notes:

This hook safety has a penalty to pay if you fail to hide the OB behind the obstructing balls. Balance this risk with careful planning. Pick a first rail target for the OB and then determine the correct aim. Pinpoint where you want to leave the OB and then visualize the path of the CB to make sure you avoid the scratch. When you can make this layout consistently, practice a few minor variations.

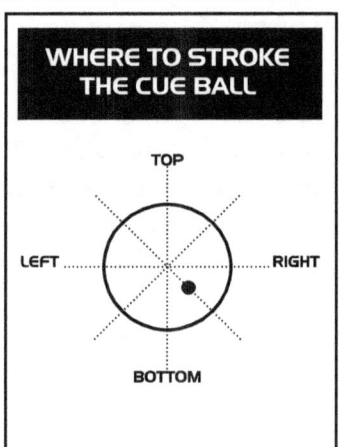

DATE	RATIO	%	DATE	RATIO	%	DATE	RATIO	%

EXECUTION

The Pro Book Reference Series — Safety #13

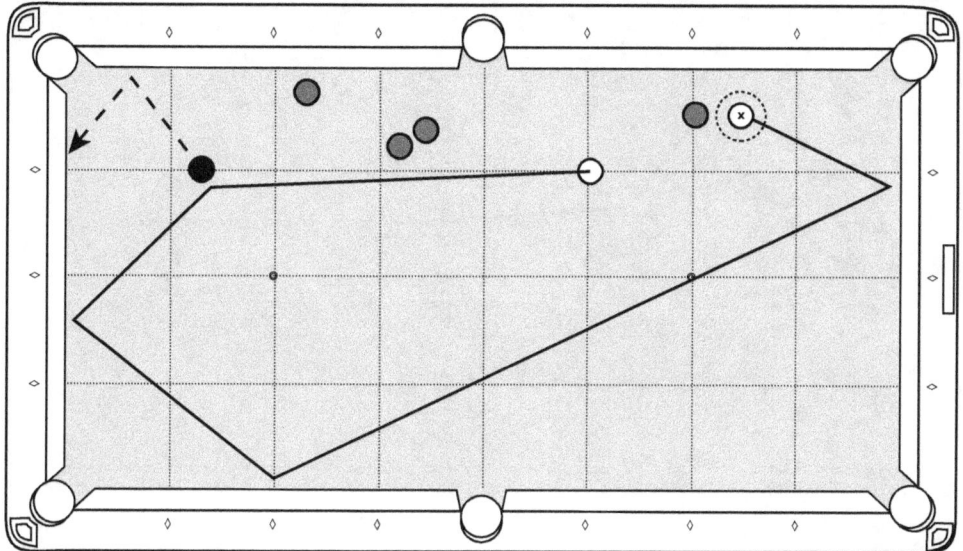

Notes:

This hook safety is a delicate balance of hit, english, and speed. The hit on the OB is thin and if the CB is much farther away than pictured, there is a possibility of missing the OB and giving up ball in hand. Pick a third rail target for the CB and work backwards to visualize your shot. This will help avoid the scratch in the corner.

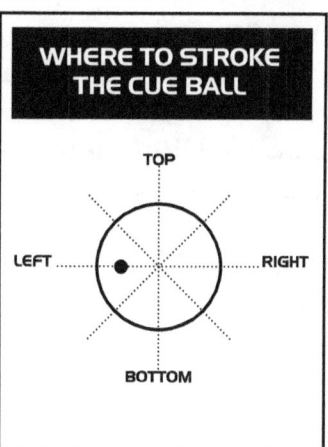

WHERE TO STROKE THE CUE BALL

DATE	RATIO	%	DATE	RATIO	%	DATE	RATIO	%

THE PRO BOOK

The Pro Book Reference Series — Safety #14

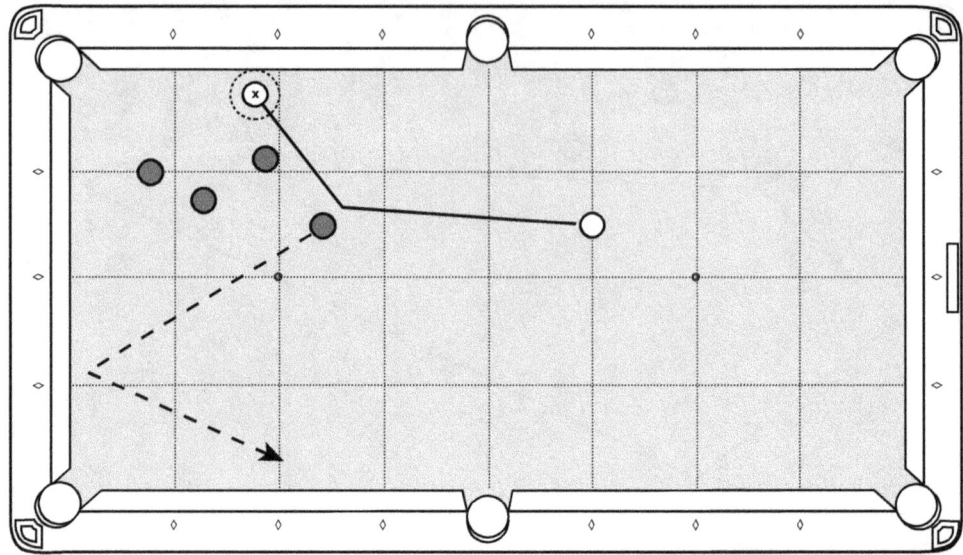

Notes:
Picking the hit and first rail target for this hook safety is crucial. CB control is limited and you want the OB to go to the middle of the lower long rail in case you fail to hide the CB. Once you know the hit on the OB, adjust your english to aim the CB for a specific point behind one of the obstructing balls. On average cloth, a draw drag shot with a little inside english is perfect.

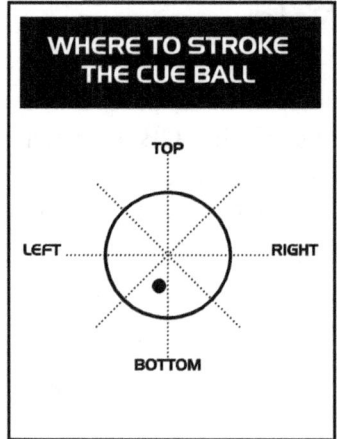

WHERE TO STROKE THE CUE BALL

DATE	RATIO	%	DATE	RATIO	%	DATE	RATIO	%

EXECUTION

The Pro Book Reference Series — Safety #15

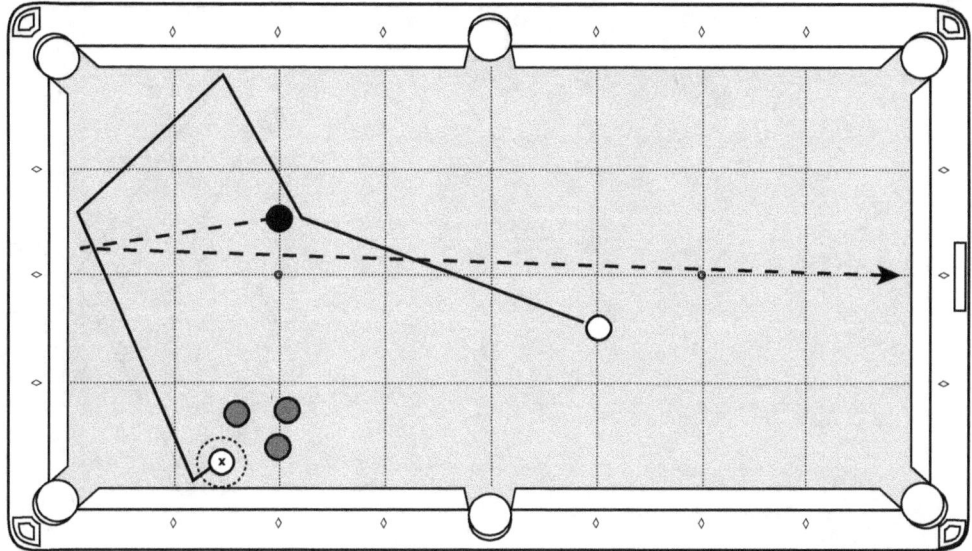

Notes:

Sometimes it is better to hide behind a cluster than to try to break it up and this hook safety presents such a situation. Hit the CB with left english and just below center. The main objective is to put the CB behind the obstructing balls, but if you do miss, you will still have the advantage of distance. Speed and cueing are the definitive factors in this shot.

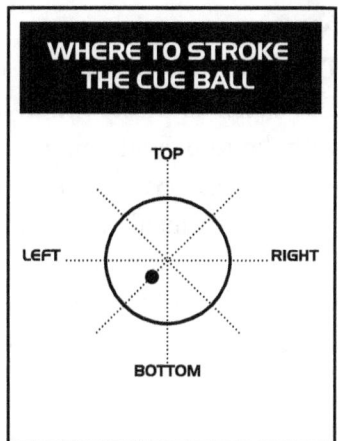

DATE	RATIO	%	DATE	RATIO	%	DATE	RATIO	%

THE PRO BOOK

The Pro Book Reference Series — Safety #16

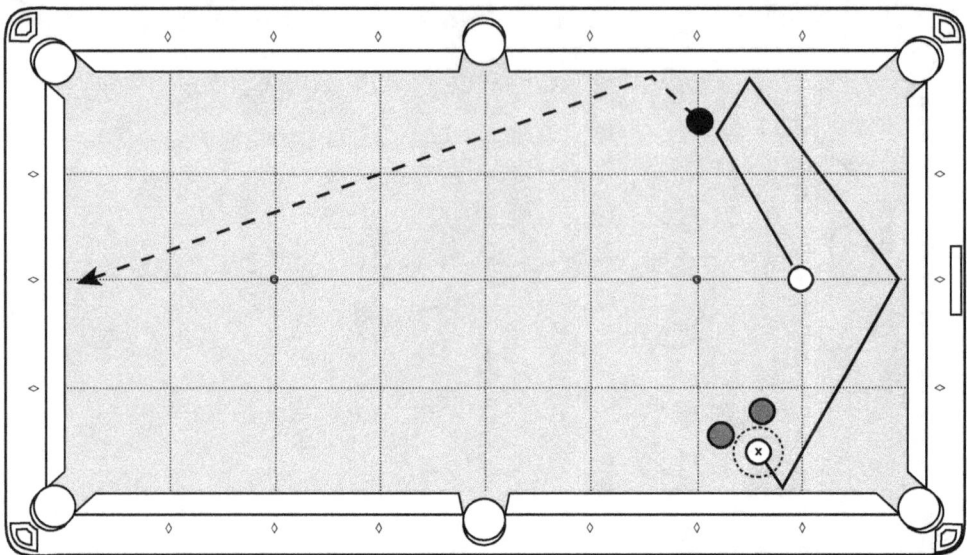

Notes:

This safety is a perfect way out of a bad situation and easier to execute than it looks. A 1/3 ball hit with bottom-right english is all it takes. It is better than trying to slice the OB into the far corner with inside english for position. It is also better than attempting to bank the OB back behind the obstructing balls and send the CB up table. Focus on the hit and on CB speed.

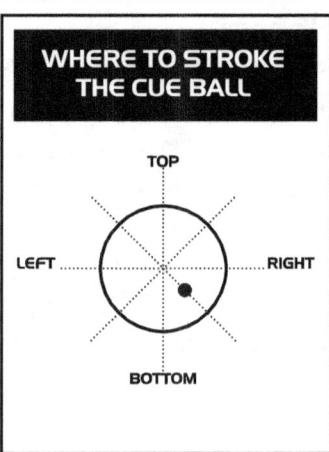

WHERE TO STROKE THE CUE BALL

DATE	RATIO	%	DATE	RATIO	%	DATE	RATIO	%

EXECUTION

Kicks

The importance of kicking in pool today cannot be overemphasized. When *runout players* are playing, kicking ability often determines the winner. Your ability to kick can either reward or destroy the defensive ability of your opponent. If he hides the ball from you so that you can't get a legal hit, you have few options. You can intentionally foul and tie balls up, or you can jump, curve, or kick the cue ball. You should practice all of these options, however, only the kick will be addressed in the *Pro Book*.

Some kicks are easier to judge than others. If the cue ball and the object ball lie on a path between two long or two short rails, it is a simple task to calculate a one rail kick by using the diamonds. Simply find the striking point on the far rail that is 1/2 of the distance between the cue ball origination and the cue ball destination if both of those points were extended to the near rail. Two rail kicks from long rail to long rail are also relatively easy. They are a simple calculation of the *corner five* system. If you don't know that system, it is recommended that you get a copy of Jack Koehler's *Science of Pocket Billiards* and learn it as soon as possible. It is accurate and dependable.

Most of the *Pro Book Reference Kicks* address the *difficult to judge* situations when the target point cannot be determined by simple diamond or system calculation. Many of these kicks are when the cue ball comes *from* a short rail to a long rail or *from* a long rail *to* a short. One very important destination point for kicks is the *center of the short rail*. This is the number one position your opponent will attempt to leave the object ball when he plays *safe*, so it is the number one place that you need to be able to hit when kicking.

Fourth Printing Update: Establishing a uniform speed and cueing for kicks will greatly help build your consistency. Try a natural lag stroke with 1/2 tip follow and 1/2 tip natural english and alter this only when you must. The *Pro Book Reference Kicks* have been changed to reflect this update.

THE PRO BOOK

The Pro Book Reference Series — Kick #1

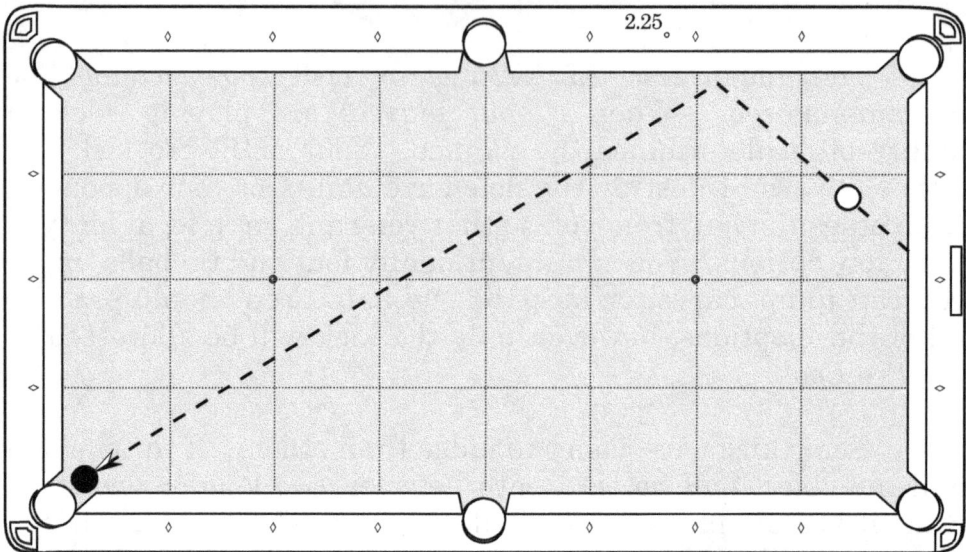

Notes:

This kick is hit with regular speed. You may find that some tables play a little different and the way to adjust is by changing your aim point. Keep your english consistent. When you can sink an OB sitting in the jaws on a regular basis, practice altering the first rail hit to strike targets slightly long and short of the pocket. Start with the CB anywhere on the track line.

(Kick 1 is slightly changed from the first three printings of the PB. See note on page 57.)

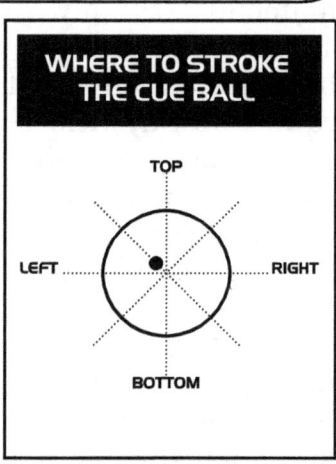

DATE	RATIO	%	DATE	RATIO	%	DATE	RATIO	%

EXECUTION

The Pro Book Reference Series — Kick #2

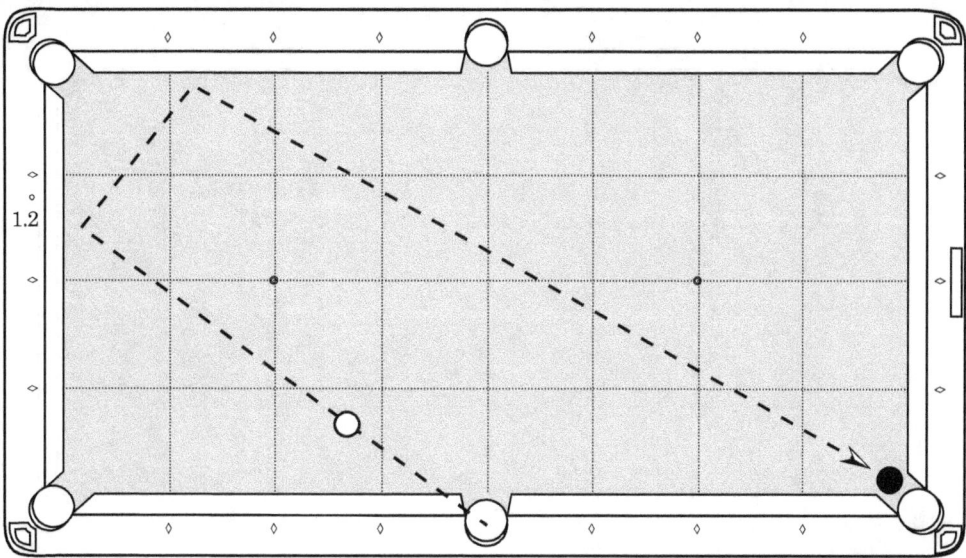

Notes:

This kick is normally hit with regular kicking speed, but if you need to hit it more firmly, the trick is to hit closer to the long rail. This kick also adjusts easily up and down the table. When moving the line of the kick closer to the target pocket, adjust with a parallel line until you run out of short rail. To go the other way, adjust with 1/2 of the parallel line distance.

(Kick 2 is slightly changed from the first three printings of the PB. See note on page 57.)

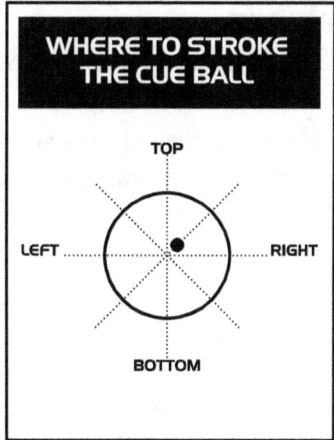

WHERE TO STROKE THE CUE BALL

DATE	RATIO	%	DATE	RATIO	%	DATE	RATIO	%

THE PRO BOOK

The Pro Book Reference Series — Kick #3

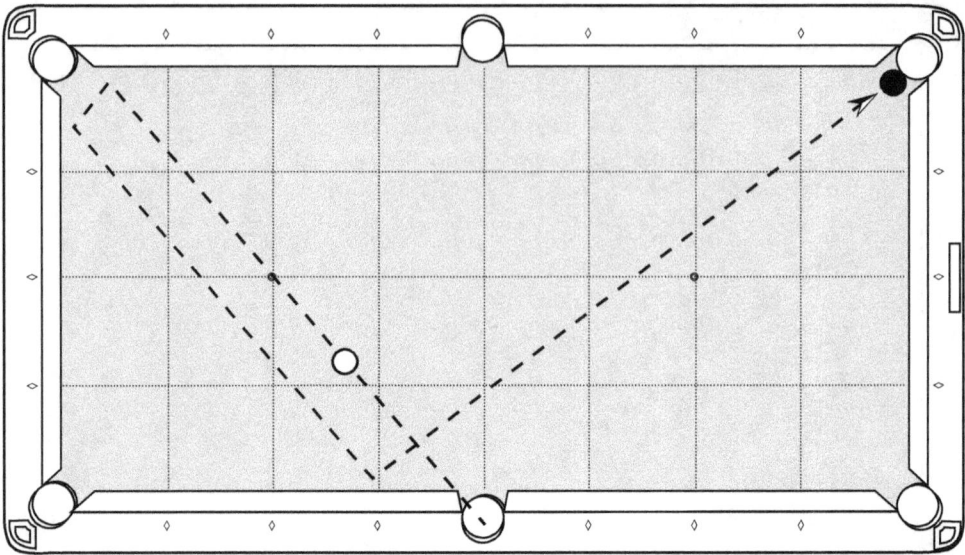

Notes:

This kick is important because it is one of the boundaries for the three rail kick to the corner. Adjust for discrepancies on different tables and slightly different targets by changing your aiming point. Keep your english consistent if possible. Hitting more of the first rail will bring the CB short of the pocket at an approximate ratio of 1:2.

(Kick 3 is slightly changed from the first three printings of the PB. See note on page 57.)

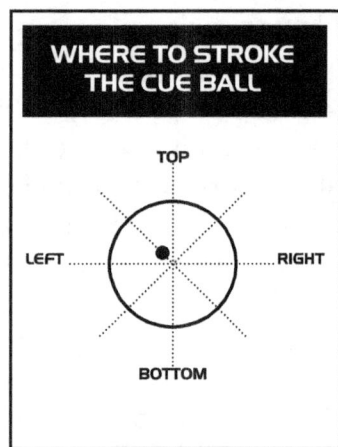

DATE	RATIO	%	DATE	RATIO	%	DATE	RATIO	%

EXECUTION

The Pro Book Reference Series — Kick #4

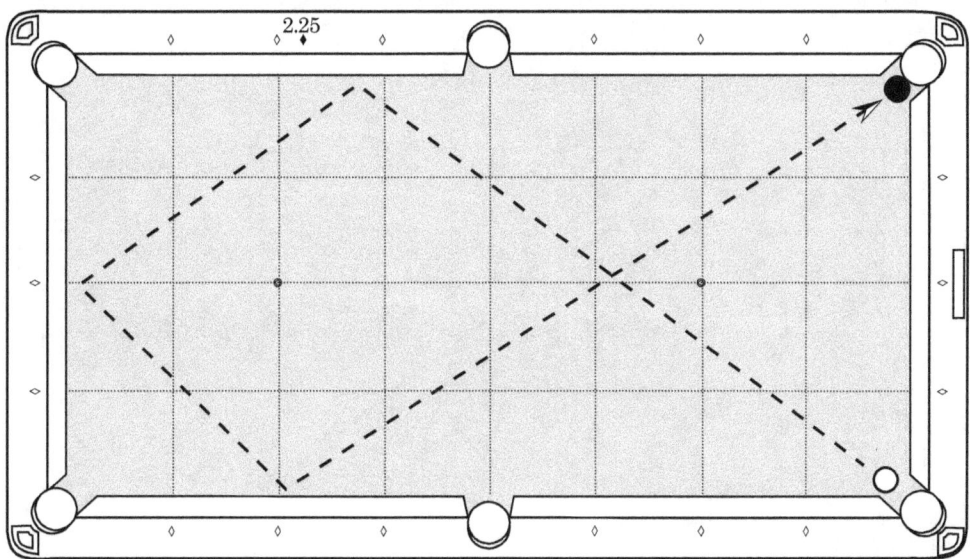

Notes:

This is a very important kick shot. It takes the CB from corner to corner and hits a strategic *middle of the rail* spot three separate times. In addition, this kick shot works in conjunction with Kick 3 to extrapolate three rails to the corner for any starting position between the side pocket and the corner. It also adjusts at a ratio of 1:1 for targets both long and short of the corner.

(Kick 4 is slightly changed from the first three printings of the PB. See note on page 57.)

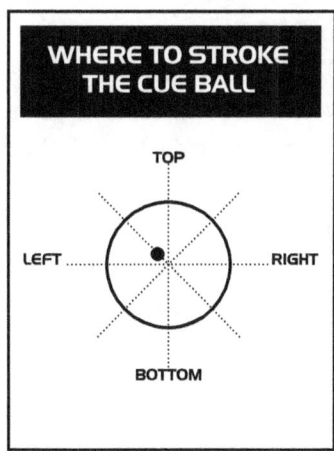

WHERE TO STROKE THE CUE BALL

DATE	RATIO	%	DATE	RATIO	%	DATE	RATIO	%

THE PRO BOOK

The Pro Book Reference Series — Kick #5

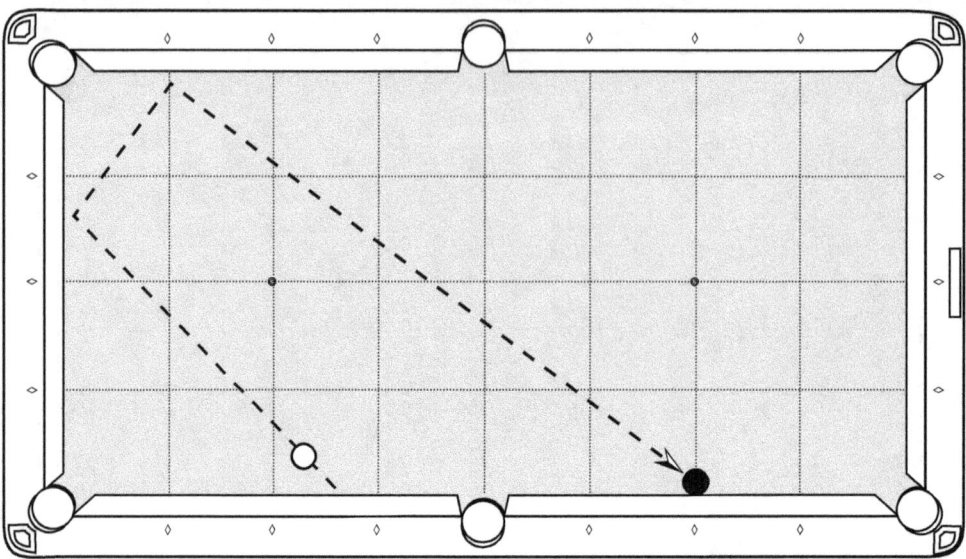

Notes:

This kick adjusts for different tables by changing your first rail aiming point. Adjust for a firmer hit by striking less of the first rail. Aiming 1/3 diamond to the left goes 1 diamond long and aiming 1/2 diamond to the right goes 1/2 diamond short. Adjust for CB positions to the right with a parallel line and to the left with 1/2 of a parallel line distance.

(Kick 5 is slightly changed from the first three printings of the PB. See note on page 57.)

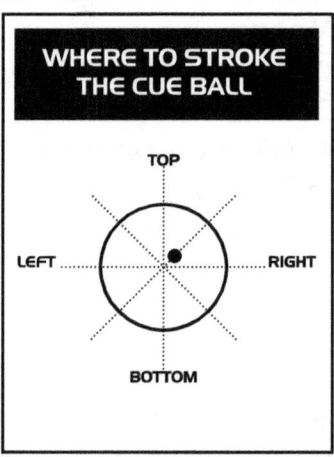

DATE	RATIO	%	DATE	RATIO	%	DATE	RATIO	%

EXECUTION

The Pro Book Reference Series — Kick #6

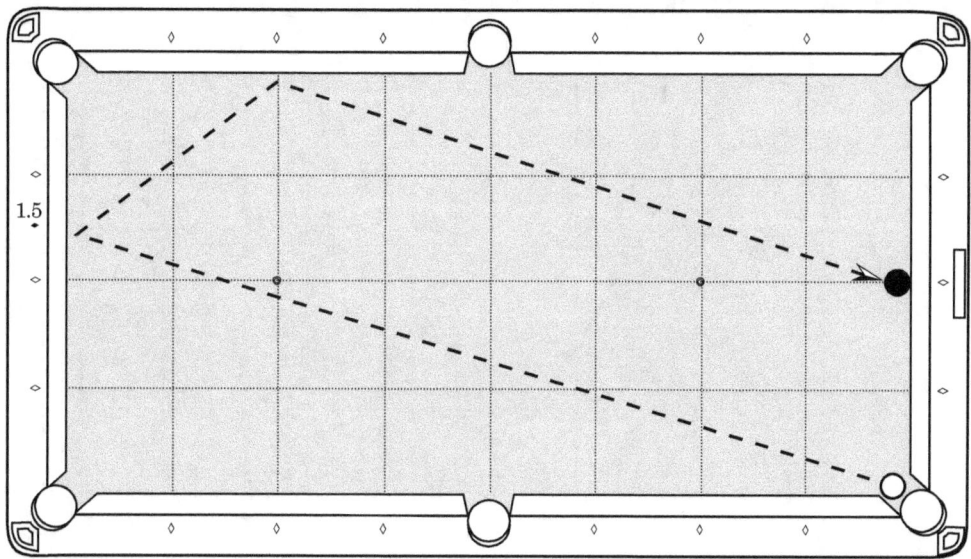

Notes:

This shot is a sensitive one to develop accuracy with, but when your opponent leaves the OB in the middle of the rail with no other way to hit it, you'll be glad you took the time to learn it. It adjusts left and right with a parallel line and is best learned at a medium speed. Normal kicking speed will leave the CB and OB lined up for an easy shot in the corner.

(Kick 6 is slightly changed from the first three printings of the PB. See note on page 57.)

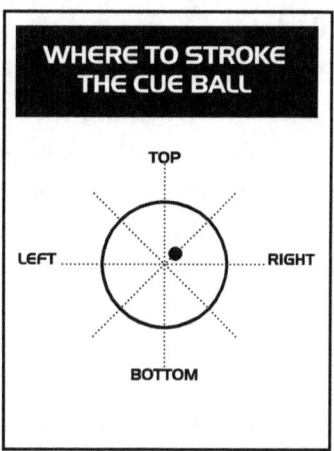

DATE	RATIO	%	DATE	RATIO	%	DATE	RATIO	%

THE PRO BOOK

The Pro Book Reference Series — Kick #7

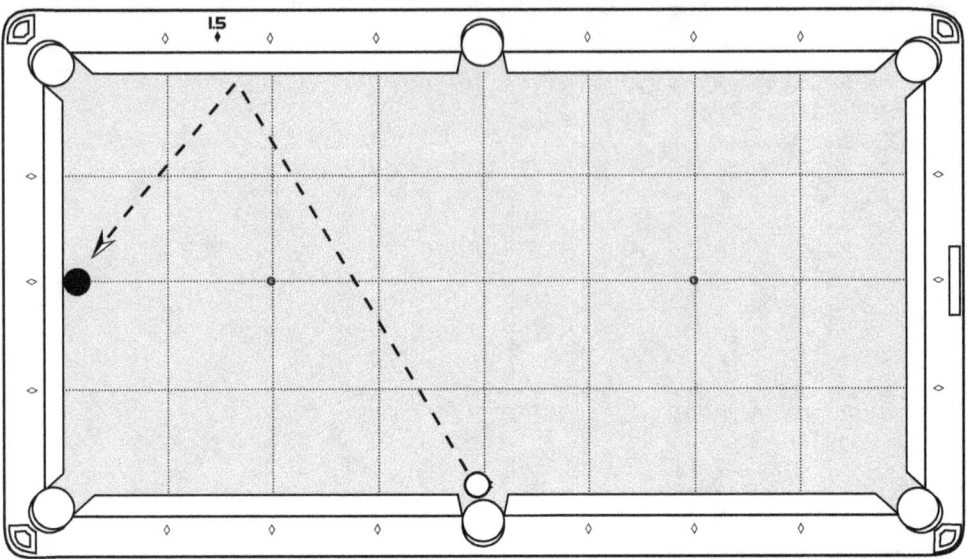

Notes:

Practicing this shot will give you a lot of confidence in kicking your way out of short table hooks. This kick is dead on if you aim at 1.5 diamonds with regular kicking english. You can often kick the OB in the corner and if you miss, you will usually be safe as the CB normally continues down to the other short rail.

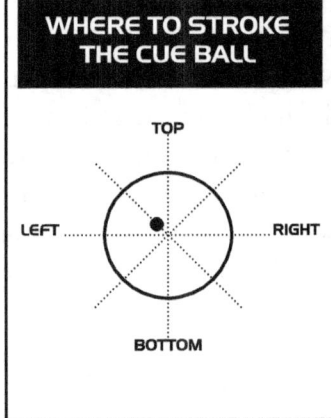

(Kick 7 is slightly changed from the first three printings of the PB. See note on page 57.)

DATE	RATIO	%	DATE	RATIO	%	DATE	RATIO	%

EXECUTION

The Pro Book Reference Series — Kick #8

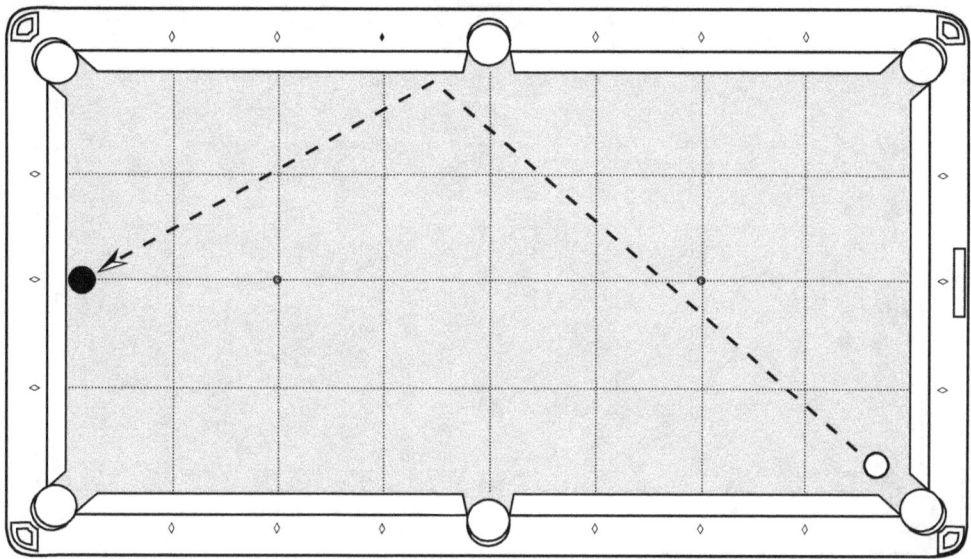

Notes:

This is a great kick shot. You can use it with Kick 7 to extrapolate CB positions all the way from the corner to the side pocket. The CB will often hit the OB square and double-kiss, leaving the OB in place and sending the CB down to the other short rail. For CB positions further up the short rail, adjust by aiming 1/2 of the parallel line distance.

(Kick 8 is slightly changed from the first three printings of the PB. See note on page 57.)

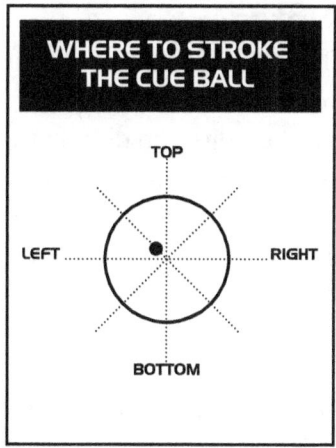

DATE	RATIO	%	DATE	RATIO	%	DATE	RATIO	%

THE PRO BOOK

The Pro Book Reference Series — Kick #9

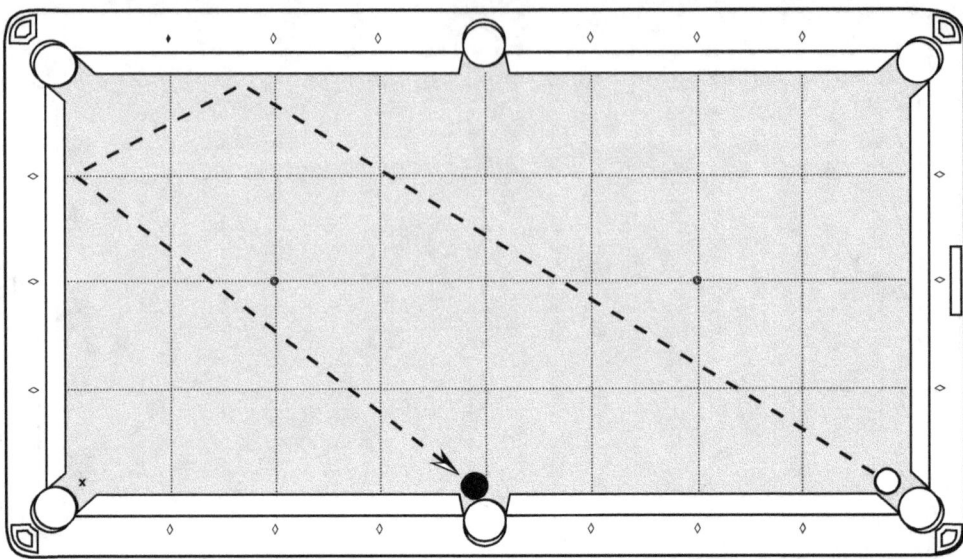

Notes:

This is a standard two rail kick from the corner to the side with regular kicking english and speed. Adjust on different tables with the hit, not english. You can move the CB position almost a diamond down the long rail by aiming with a parallel line. You can adjust diamond for diamond going up the short rail if you cue the CB closer to center as you go.

(Kick 9 is slightly changed from the first three printings of the PB. See note on page 57.)

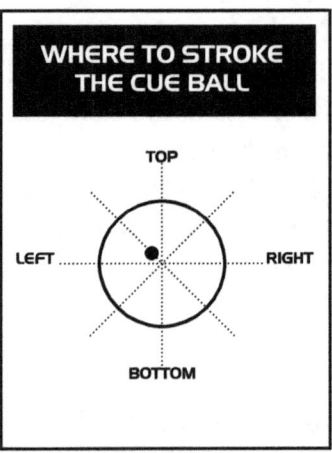

DATE	RATIO	%	DATE	RATIO	%	DATE	RATIO	%

EXECUTION

The Pro Book Reference Series — Kick #10

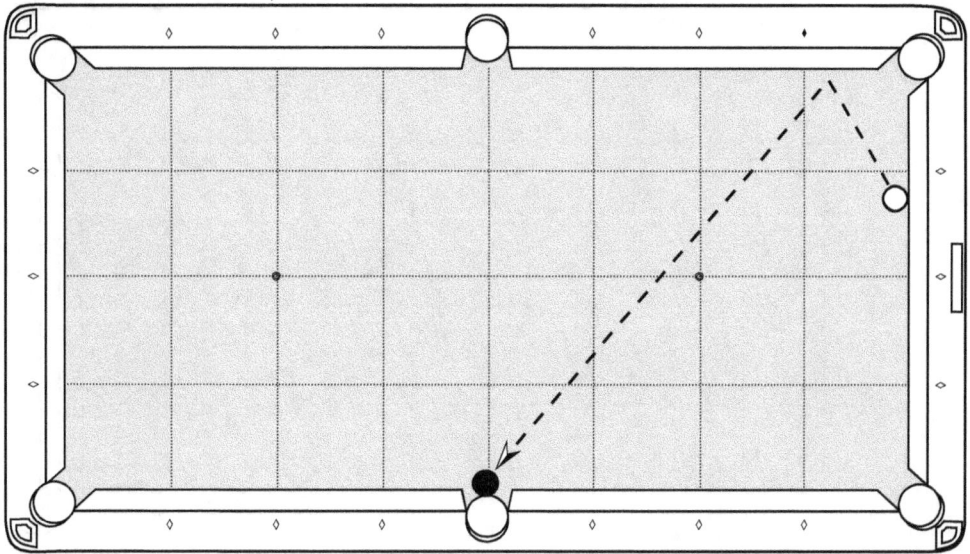

Notes:

This kick to the side pocket from the short rail is difficult to judge, so it makes sense to practice it. It is most consistent at slow speed, and you adjust on different tables with aim, not english. You can move the CB starting position down the short rail, a diamond or so by adjusting in a ratio of 2:1 (short rail to long rail.)

(Kick 10 is slightly changed from the first three printings of the PB. See note on page 57.)

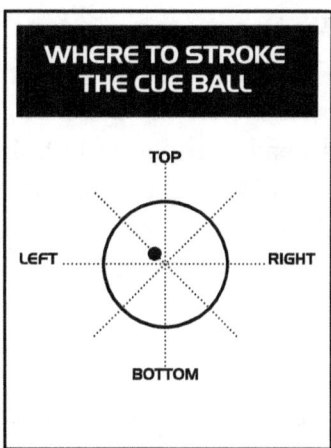

DATE	RATIO	%	DATE	RATIO	%	DATE	RATIO	%

THE PRO BOOK

The Pro Book Reference Series — Kick #11

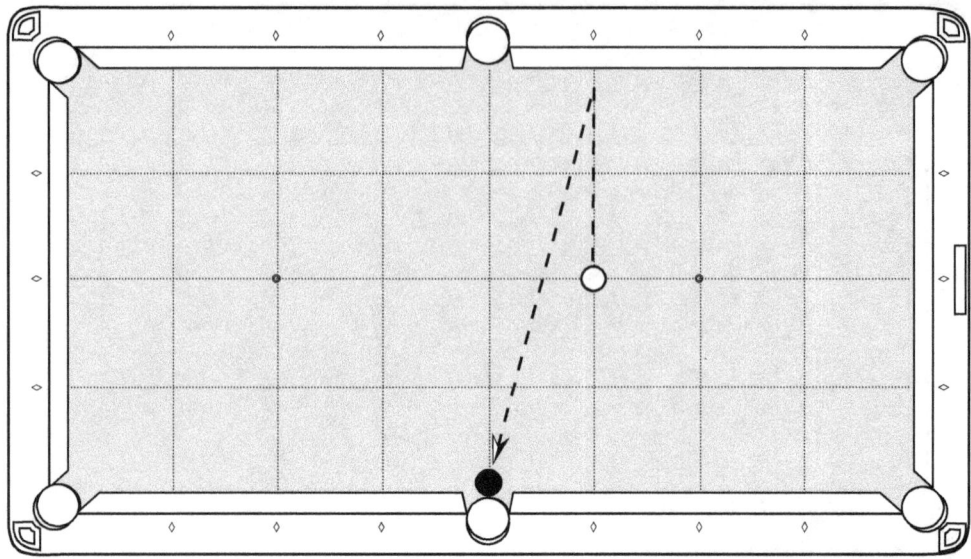

Notes:

This kick can be used in many different positions on the table. It gives a standard and dependable angle of 11 to 12 degrees (a spread of one diamond across the width of the table.) Cueing is different from normal kicking with the cue tip centered on the horizontal axis of the CB with 1/2 tip of english. Aim perpendicular into the rail and let the english do the work.

(Kick 11 is slightly changed from the first three printings of the PB. See note on page 57.)

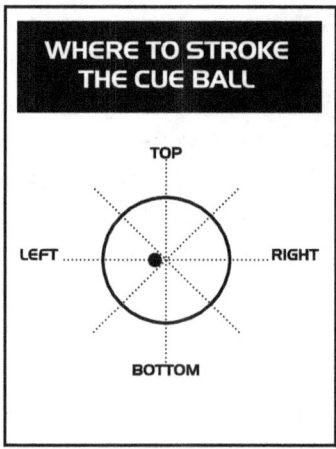

DATE	RATIO	%	DATE	RATIO	%	DATE	RATIO	%

EXECUTION

The Pro Book Reference Series — Kick #12

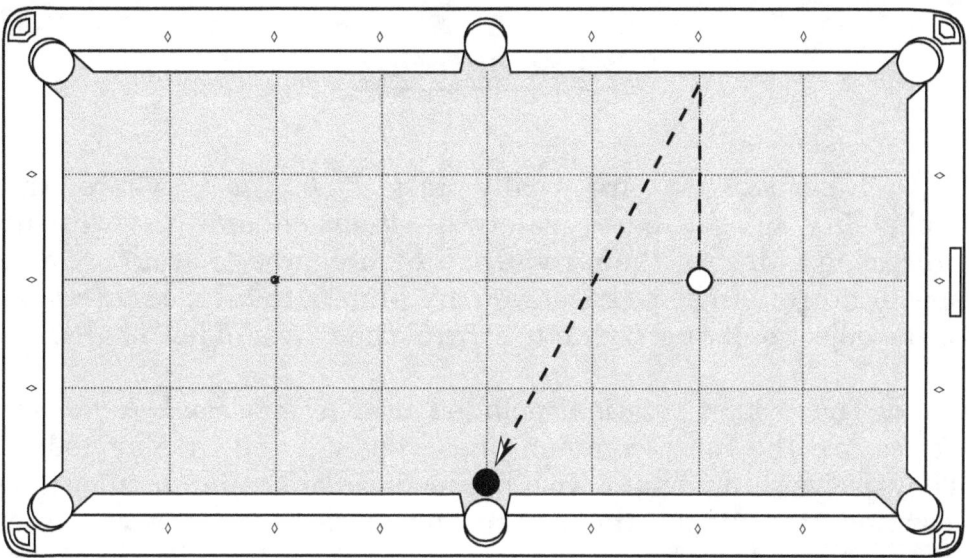

Notes:

This kick can also be used in many different places on the table. It gives a dependable angle of approximately 23 degrees (a spread of two diamonds across the width of the table.) Cue on the horizontal axis about one cue tip from the edge of the CB. This shot can be used with Kick 11 to extrapolate a whole range of english kicks.

(Kick 12 is slightly changed from the first three printings of the PB. See note on page 57.)

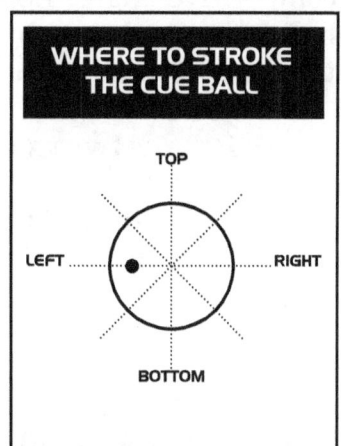

DATE	RATIO	%	DATE	RATIO	%	DATE	RATIO	%

Kick Safeties

Kick safeties are really just *kick shots* where the probability of getting a safety is high enough to warrant practicing. Most of them require a high degree of accuracy and speed control. In some cases you are aiming to hit a *certain part* of the object ball *and* trying to control the travel of both balls.

The 8 kick safeties included in *The Pro Book Reference Series* are the most common ones you will see in play today. They are very important with the modern *ball in hand* rules and learning to judge them can dramatically improve your competitive edge. Learn them by name first, by rail and object ball hit second, and by speed last. Other principles which apply to kick safeties are:

1. Always choose rail targets.

2. In a 1/2 ball hit without english, the cue ball and object ball travel the same distance.

3. Low-reverse english limits the travel of a cue ball striking an object ball after a cushion.

4. Natural english promotes cue ball travel.

5. Avoid making the ball and *hooking yourself*.

6. Avoid scratching.

7. Control is easiest when you can hit the object ball *fully* and *close to the rail*.

EXECUTION

The Pro Book Reference Series — Kick Safety #1

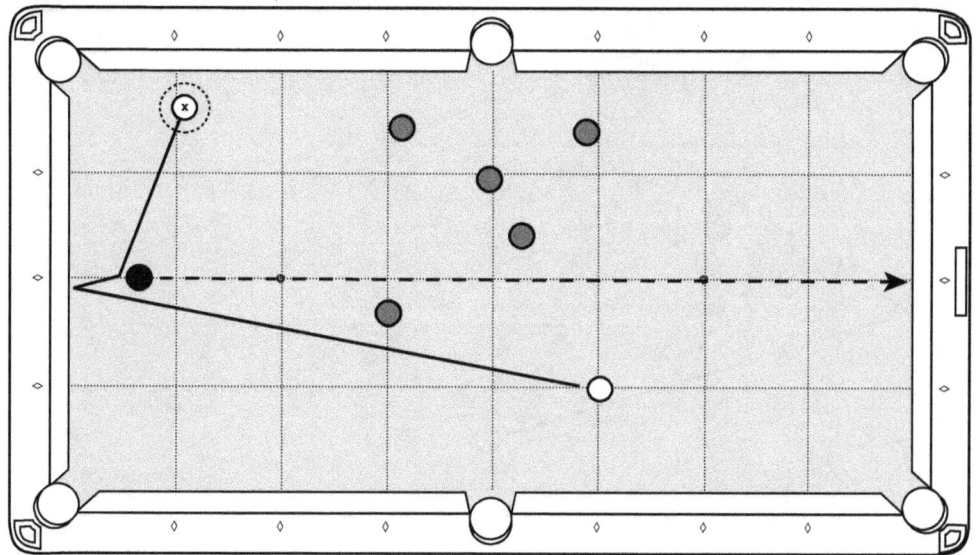

Notes:

This is a tricky kick safety that comes up frequently. You have to spin the CB to hit the OB correctly and it is wise to practice hitting it both dead center and slightly left and right. The objective is to take advantage of any blocking balls and leave the OB just off the short rail. Use just enough speed to get a ball to the rail and make sure you do not accidently make the OB and end up hooking yourself!

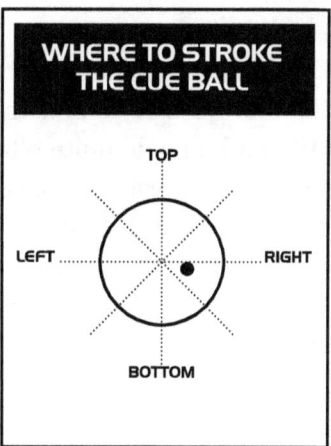

DATE	RATIO	%	DATE	RATIO	%	DATE	RATIO	%

THE PRO BOOK

The Pro Book Reference Series — Kick Safety #2

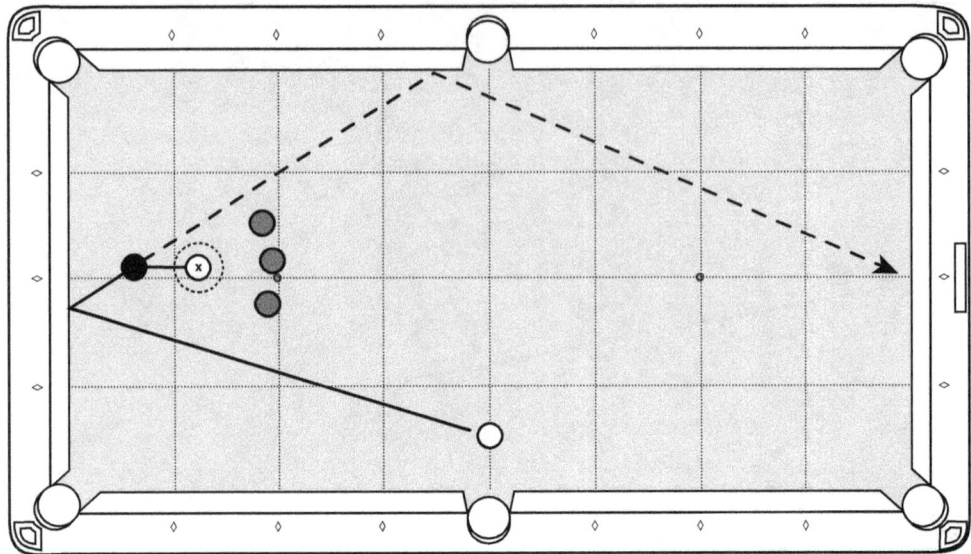

Notes:

Precision speed and follow are crucial to stop the CB and keep it behind the blocking balls. The OB can be made quite often in the side pocket, so go for it if you will have position on the next ball and avoid it if you will not. When you can make this shot consistently, practice slightly different variations between the CB, the OB, and the blocking balls.

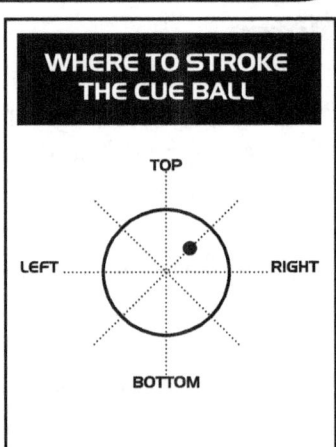

DATE	RATIO	%	DATE	RATIO	%	DATE	RATIO	%

EXECUTION

The Pro Book Reference Series — Kick Safety #3

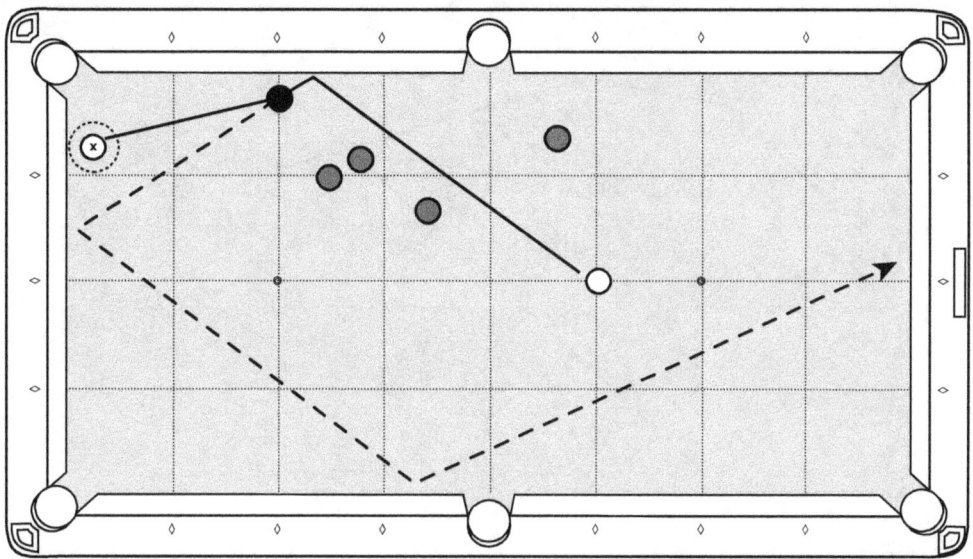

Notes:

This is a dependable kick safety once you get the feel for it. It is best to use low reverse, as that has a tendency to kill the CB. High reverse will float the CB down towards the corner pocket. The tendency with this shot is to undercut it by hitting the rail too far away from the OB. Also, make sure you hit it firmly enough, the OB has a long way to go.

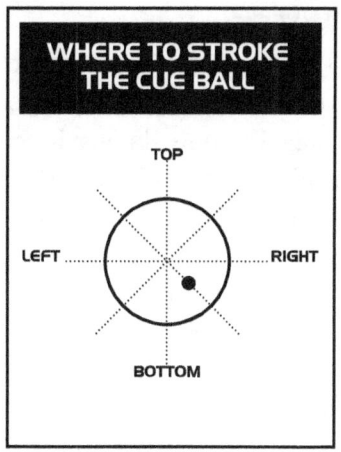

DATE	RATIO	%	DATE	RATIO	%	DATE	RATIO	%

THE PRO BOOK

The Pro Book Reference Series — Kick Safety #4

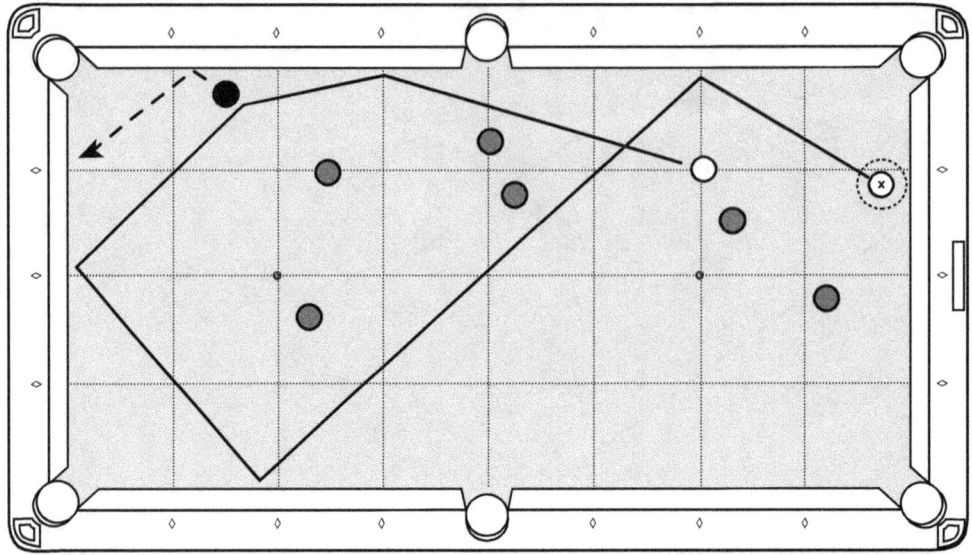

Notes:

This is a versatile and effective kick safety. Once you know where to aim, you can make it all day long. The only danger is scratching in the corner and you can eliminate that with good speed control. Also, if you put more english on the CB, you will bring it back to the long rail short of the pocket. If you use less english, you will hit the short rail first. The first option is best if the blocking balls allow it.

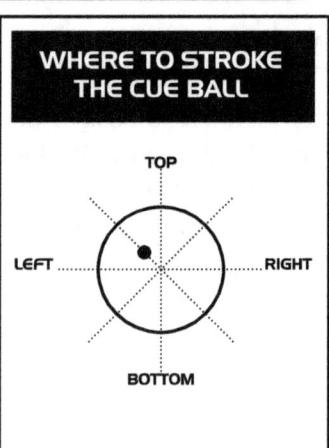

WHERE TO STROKE THE CUE BALL

DATE	RATIO	%	DATE	RATIO	%	DATE	RATIO	%

EXECUTION

The Pro Book Reference Series — Kick Safety #5

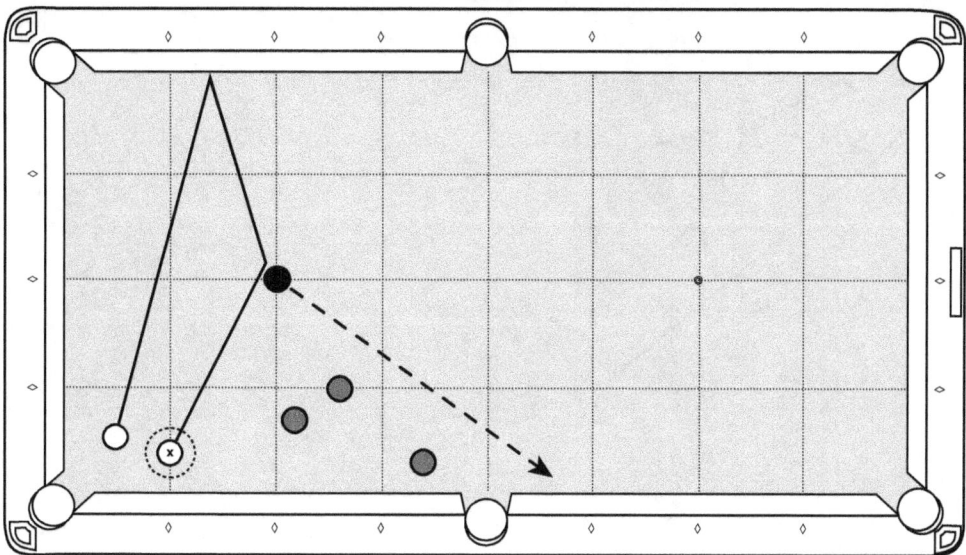

Notes:

This short table kick safety is seen quite often in modern competition. It is very sensitive to aim and speed and is tougher than it looks. Any left or right english will only confuse your judgement, so strike the CB on the vertical axis. Decide which ball is going to hit a rail before you shoot. If you will have a shot on the next ball, you might even want to try to make the OB in the side.

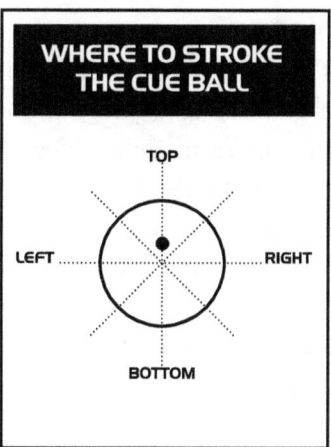

DATE	RATIO	%	DATE	RATIO	%	DATE	RATIO	%

THE PRO BOOK

The Pro Book Reference Series — Kick Safety #6

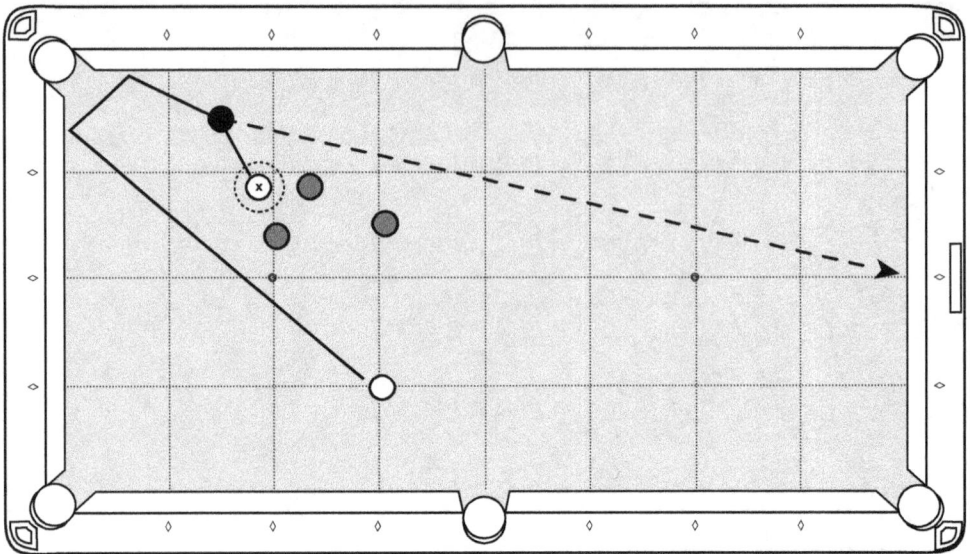

Notes:

This kick safety is difficult to hit accurately, but it gets easier to judge after you practice it a few times. Your first objective is to stroke firm enough to get the OB to the short rail. Your second objective is to hide the CB behind the blocking balls. The OB will sometimes go into the corner, so make sure to consider that in your strategic thinking.

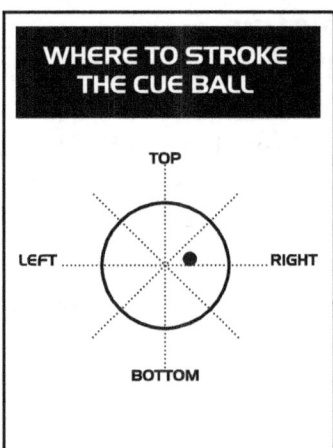

DATE	RATIO	%	DATE	RATIO	%	DATE	RATIO	%

EXECUTION

The Pro Book Reference Series — Kick Safety #7

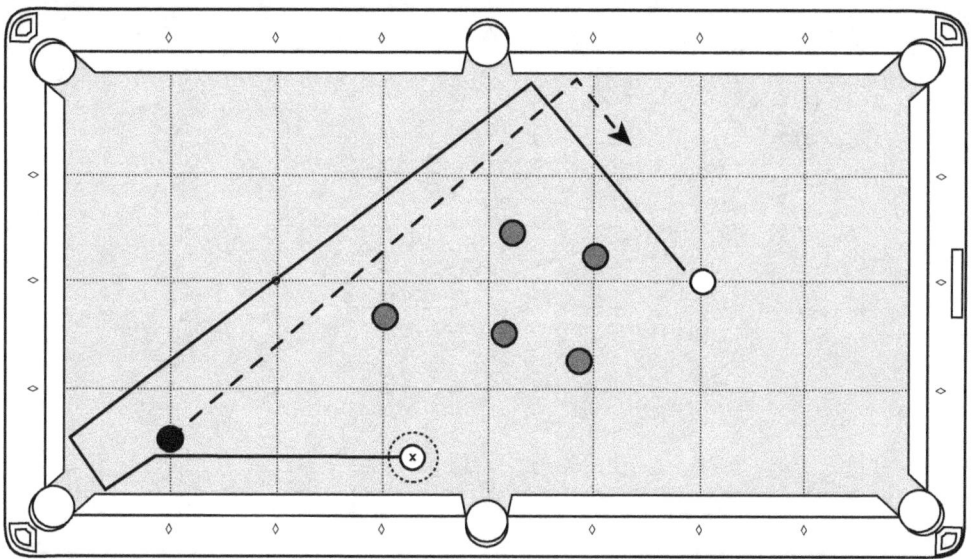

Notes:

Sometimes it is better to kick a ball away from a pocket than to try to kick it in. In this layout the hooking ball is too far to jump and other blocking balls are in good position for the safety. The key to this shot is to pick your second rail target and work your way backwards to the first. Make sure to avoid scratching in the corner and do not make the OB in the side unless you have a shot on the next ball.

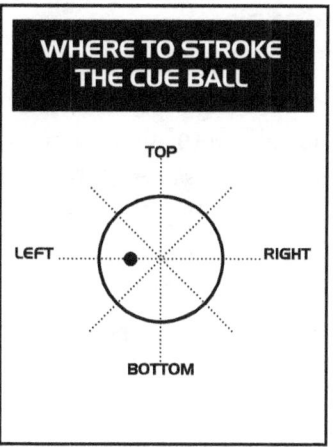

WHERE TO STROKE THE CUE BALL

DATE	RATIO	%	DATE	RATIO	%	DATE	RATIO	%

THE PRO BOOK

The Pro Book Reference Series — Kick Safety #8

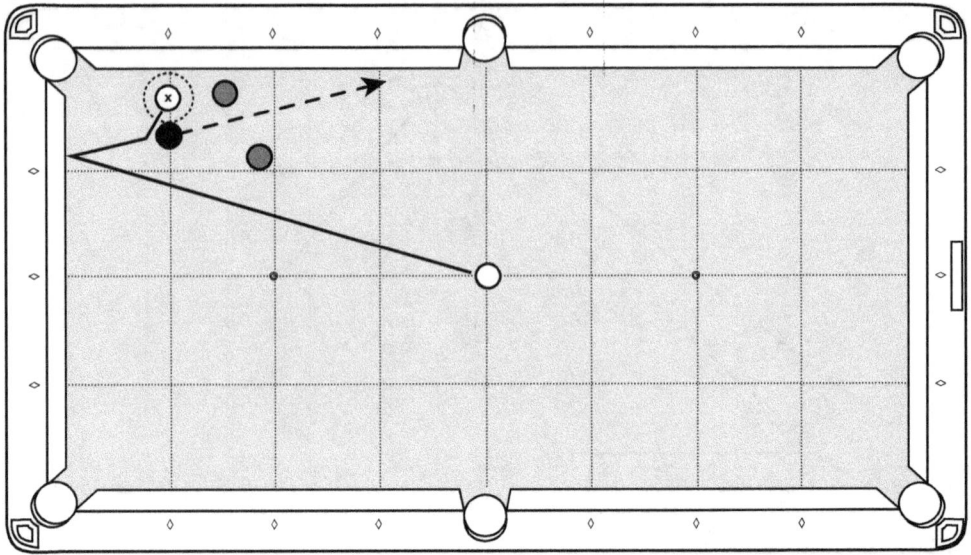

Notes:

This soft hit kick safety is very sensitive to aim and speed so a center ball hit on the CB will help simplify your judgement. The key is to pick your first rail target with precision, because a little bit of error will give a dramatically different result. Make sure the CB hits the second rail and hides behind the blocking balls. Practice this shot in several different positions.

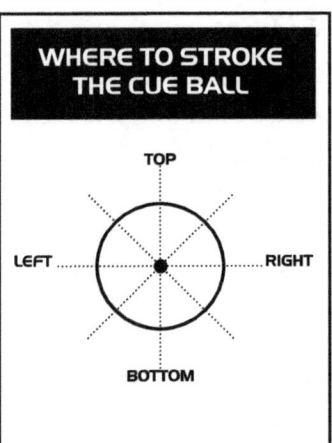

DATE	RATIO	%	DATE	RATIO	%	DATE	RATIO	%

EXECUTION

Banks

There are 8 standard banks in *The Pro Book Reference Series*. They are the most important strategic banks in pool, not counting specialty games like One Pocket and Banks. Most of them are shots where it is difficult to judge the aim by using the diamonds or by *seeing* the angle.

Some bank shots come up in game situations where your opponent will have to shoot the same ball if you miss. In these situations, speed of the shot and cue ball position are sometimes more important objectives than making the bank. With many bank shots it is to your advantage to aim either slightly short or long to control the position of the object ball if you should miss. Train accordingly.

Learn to recognize each shot by name first. Then learn to make it and keep the cue ball on the position line. Adjusting speed control is the last thing to learn. Other principles which apply to banks are:

1. **Inside english or a firmer hit will *shorten* the rebound angle.**

2. **Outside english or a lighter hit will *lengthen* the rebound angle.**

3. **A good aiming technique when the object ball is close to the rail is to concentrate on the relationship between the edge of the cue tip and the edge of the object ball.**

THE PRO BOOK

The Pro Book Reference Series — Bank #1

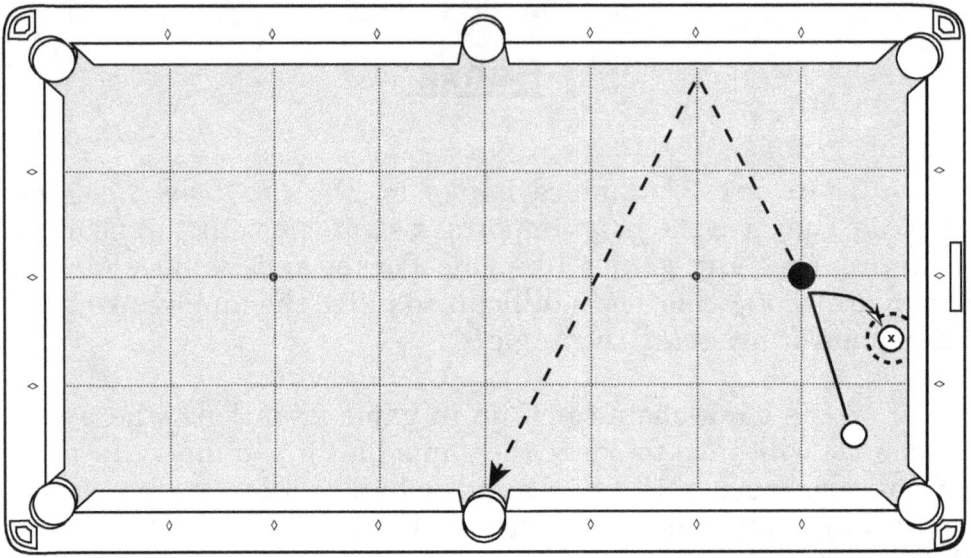

Notes:

This is a very important bank shot in both Eight Ball and Nine Ball because the game ball has a tendency to remain in the vicinity of the rack. Your first objective is to leave the CB on the short rail and a tough shot on the OB in case you miss the bank. Your second objective is to make the bank shot! Practice this shot in slightly different positions with those priorities in mind.

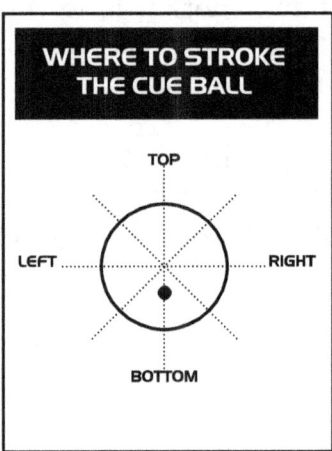

DATE	RATIO	%	DATE	RATIO	%	DATE	RATIO	%

EXECUTION

The Pro Book Reference Series — Bank #2

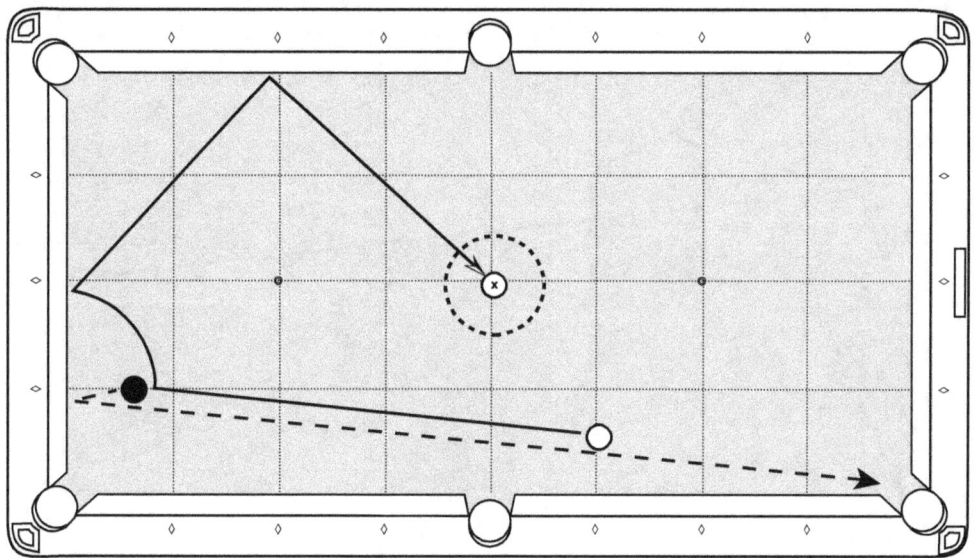

Notes:

This bank is easy after you get the feel for it and bringing the CB to the center of the table is a natural result of proper speed. Aim to error short, as this reduces your liability if you miss. A good way to judge the hit on this and most *close to the rail banks* is to gage the distance off the rail and then aim by concentrating on the relationship between the edges of the cue tip and the edges of the OB.

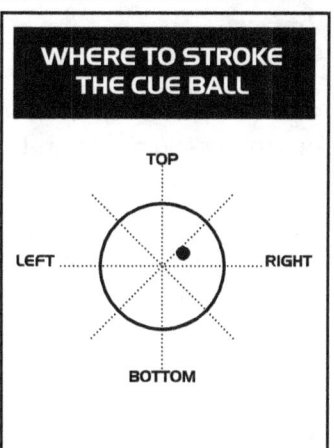

DATE	RATIO	%	DATE	RATIO	%	DATE	RATIO	%

THE PRO BOOK

The Pro Book Reference Series — Bank #3

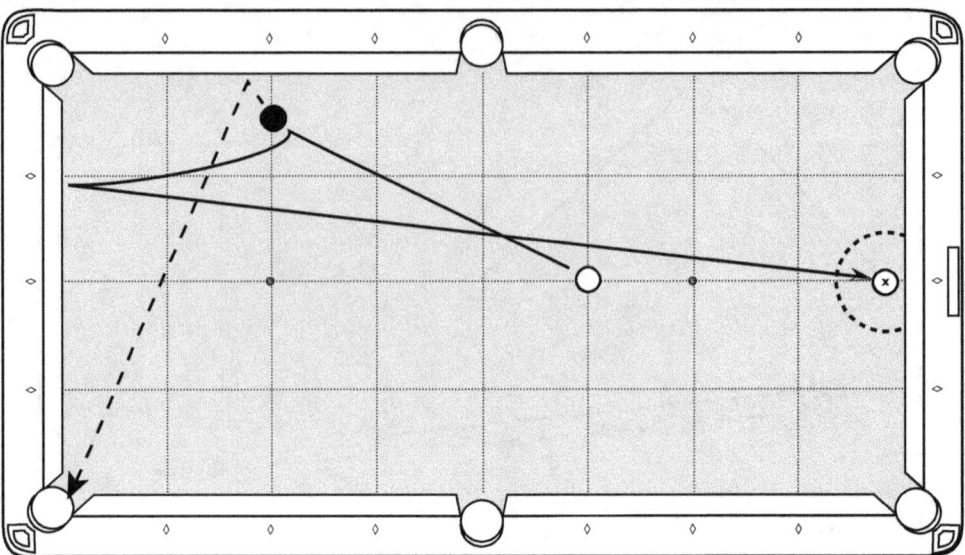

Notes:

This bank comes up in game situations where you need to get the CB down table for position. Aim to the short side and you will get Safety 9 if you miss. Aim the *entire* cue tip just inside the edge of the OB. Practice slightly different layouts to learn when the balls will kiss. If you move the OB out to 1/2 of a diamond from the rail, the aim is the center of the cue tip to the edge of the OB.

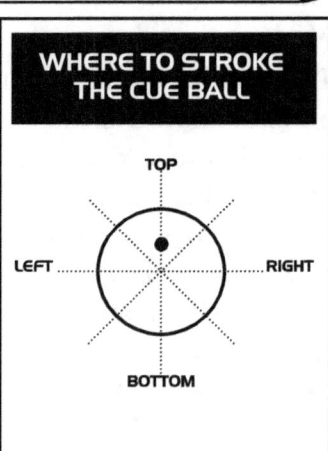

DATE	RATIO	%	DATE	RATIO	%	DATE	RATIO	%

EXECUTION

The Pro Book Reference Series — Bank #4

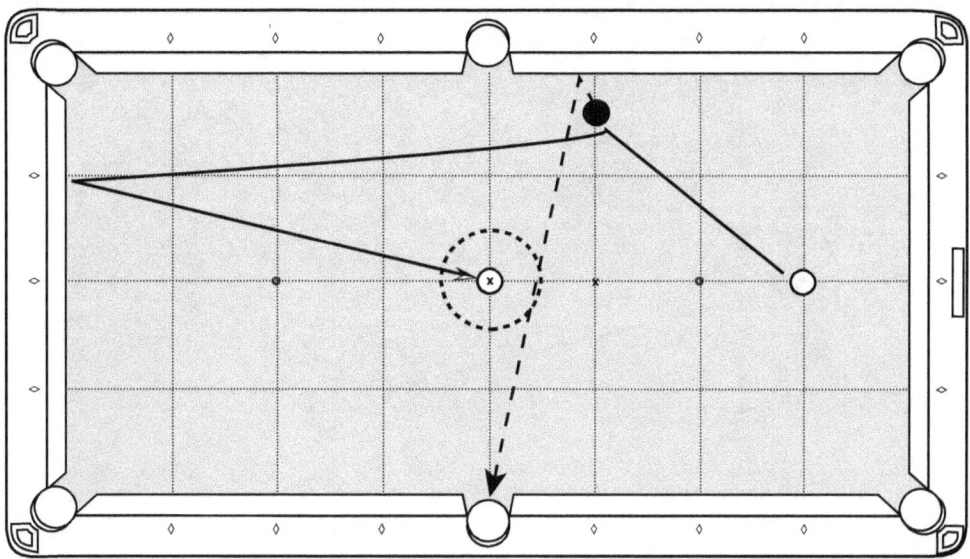

Notes:

The aim on this bank is with the center of the cue tip aligned with the edge of the OB. The key to CB placement is to pick a first rail target before you shoot. Also, be aware that if you hit the OB with a rolling CB, you are likely to scratch in the corner. When you can make this bank consistently, move the positions of the balls slightly to discover the limitations of the shot.

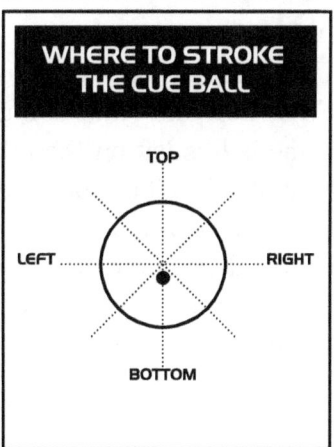

DATE	RATIO	%	DATE	RATIO	%	DATE	RATIO	%

THE PRO BOOK

The Pro Book Reference Series — Bank #5

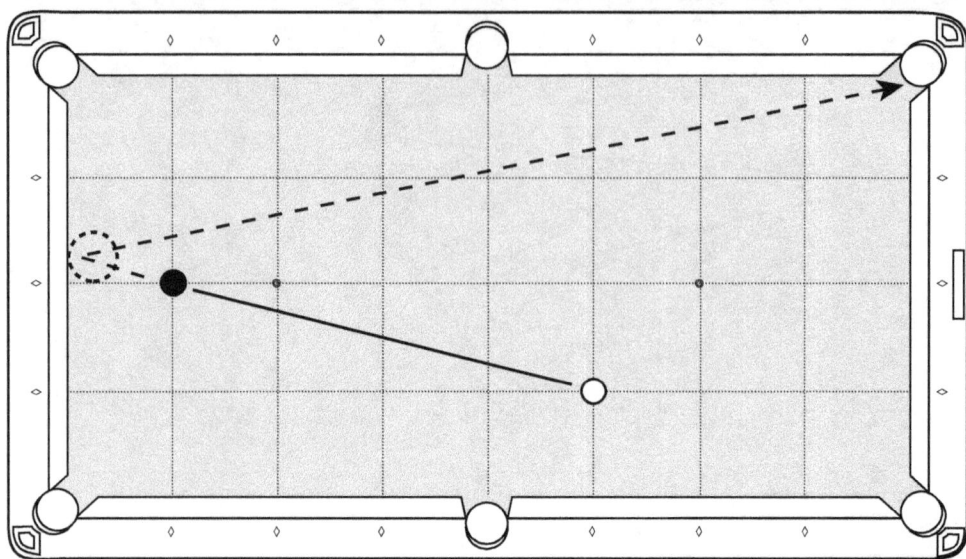

Notes:

This bank shot is a common sight at the end of Eight Ball and Nine Ball games when only the game ball is left on the table. The angle of this bank needs to be shortened and the proper way to do this is with a mixture of speed and english, not by altering the aim. Shoot to pocket the OB, but *float* the CB up to the rail to minimize your liability if you miss.

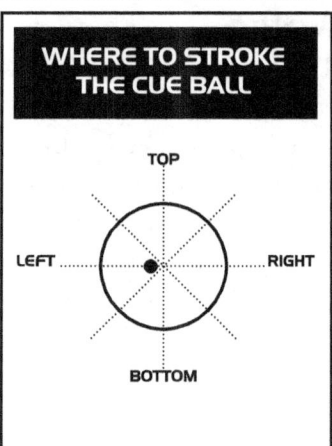

DATE	RATIO	%	DATE	RATIO	%	DATE	RATIO	%

EXECUTION

The Pro Book Reference Series — Bank #6

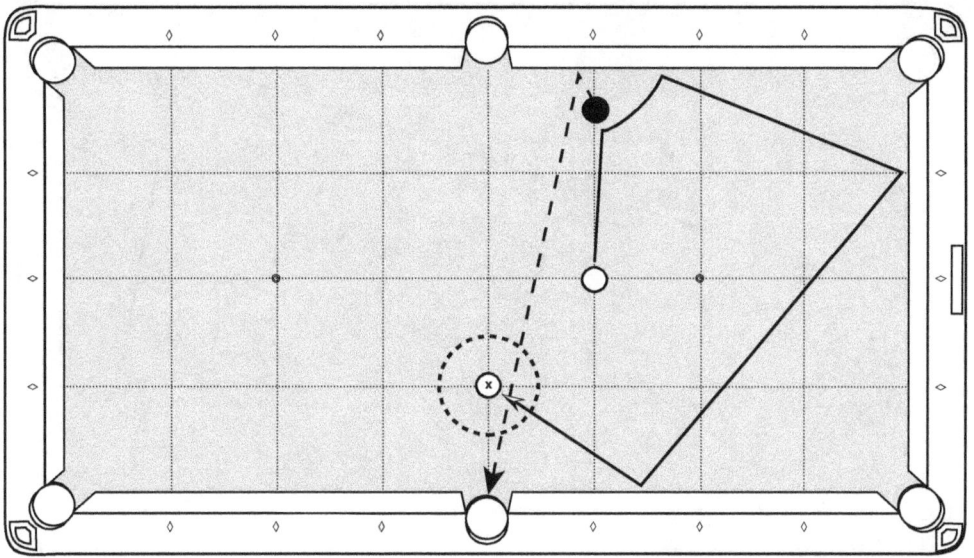

Notes:

This is a common bank shot that is so dependable that good players will often play position for it. A lot of follow or natural running english on the CB will not significantly alter its final destination point. It is best to hit this bank with a firm, authoritative stroke at center ball as the CB will pick up the necessary english from the collision with the OB. You can send the CB down table by adding speed.

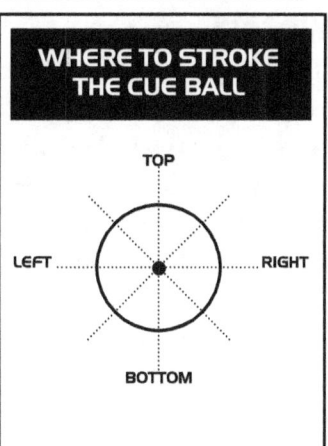

WHERE TO STROKE THE CUE BALL

DATE	RATIO	%	DATE	RATIO	%	DATE	RATIO	%

THE PRO BOOK

The Pro Book Reference Series — Bank #7

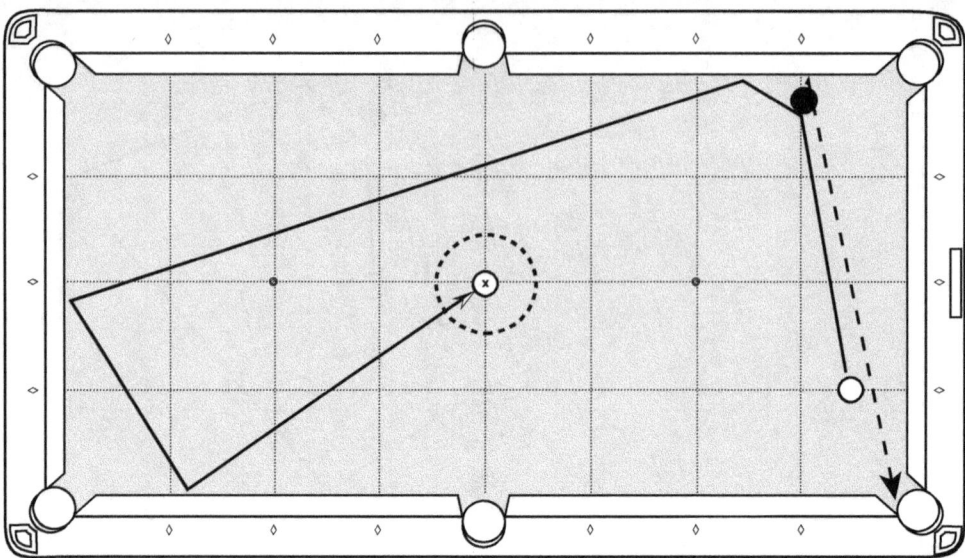

Notes:

This important bank shot is aimed with the center of the cue tip lined up with the outside edge of the the OB, a 1/2 ball hit. Stroke the CB at center ball and it will take a natural path to the middle of the table. The contact with the OB and the rails will supply the necessary english. Aim to error short and you are likely to be safe if you miss the bank.

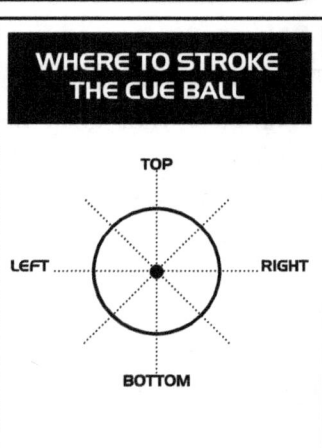

DATE	RATIO	%	DATE	RATIO	%	DATE	RATIO	%

EXECUTION

The Pro Book Reference Series — Bank #8

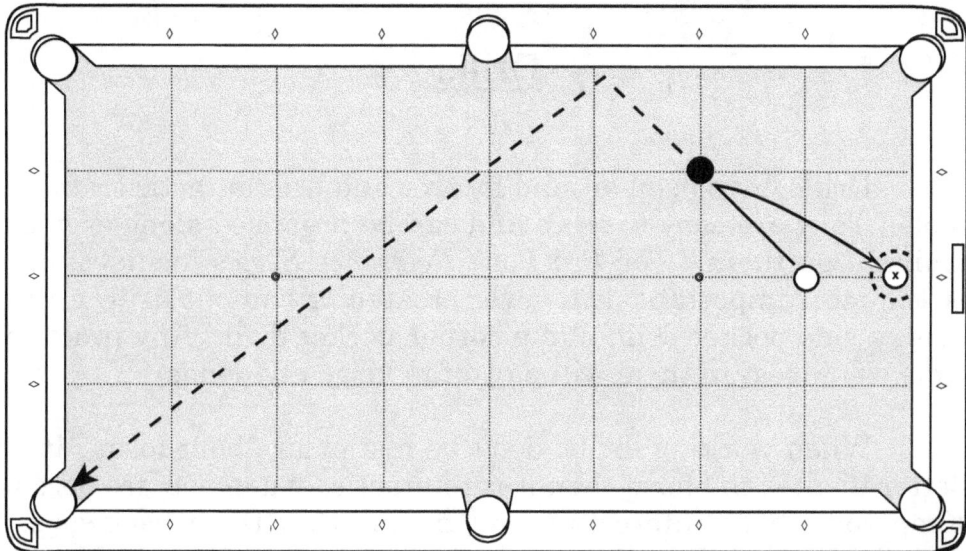

Notes:

This OB is possible cross-side, but the kiss is big and you leave a shot if you miss. The layout is the same as Shot 11b, which also may leave a shot if you miss. For game ball situations, the best option is often to bank the OB into the corner. A key objective is to draw the CB back with just enough speed to leave it touching the short rail. Aim is a full ball hit with english as shown.

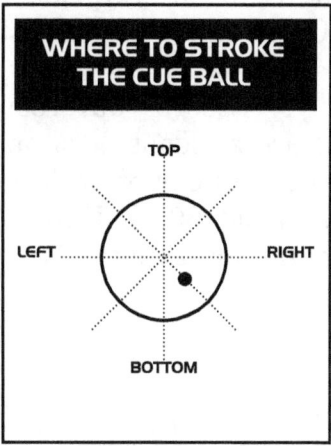

WHERE TO STROKE THE CUE BALL

DATE	RATIO	%	DATE	RATIO	%	DATE	RATIO	%

Drills

Drills have been around forever and are fantastic training tools. They are easy to score and can be practiced alone or with training partners. *The Pro Book Reference Series* includes four of the most important drills ever created, a run-out drill, a rail drill, a side pocket drill, and a corner pocket drill. Any practice time you invest in them will pay off in large dividends.

When working drills, don't be a stickler about form. It is better to alter the form then it is to practice when you are bored. Keep your drills interesting and fresh. Run them backwards; start in different locations; and add or subtract additional balls. Challenge yourself with result goals for each practice session.

Score your results and track your progress. If you can't score at least 60% on a drill, it is too difficult for you. Reduce the number of balls in the drill until you can consistently score at least 60%. Don't move to a more difficult version until you can score at least 75% on a consistent basis.

EXECUTION

The Pro Book Reference Series — Drill #1

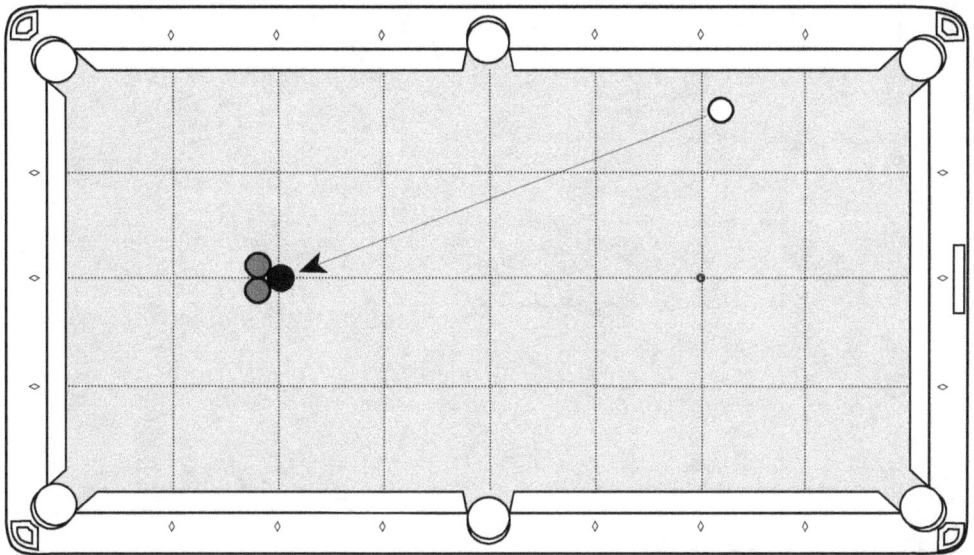

Notes:

This *pattern play drill* is great practice for run-out Eight Ball and Nine Ball. Rack three balls and shoot a normal break shot. Take ball in hand and run them out in sequence. *No tough shots or getting out of line allowed.* Shoot sets of 20 and when you can consistently run 15 out of 20, (75%), move to four balls, then five balls, then six balls, etc.

(Jerry Briesath, of The Pool School, first shared this very productive drill with the author.)

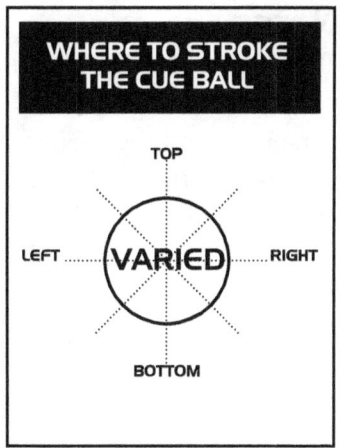

DATE	RATIO	%	DATE	RATIO	%	DATE	RATIO	%

THE PRO BOOK

The Pro Book Reference Series — Drill #2

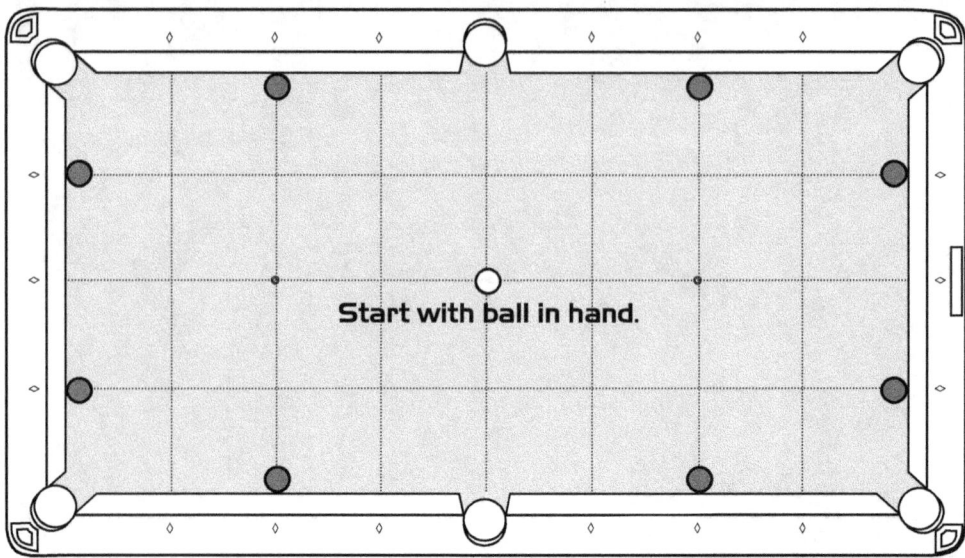

Start with ball in hand.

Notes:

This *rail drill* will strengthen your ability to tie patterns together and dramatically raise your run-out percentage. Set up eight random balls as shown. Start with the lowest numbered ball, take ball in hand, and run them out in sequence. When you miss, take ball in hand and move to the next shot. Shoot five sets and score yourself as a ratio of successful shots out of 40. 35 out of 40 is *very good*.

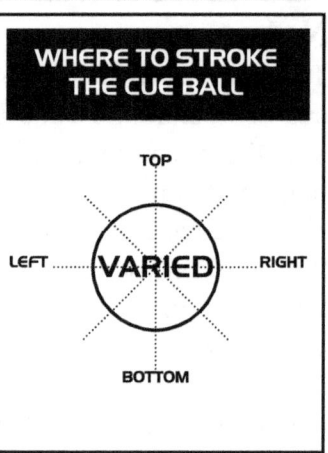

DATE	RATIO	%	DATE	RATIO	%	DATE	RATIO	%

EXECUTION

The Pro Book Reference Series — Drill #3

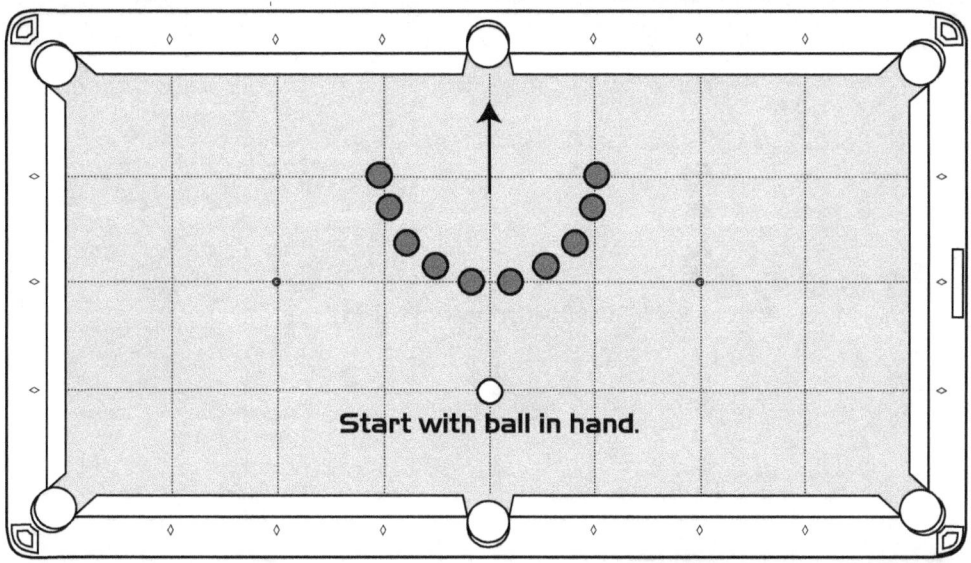

Start with ball in hand.

Notes:

Working this *side pocket drill* will develop your control of side pocket patterns and train your concentration. Start with ball in hand and shoot each one into the side pocket. Use whatever rails and english is necessary and avoid moving any of the remaining balls. Shoot at least three sets and score yourself. If it is too tough for you at first, set up fewer balls. When it gets too easy, start with more balls.

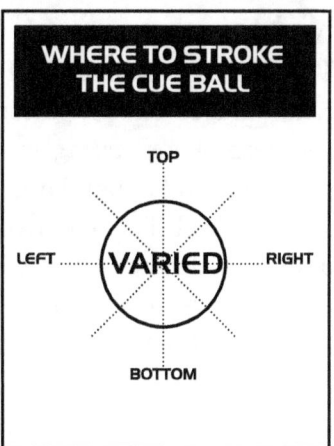

WHERE TO STROKE THE CUE BALL — VARIED (TOP, BOTTOM, LEFT, RIGHT)

DATE	RATIO	%	DATE	RATIO	%	DATE	RATIO	%

THE PRO BOOK

The Pro Book Reference Series — Drill #4

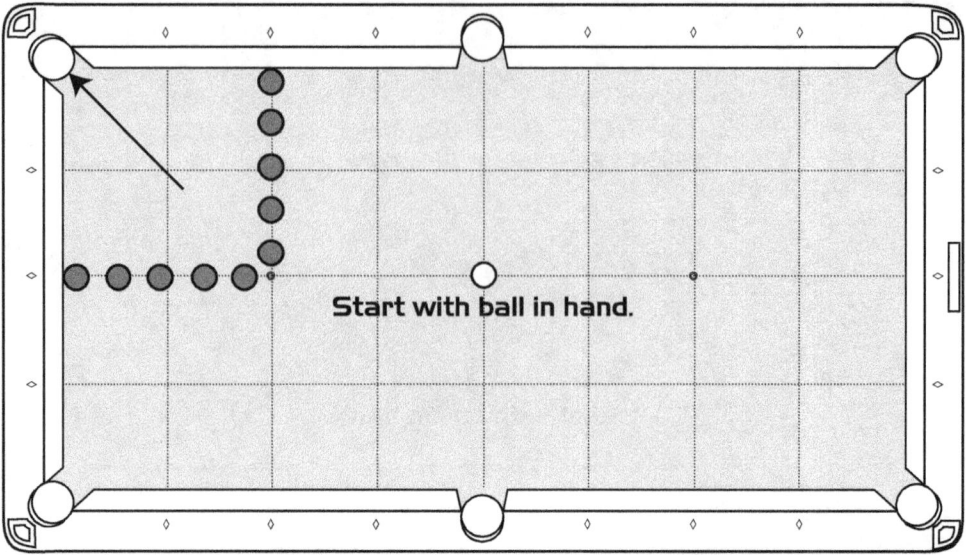

Notes:

This corner pocket drill will increase your command of corner patterns and really teach you respect for *getting on the right side of the ball.* Take ball in hand and start with the ball on the short rail. The objective is to shoot each ball, in order, into the corner without disturbing any of the others. If you miss, take ball in hand and move on to the next shot.

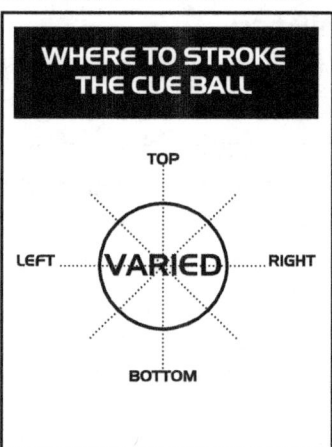

DATE	RATIO	%	DATE	RATIO	%	DATE	RATIO	%

Equipment

*"Things have their laws as well as men;
things refuse to be trifled with.*

—Ralph Waldo Emerson

The Truth About Equipment

Everybody wants to play with good *equipment*. They want to play their best and the best is easiest to produce with top-of-the-line equipment. From the perspective of a competitive event, however, the condition of the equipment is irrelevant. The only important thing is who has better command of the playing field.

If *your* personal equipment is dependable, you won't need to have your attention on it. It will be transparent for you. If *you* can quickly adapt to unknown tables and conditions, *you* can take an early lead.

Your personal equipment includes your cue, chalk, shapers, powder, and whatever else supports your game. This book assumes you have handled these items and will focus strictly on playing conditions. If you need help with selecting a cue, Mark Wilson wrote a fine article on that subject which is published in *The Blue Book of Cues.*

Playing Conditions

You will learn about table conditions faster if you practice on high quality and consistent equipment during your practice periods. This will allow you to establish a reference point from which to judge others. If you practice on different tables, you will eventually learn to adapt, but the process will take longer.

There are several parts of the playing field that need to be examined by an astute competitor. These are the *table bed,* the *cloth,* the *rails,* the *pockets,* and the *balls.* Another important variable to take into account is *humidity.*

Inspecting The Table Bed

The major thing you want to know about a strange table is where and how badly does it *roll.* A good way to discover this is to slow roll a ball from each corner pocket diagonally across the table to the opposite corner. Keep in mind that there is only one slate on a seven-foot table, but three separate ones on eight and nine-foot tables. You are looking for roll on each slate.

Roll each ball so that it has just enough force to reach the far corner. As it slows down, any table error will show up dramatically. You are checking the center slate and the far slate with each ball you roll. Observe where "down hill" is for each separate slate. Measure it and describe it to yourself in terms of a table length roll. For instance, *"1/2 ball roll toward the door,"* or *"1/4 ball roll toward the window, etc."* You can recheck any significant roll you find by slow rolling a ball across the width of the table right down the center of each slate.

EQUIPMENT

The other thing to know about a table bed is whether there are any holes, ledges, cracks, or bumps significant enough to affect play. You can find these by simple observation of stress points on the cloth, or by running your hand across the table bed. Ledges and cracks usually show up where the slates are joined together and it's not unusual to find one bad enough to turn a slow rolling ball 20 or 30 degrees. Humps are usually located in the same general vicinity and are usually pieces of seam filler that have worked their way out of the seams. Holes are much rarer and are usually close to the rails.

Assessing The Cloth

The most important thing to know about the cloth you are playing on is how *fast* it is. This is largely a function of the nap. The heavier the nap, the slower the cloth. Dirt, powder, and other foreign matter on the cloth will also slow it down. The best way to determine the speed of cloth is to shoot a few shots that involve significant cue ball travel. It is a judgment call on your part, and if you have been practicing on fast cloth like Simonis 860, it will be easier to judge and to adjust to slower cloth. It is easier to adjust down than it is to adjust up.

Fast cloth is slippery. The break is more important with fast cloth because the balls will move further. Also the action between balls, throw and skid, will be slightly more pronounced due to the lack of resistance from nap. The more developed your sense of touch, the more you will like playing on fast cloth.

There are a couple of other things to be aware of with cloth. Obviously any tears or holes in the cloth could spell disaster and need to be noted. Rail tracks, if well worn, are actually grooves in the fabric and these grooves will sometimes hold balls which are shot gently. This can sometimes be used in your favor. Also, on an unfamiliar table, you can tell by looking at the cloth where players who are familiar with it are breaking from. Just look for the marks made by the cue ball as it bounced its way to the rack.

THE PRO BOOK

Knowing the Rails

Rails can also be thought of in terms of *speed*. The more force absorbed by a rail when a ball strikes it, the slower the rails are considered and the less distance you will get on any particular shot. Even more important than speed, however, is the consistency of the rails. Do they play the same no matter where you hit them? Shoot a few multiple rail kick, bank, or position shots and look for dead spots.

Another important aspect about rails is whether they play long or short. Rails are fastened to the table bed with bolts and there is slop and manufacturer's tolerances to contend with. Rail position, in reality, always differs somewhat from what is considered *mathematically perfect*. Discover how the rails play by shooting a few kick shots. Kick #4 is excellent for this purpose. What you are looking for is how the balls come off the rails relative to the angle of approach. Do they come off wider or narrower than you are used to? You want to know exactly what the difference is and communicate it to yourself in terms of diamonds. For instance *"this table plays 1/2 diamond long."*

Understanding Pocket Strategy

Pockets are either *tight, normal,* or *loose*. You can tell by taking two object balls and measuring the width of a corner pocket at the mouth. If the two balls will not go in side by side, the table has very tight pockets. Normal pockets will accept two balls side by side with about 1/4" of clearance. Anything more than that designates a loose pocket. Other variables determining the *size* of a pocket are the cut of the jaws and the depth of the slate. Check all these variables because pocket size is a very important factor in considering strategic choices.

Loose Pockets:

1. Favor a shotmaker.

2. Favor more aggressive play.

EQUIPMENT

3. Make the break more effective.

4. Increase the chance of scratching if you *let the cue ball loose.*

5. Allow balls to be hit firmer.

6. Reduce the effectiveness of distance for defense.

7. Favor the long bank over playing safe.

Tight Pockets:

1. Favor more conservative play.

2. Reduce the effectiveness of the break.

3. Increase the effectiveness of distance for defense.

4. Penalize you for shooting hard.

5. Favor playing safe over the long bank.

Playing With Balls

There are several things to know about the *balls* you are using. Are they consistent in size? Are they consistent in weight? Are they clean, dirty, or sticky? All of these variables will affect play.

Size Consistency

Balls of the same *size* will rack consistently and the same hit on any ball will produce the same result. If you have noticeable size inconsistencies between two object balls the same

THE PRO BOOK

hit with the same cue ball will have different results. This is due to the spherical nature of the balls.

The main concern is between the cue ball and the object balls. The cue ball gets banged around with every shot, but object balls do not. Subsequently, over time, the cue ball will tend to get smaller than the object balls. If the cue ball is noticeably smaller than the object balls, that will influence the hit and aim of shots. You have to undercut slightly on cut shots.

The opposite happens if you play on tables requiring an oversize cue ball. Jack Koehler, in his book *The Science of Pocket Billiards,* has a whole chapter on playing with the oversize cue ball. If you are willing to play on such substandard equipment, make sure you know what you're doing.

Weight Consistency

Weight is related in part to size. Bigger balls normally weigh more. The most important inconsistencies to be aware of are once again between the cue ball and the object balls. If the cue ball is lighter than the object ball it will draw easier and farther, but will follow less easily. It will also tend to bounce off of the heavier object balls and exaggerate carom angles. A lighter cue ball is fun to play with for most players, because most players favor draw.

If the cue ball is heavier than the object balls, it will be harder to draw and easier to follow. It will want to plow right through the collision with an object ball and by so doing, reduce the natural carom angle. It will also tend to rebound at wider angles after hitting a rail. These effects can dramatically effect position outcomes.

Cleanliness

Clean balls play naturally, but dirty and sticky balls require adjustment. When balls are sticky, they tend to *stick together* more at impact. Many players refer to this as *skidding* and it is most noticeable on 1/2 to 3/4 ball hits. A slight overcut is often required to compensate.

EQUIPMENT

Another effect of sticky balls is an exaggeration of *throw*. English on the cue ball will transfer more spin to the object ball and frozen balls will throw the end ball more dramatically. Experiment with this during practice and you will be able to adapt more quickly during competition.

The Effect of Humidity

Wetness slows everything down and dryness speeds it up. When the humidity is high, tables play slower. Sitting moisture on the cloth slows balls down just like sitting water on a road slows cars down. You have to expend more force to get the same distance.

The dampness also makes things slippery. Balls pick up moisture and will not *cling* as dramatically. This can reduce throw. Balls can also plane and slide on the moisture after contact and this can widen, or skid, a shot. Results are not dependable when it is damp. Play with caution.

Set Ups & Sabotage

If you play challenge matches, it is always to your advantage to play on *your* table. It is normally considered a disadvantage to play on your opponent's table. He is used to his equipment and its peculiarities just like you are with yours. If you have to play on his table, make sure you have plenty of time to warm up and get used to it.

People have also been known to do things to diminish or increase the advantage of the home court and you need to protect yourself from that. There are quite a few stories floating around about players *fixing* the equipment. Certain players, as one story tells, used to come early to the Johnston City Hustler's Tournament in the 1960's and insert strategically placed straight pins into the lips of the rails. This made One Pocket banks very unpredictable except for those who knew where the pins were.

THE PRO BOOK

Another player sneaked into a private club room the day before a One Pocket match and moved the action table just a fraction of an inch. The next day, the home boy, who knew where the multiple rail aim spots were located on the walls, couldn't understand why his game was off. He lost $45,000.

The Power of Rules

Most people do not think of *the rules* as part of their *equipment*. At first examination, many would think that the rules should be in the *Mental Game* section. However, if you look closely, you will see that the rules are part of the *playing field*. If you look even closer, you will see that the rules are actually the very *foundation* of the playing field.

In pool, it is necessary to have a thorough knowledge of the rules. They make you sharp and able to recognize where the power is at any given moment. They tell you what your opponent is allowed or not allowed to do and what you can or cannot do. There are penalties for breaking the rules and you want to capitalize on that whenever possible. You demonstrate authority in the game by knowing the rules.

For instance, if you are distracted by an opponent who is walking around during your inning, you can say, with authority, "*take a chair!*" He *has* to take a seat in the player's chair because *the rules say he has to*. The rules provide a penalty if he refuses, up to and including forfeiture of the match. Knowledge of the rules gives you power to act instead of reacting. Remember, acting is associated with winning and reacting is associated with losing. Learn the rules, they are part of your physical game.

Conditioning

*"The race is not always to the swift,
nor the battle to the strong, but that's the way to bet."*

—Damon Runyun

If two players of equal skill, mental ability, and emotional maturity meet in competition, the outcome will be largely determined by the *physical condition* of the combatants. The contender who can best manage physical energy, when all other things are equal, is most likely win. There are three components that relate to conditioning.

1. **Exercise**

2. **Relaxation**

3. **Diet and Nutrition**

As in all other areas of training, the goal is to find out what works for you. There are thousands of books written on each of these areas and hundreds of people who profess to be experts. Explore whatever resources present themselves to you and use your common sense to determine what will maximize your own competitive performance. You are an individual, with unique physical attributes and unique requirements. It is your responsibility to seek out and discover what works best for you.

Exercise

The Needs and Benefits

Exercise is one of the most overlooked areas that affect competitive billiards. Pool is more physically demanding than most people think and many players have paid the price for being out of shape.

Your brain requires glucose and oxygen to maintain concentration. The muscles in your stroking arm require a consistent flow of blood and oxygen to work efficiently. Your eyes have needs which must be fulfilled if they are to perform flawlessly. On a physical level, you are a machine and only an efficient machine delivers an efficient effort.

The 1972 World Chess Championship between Bobby Fisher and Boris Spasky is a great example of this idea. In his pre-match strategy, Bobby knew that Boris tended to lose matches if they lasted longer than 9 or 10 hours. He studied photographs of previous competitions and saw that Boris slouched in his chair. The longer the match, the worse he slouched.

Bobby knew that the human brain feeds on glucose and oxygen and the less oxygen it gets, the slower it works. He knew that people tend to make dumb mistakes when their brains run low on oxygen.

Bobby trained extensively for the 1972 match, but not by sitting in front of a chess board. He ran, swam underwater laps, and engaged in other aerobic activities to build up the power of his lungs. He knew a peak performer needs a reservoir of physical energy to handle the mental and emotional stress of competition and he knew the key to energy was physical exercise. His understanding and training won him the World Championship.

CONDITIONING

You, as a competitive pool player, have the same needs as Bobby Fisher. You need to maximize your capacity to store and deliver glucose and oxygen to your brain and muscles. You need to exercise!

1. **It will increase your confidence.**

2. **It will improve your technique.**

3. **It will increase your power.**

4. **It will delay fatigue.**

5. **It will promote fast recovery.**

If you already have a physical training program and are using it, congratulations. If you don't have an organized program, start one today.

(Publisher's Note: You are advised to consult a physician before beginning any type of exercise program.)

Stretching

Stretching will wake up your muscles. It prepares the muscles for activity and opens the capillaries to allow the free flow of blood. It warms and limbers the muscles and assists you in preparing for exercise or competition. It is advised that you get a good resource book on stretches and train yourself to use them. A regular stretching program will maintain the flexibility of your body and favorably impact the consistency of muscular response, which every pool player should appreciate.

Stretch after sleeping or long periods of inactivity. Stretch before competition and even while you are sitting in the chair and your opponent is shooting. It will keep you flexible and ready to play your best when you get your chance. Stretch in the evening before you retire and you will sleep better, wake up loose, and be ready to go in the morning. Always stretch before and after heavy exercise.

THE PRO BOOK

Never stretch any muscle or limb in a vigorous or sudden manner. All stretching should be done easily and slowly after you have warmed up with light exercise. Think of it as pleasure, not as work. There are no goals to achieve and no better way to be than the way you are. You are simply taking care of your body. Be aware and make sure never to tear or overtax any muscle or ligament. Be especially gentle—you are a pool player and require exquisite and consistent muscular responses.

Aerobic and Anaerobic

Most experts agree that there are two basic types of exercise: *aerobic and anaerobic*. *Aerobic* is associated with cardiovascular fitness and jogging, lap swimming, and biking are examples. An athlete who trains heavily with aerobic exercise will develop the capacity to withstand a continuous, low intensity work load for a long period of time. In the body, the aerobic system is an energy system associated with the intake and delivery of oxygen.

Anaerobic exercise, on the other hand, increases the ability of the anaerobic energy system. In this system, the body derives the energy required for an activity from energy already stored in the muscles. The names for these energy sources are adenosine triphosphate (ATP) and phosphocreatine (PC), as well as glucose, which is broken down to lactic acid. An athlete who trains anerobically will increase the capacity of his anaerobic system to replenish itself over and over. Any exercise done for short, high intensity periods followed by short rest periods, is anerobic.

A Physical Training Program

An exercise program designed for a specific sport is called a *physical training program*. The first thing is to look at the demands of the sport and design a program to increase your ability to meet those demands.

CONDITIONING

At first examination, billiard performance seems to be an aerobic activity. It is low intensity and continues for long periods of time. Most pool players who exercise do so aerobically. Many are joggers, swimmers, and bike riders. Serious players are also known to practice for three of four hours at a time, continuously walking around the table, bending, and shooting. This appears to be a low level aerobic activity.

Let's look at it from a different perspective. Imagine you are in a match. First, you are up and at the table. A few minutes later, you are in the chair. Soon, you are back at the table. While at the table, you walk, stop, walk again, stop, bend over and stroke a few times, then stand back up. You move to the next shot, line up, bend down, stroke, shoot, and stand back up. From the perspective of your body, the physical demand is on and off, on and off, on and off, on and off. If we just look at your stroking arm, we will see that the demand for energy by the muscles involved is low intensity, but it's not continuous. If you were strumming a guitar, that would be continuous. A p*hysical training program* which is *entirely aerobic* is inconsistent with the demands of billiard competition.

In Fox and Matthew's *Interval Training*, there is a chart showing the type of energy system required for forty different sports. Pool is not listed, but golf, which has similar physical demands, is listed as *100% anaerobic* and 0% aerobic. Volleyball and wrestling are also listed as *100% anaerobic*.

The best form of anaerobic exercise for pool players is Interval Training. With this type of training, you do a series of exercise sessions back to back. Each session is composed of a short period of high intensity exercise followed by a short rest. Recommended activities are rope jumping, sprints, power swims, calisthenics, and anything else you enjoy doing that can be maintained for a short period at high intensity loads. Time your activity period to be slightly longer than an average inning at the table. Three to five minutes is a good rule of thumb. Time your rest periods at about one-half the length of your activity periods. Keep your aerobic exercise for general tone and fitness, but stress the anaerobic for developing a strong physical foundation for your game.

What About Lifting Weights?

There is controversy, in billiard circles, about exercising with weights. Some people believe that the use of free weights and resistance machines will harm your performance. Others believe it will improve it.

The players who are opposed to it believe that exercising with weights strains the muscles and reduces their sensitivity. There are good players so convinced of this that they *never pick up anything heavier than a pool cue.*

On the other hand, there are accomplished players who believe that working out with weights builds overall strength, and this in turn, builds confidence. Some of these players follow a regular weight program, but most workout on a casual, infrequent basis. Sometimes, it they are playing poorly, they will work out for a few days as a corrective measure. One top player works out with a hand grip for hand strength and a barbell for arm strength, but only for his stroking arm!

It will probably not hurt your game if you work out with weights intelligently. Be aware that weight training can tear tissue and effect muscle sensitivity. In fact, if you do short repetitions with *heavy* weight, you are actually training to build muscle and the first step in building muscle mass requires the tearing of muscle fibers. If, however, you do a conditioning workout, which is longer repetitions of *light* weight, your pool game will most likely benefit.

Any weight work or muscle stress right before a performance, however, is not a good idea. Make sure there is enough time between exercise and competitive performance for your muscles to fully recover.

CONDITIONING

Relaxation

Relaxation has physical, mental, and emotional components. On the strictly physical plane, relaxation is biochemical. Your level of physical relaxation is determined by the types and quantities of hormones and chemicals released into your brain and bloodstream.

When you are faced with a stress situation, hundreds of thousands of years of biological evolution begin immediately to prepare you to flee or fight. At this time, however, you may want to play your best pool instead! You need a high level of concentration and smooth physical motion, and that comes best from a relaxed body.

Your goal as a sports competitor is to learn to override the evolutionary response to stress. You want the relaxation level of your body to be a response to inner direction, not from outside events. You want to control your physical state.

The Importance of Breathing

You can live for weeks without food and days without water, but you will only last about five minutes without breathing. It is the first thing you do when you come into the world and the last thing you do when you leave. The next breath you pull is not happening in the past or in the future, but in the present moment—*right now*.

This truth has made the study and use of breath a major facet in most of the great disciplines of history. Great sages, warriors, and athletes of the past have recognized the importance of breathing and went to great lengths to learn to control it. If you can control your breathing, you can control stress. If you can control stress, you can control the flow of life itself.

In competition, the way you breath will directly effect your performance. Breathing that is short, shallow, and irregular will give an irregular performance. It is estimated that 1/4 of each breath you take goes directly into the central nervous system and a great portion of this goes right into the brain. The better you can store and process oxygen, the better you can play.

Choking is directly related to the fight or flight syndrome. When you miss a shot within your skill capacity in a pressure situation, you have surrendered to the effect of stress. If you look back on this moment, you will see that your breathing was not even, peaceful, and relaxed.

Breathing Exercises

Build up your capacity and control of breath and you will be a *better performer*. You will fare better under stressful situations and play with greater consistency. You can do this by learning the basic breathing principles and by the regular practice of breathing exercises.

Basic Breathing Principles

1. **Breathe from your belly to utilize the blood that pools in the lower lungs due to gravity. Belly breathers perform better.**

2. **The key to breathing is the exhale because muscle tension drops when you exhale. The longer the exhale, the more pronounced the relaxation.**

Breathing Exercise #1

Do this exercise for five minutes a day, everyday for two weeks. Find a place that is quiet and where you will not be disturbed. Sit comfortably, but upright. Place your feet flat on the floor and rest your hands on your thighs. Follow the steps.

CONDITIONING

Step #1: Close your eyes and listen to your breathing. Breathe in through your nose and out through your mouth. Don't try to force how you are breathing, just accept what is natural.

Step #2: After a couple of moments, consciously breathe in through your nose and into your belly at a slow count of four—1...2...3...4. Let your belly expand naturally. Breathe in fully without forcing.

Step #3: Hold the breath (no more than a count of two) and then exhale through your mouth at a count of six—1...2...3...4...5...6. Make a slight sound as you exhale and listen to this sound.

Step #4: After about ten repetitions, stop counting and just breathe naturally. Keep listening to the sound of your breath.

Step #5: After a moment or two, return to Step #2 and do another set. Continue throughout your session.

Breathing Exercise #2

This exercise is similar to #1 and begins the same way. You can do this one with your eyes open. This exercise pushes oxygen into your bloodstream and muscles. During the breath holding period you may feel the urge to stretch or yawn. Go ahead and do so, but continue the breathing count.

Step #1: Breathe in through your nose and out through your mouth. Don't try to force how you are breathing, just accept whatever is natural.

Step #2: After a couple of moments, consciously breathe in through your nose and into your belly at a slow count of four—1...2...3...4. Let your belly expand naturally. Breathe in fully without forcing.

Step #3: Hold the breath as you continue to count from five to sixteen— 5... 6... 7... 8... 9... 10... 11... 12... 13... 14... 15...16. Exhale through your mouth for an additional count of eight—17... 18... 19... 20... 21... 22...23...24. Listen to your breathing.

Step #4: After about ten repetitions, stop counting and just breath naturally. Keep listening to the sound of your breath.

Step #5: After a moment or two, return to Step #2 and do another set. Continue throughout your session.

Relaxation Recognition

The second way to gain mastery over the fight or flight syndrome is to increase your level of recognition. Learn to detect unwanted tension in your body and you can learn to control it. Recognize when you are relaxed and when you are not. Practice relaxation so you can duplicate it whenever you want, even under pressure.

The deeper your understanding of how tension shows up in your body, the more control you will have over it. The more clearly you recognize your own state of relaxation, the easier it will be for you to reproduce it. The following exercises can help tremendously if you do them on a regular basis.

Relaxation Exercises

There are two basic types of relaxation exercises. The first type requires tensing individual groups of muscles, holding the tension for a while, and then releasing it. The second type of exercise works by going through groups of muscles and focusing your attention on different sensations such as weight and warmth.

CONDITIONING

Relaxation Exercise #1

This is a short tension-release exercise you can use just about anywhere, including during competition.

Step #1: Take a couple of deep belly breaths. In through your nose at a count of four, hold for a count of two, and exhale through your mouth for a count of six. Listen to your breath.

Step #2: On the next intake, hunch your shoulders upward with tension. Feel the tension all the way down to your hands. Clench your hands.

Step #3: Hold the breath, and the tension, for a full count of twelve. Then expel the breath through your mouth as you release the tension. Unclench your hands and drop your shoulders.

Step #4: Repeat as necessary. (Breathe from your belly.)

Relaxation Exercise #2

This is also a tension-release exercise, but of longer duration. Do this where you will be undisturbed for at least fifteen minutes. Loosen your clothes, lie flat on your back with your legs slightly apart and your arms by your side. Shake your limbs gently to relax them and roll your head back and forth for a few seconds. Then let your entire body go limp.

Step #1: Raise your **left leg** up about 8 inches with the toes pointed back at you. Hold this position until the muscles begin to tremble. Say to yourself — *Relax...*Stop flexing and let the leg drop. Rest for about 10 seconds and focus on the tension draining out of your leg. Repeat: *My leg is completely relaxed... my leg feels warm and relaxed, etc.* Repeat the step one time.

THE PRO BOOK

Step #2: Do Step #1 with your **right leg**.

Step #3: Tighten your **buttocks and thighs** as much as possible. Hold it as long as you can. Say—*Relax*...and release the tension. Pause for 10 seconds and focus on the tension draining away. Talk to yourself. Repeat.

Step #4: Do the same procedure for your **stomach.**

Step #5: Arch your spine, tightening all along your **back and neck**. Finish by saying *Relax*... Repeat.

Step #6: Raise your arms straight up in the air and flex the muscles in your **arms and shoulders**. Hunch your shoulders tightly. Hold as long as you can and then—*Relax*... Rest for 10 seconds and focus on the tension draining away. Repeat.

Step #7: Tighten your **jaw** muscles and clamp down with your back teeth. Say— *Relax*...and release the tension. Repeat.

Step #8: Do the same process with your **face.**

Step #9: Roll your **eyes** to the left, to center, to right, and back to center. Repeat again. Rub your hands together to warm them and say —*Relax*... Let your eyes close. Put your hands over your eyes and feel the warmth. Focus on the tension draining away and say —*My eyes are completely relaxed, etc.*

Step #10: Do the procedure with your **whole body**. Hold the tension as long as you can and then say— *Relax*... and let the tension go. Lie there for as long as ten minutes. Talk to yourself: *I am completely relaxed...this is how I feel when I am relaxed, etc.*

CONDITIONING

Relaxation Exercise #3

Start this exercise sitting in a chair with your feet flat on the floor and your hands resting on your thighs. Close your eyes and do the first three steps of Breathing Exercise #1.

Step #1: Focus your attention on your right arm and say to yourself — *My arm is feeling warm and heavy... Very warm and very heavy.* Continue until your arm actually feels warm and heavy. Then do the same with your left arm and end with—*My arms feel warm and heavy ... heavy as lead...etc.*

Step #2: Then do the same with your right leg, then your left leg, then both legs. End with— *My arms and legs feel heavy and warm...very heavy and very warm, etc.* Do not move to the next step until you actually have these feelings.

Step #3: Take a deep breath and focus on your chest area. Say— *My chest feels warm and pleasant.* Continue this focus until you have the sensation.

Step #4: Focus on your heartbeat. Say — *My heartbeat is calm and steady.* Continue until it is.

Step #5: Move your focus to your stomach. Say— *My stomach feels warm and soft...very warm and soft.*

Step #6: Focus on your face and drop your jaw. Relax all the muscles in you face and say — *My face is completely and totally relaxed.* Feel the weight of your skin and muscles as they relax.

Step #7: Focus on your whole body. Say— *I am completely and totally relaxed... This is how I feel when I am completely and totally relaxed...I am relaxed.*

Diet & Nutrition

Diet refers to the foods you eat and when and how you eat them. *Nutrition* refers to the makeup of the foods you eat and how it relates to your specific nutritional needs. The cause and effect relationship between diet, nutrition, and good health is well established and accepted. The condition of your body and your bodily processes, which includes your brain, is determined in large part by what and how you eat.

Nutrition and Performance

The idea that what you eat impacts your competitive performance is no longer questioned. Every serious and well financed athlete in professional sports has a nutritional plan and most likely a trained nutritional coach. Robert Haas was coaching Martina Navratilova and a dozen other world-class athletes as early as 1982. His book "*Eat to Win: The Sports Nutrition Bible,*" sold in excess of 2 million copies by 1989. There are also many other books available on sports nutrition.

It is safe to assume that if you are playing serious pool, you are competing with people who are managing their nutritional plan with the intention of beating you. Don't you think it's time for you to take control of yours? Eating right will help you manage energy. It will stabilize moodiness and significantly improve concentration.

(Publisher's Note: The author is not a *clinical nutritionist*. You are advised to seek the assistance of a health professional to develop your nutritional plan.)

Are you an Athlete?

Who you consider yourself to be will determine, in part, who you will become. Different people represent pool in different ways. Some players consider it a sport, think of

CONDITIONING

themselves as athletes, and train accordingly. Others consider pool a game and themselves as game players. Gamblers see it as a wager and ball bangers see it as a pastime.

Ewa Mataya, one of the top women pros, thrilled thousands when she was on Dave Letterman's show. While the two of them were at the pool table, Dave assumed the demeanor of a loud-mouthed buffoon and called for "a couple of beers over here." "I don't drink, Dave," Ewa said quietly, "I'm an athlete."

According to the experts, playing billiards will burn about 235 calories per hour for the average 154-pound man with an average *Basic Metabolism Rate*. For comparison, the same man playing basketball will burn about 560 calories per hour. Washing and shaving will knock out about 150 calories and reading a book about 105. The closest sport to pool is gymnastics. An average 154-pound man doing gymnastics will burn 257 calories per hour. See—you are engaged in a sport!

How does all this relate to diet and nutrition? Simple. If you consider yourself an athlete, train accordingly.

A Competitor's Diet

A key concept to understand about *diet* is that *different people* have *different needs*. It is your responsibility to manage your diet and to be continually looking for feedback and the opportunity to improve. A good place to start is to look at the goals of a high-performance competitor's diet. They are to:

1. **increase energy.**
2. **build strength and power.**
3. **enhance general health.**
4. **improve general functioning.**
5. **stimulate mental concentration.**

THE PRO BOOK

The Basic Building Blocks

The *basic building blocks* of any diet are *carbohydrates, fats,* and *proteins*. The average American diet is way to high in fats and simple carbohydrates. The daily calorie intake for peak performance seeking competitors should be made up of:

1. **60 to 80 % complex carbohydrates** (starches)

2. **5 to 10 % simple carbohydrates** (sweets)

3. **10 to 15 % protein** (animal and vegetable)

4. **5 to 20 % fat** (animal and vegetable)

Carbohydrates

Carbohydrates are the primary source of energy for bodily functions and muscular exertion. Your body easily burns carbohydrates to fuel your nervous and muscular systems. Compared to burning proteins and fats, there is very little waste and toxic by-products. Your digestive system converts all sugars and starches to glucose, also called *blood sugar*. Some of this is converted to glycogen and stored inside muscle cells, but most of the needs of your brain and working muscles are supplied by this blood-borne glucose. If there is any glucose left over after a period of about two or three hours after eating, it is converted to stored energy.

Important: The *complex carbohydrates* found in whole grains, nuts, vegetables, and some fruits become sugar at a *slow and stable* rate, yielding energy over a prolonged period of time.

Simple carbohydrates, on the other hand, become blood glucose very rapidly. If you eat a snack loaded with sugar and processed white flour, you will experience an initial rush of energy as your blood sugar soars. Unfortunately, it will soon plummet in equally dramatic fashion and you will be left feeling dizzy, fatigued, and nervous.

CONDITIONING

Keep your fuel supply steady, consistent, and sufficient to maintain a consistent performance. Shun the simple carbohydrates for what a pool player's body really needs—complex carbohydrates—wholes grains, fruits, raw and steamed vegetables, legumes, nuts and seeds, and pasta.

Proteins

Protein is the primary structural material for your body, but it is a poor source for immediate energy. Your body can burn proteins for fuel, but doing so yields toxic by-products that inhibit performance. Proteins also require more water to digest. If you have a lot of protein sitting in your stomach, water will be pulled away from other body parts including the muscles. This inhibits peak muscular performance.

The best diet for maximum achievement will be high in complex carbohydrates. However, protein *has* a connection with one of the most important brain chemicals, so always temper your carbohydrate intake with a little protein.

Fats

According to the experts, *fat* should only make up 10 to 15 percent of your total calories. Fat deficiency is practically unheard of in the United States. If you are eating anything remotely resembling the average American diet, you are getting way too much fat. Unfortunately, it is the fat in foods that provides the taste and textures we enjoy.

There are two major types of fats—unsaturated and saturated. The unsaturated fats are the nutritionally desirable and are necessary for normal growth and healthy blood and tissue. You can recognize these fats because they are liquid at room temperature. They come primarily from vegetable, nut, and seed sources. Some common examples are oil from olives, safflower, corn, sunflowers, and soy.

The other main type of fatty acid, the unsaturated, is derived mainly from animal sources. You can easily recognize it because it hardens at room temperature. Some common examples are lard and butter. They metabolize slowly and are associated with clogged arteries and heart disease.

Putting It Together

An ideal daily diet for a serious player *in training* could fall within the following guidelines adapted from Robert Haas' sport specific diet for golfers:

1. **Up to one cup of a high-fiber, low-fat, whole grain cereal with low-fat milk and fruit.**

2. **Up to 2 additional fruits.**

3. **Up to 6 oz. of juice and 1 oz. of dried fruit.**

4. **Up to 2 potatoes, 1 cup of brown rice, and 1 cup of pasta.**

5. **All the raw and steamed vegetables you want.**

6. **Up to 2 slices of whole grain bread and 2 whole grain pancakes.**

7. **A maximum of 1 low-fat, sugar-free dessert.**

8. **Up to 1 cup of low-fat milk, 1/2 cup of cottage cheese or yogurt, and 1 oz. of low-fat cheese.**

9. **Up to 5 oz. of meats.**

10. **Up to 1 cup of legumes.**

11. **Up to 1 oz. of nuts and seeds.**

12. **Up to 1 teaspoon of fats and oil.**

CONDITIONING

The Pre-Game Meal

The last meal you eat before a competitive event can send you off with a powerful boost of energy and a clear mind, or it can cut you off at the knees. The *pre-game meal* is an important aspect of competitive billiards.

The athlete who had a great performance in the morning, celebrated at lunch with a steak and fries, and bombed in the afternoon, is a common story. A meal heavy in fat requires a lot of time and effort to digest. When you add the stress of competition to the mix, it can take as long as eight hours. That's a lot of energy tied up for a long time. This is the same energy you want to focus on your pool game

Plan your pre-game meal around everyday foods that you like and associate with winning, and follow the following guidelines.

1. Eat lightly at least two hours before.

2. Eat foods that are easy to digest: non-greasy and non-spicy.

3. Limit your intake of simple carbohydrates.

4. Stick with complex carbohydrates (pasta, nuts, bread, grains, fruits, and vegetables.)

5. Avoid milk products for 24 hours preceding.

6. Go light on protein for 12 hours preceding.

7. Restrict your salt intake.

8. No alcohol within 12 hours.

THE PRO BOOK

Special Needs for Pool Players

As a sport, pool requires *finesse and accuracy* more than speed and strength. It demands extraordinary neuromuscular coordination and you will win or lose based on how well you can produce it. Under the stress of competition, a pool player's blood sugar needs to be stabilized. It is important to have carbohydrates available to you during play. Apples, bananas, and whole wheat bagels are excellent sources of portable complex carbohydrates. Snack on one of these at the <u>*first*</u> sign of fatigue or loss of concentration.

The brain chemicals that maximize concentration and brain-muscle communication must be in optimum supply. Some vital nutrients to research and keep your eye on are phenylalanine, tyrosine, choline, and B vitamins. If you take a combination free form amino acid capsule and a multiple vitamin and mineral tablet high in the B complex vitamins, you are probably doing all right. Because you may often be in smoky environments, make sure to get enough vitamin C.

Taking Supplements

There are hundreds of different *nutritional supplements* available and millions of people are taking them. There are new discoveries and promising possibilities being developed almost every day. The manufacture and distribution of supplements has become big business.

<u>Vitamins and Minerals</u>

Even the biochemists and the nutritionists don't know all the precise mechanisms by which minerals and vitamins work. Most agree, however, that nutritional supplements are usually necessary for high performance functioning.

As a high performance athlete, you should be taking a well-balanced vitamin and mineral package on a daily basis. This can be accomplished with a single combination product, but

CONDITIONING

stay away from the drug store, mass market stuff. Find the health food store in your neighborhood and do a little research.

Whatever program you initiate will show results over time. Don't expect immediate results. The real value in supplements comes from taking them on a daily basis over a period of months and years.

Performance Boosters

There are things available, not normally considered either foods or supplements, that can enhance your performance. Many have been known by witch doctors, shamans, and herbal doctors for centuries. The most common is right in your kitchen.

Caffeine

Caffeine has been *proven* to stimulate your central nervous system, mobilize the proper hormones for performance, improve muscle contraction, and improve your ability to utilize energy. The most effective dose may vary from person to person, but a rule of thumb is one to two cups of coffee about an hour before competition. The half-life of coffee is about 2 to 2 1/2 hours. That's how long it takes your body to eliminate enough to make its effect negligible.

Caffeine has *no nutritional value* and it can raise stomach acid levels about 400 percent, so don't use it if you have an ulcer. Don't take it if you are allergic to it, have adverse effects, or simply don't like it. Don't take it with niacin. (There are many new studies about caffeine use – please check with your doctor.)

Eleutherococcus

Eleutherococcus (also called Siberian ginseng) is derived from the Aaliaceae family of shrubs and is related to ginseng. It has been used extensively by athletes in the Soviet Union.

It appears that EC has the ability to relieve the effects of stress on the body. It appears to favorably impact endurance, reflexes, and concentration, particularly in long *endurance* type activities. For pool players, EC may improve stamina, motivation, coordination, and concentration.

The active compounds in EC and ginseng are called glycosides. The glycosides in ginseng are similar to the chemical structures in steroid compounds, which probably accounts for the toxic effects noted with the ingestion of large amounts of ginseng. The glycosides in EC appear to be far less toxic than the ones in other ginsengs.

Glycosides are active compounds that are able to stimulate the brain without the negative side effects of such drugs as amphetamines. It is believed that they produce a restorative effect by stimulating the secretion of stress-altering chemicals.

Chinese Herbs

There are three Chinese herbs that may be of interest to pool players. They are named Ma Huang, Fo-ti-tieng, and Radix Astregulus. They are reputed to increase competitive performance, but were originally used in meditation to increase attention and mental clarity. They can be found combined in a capsule form called Chi Power. The manufacturers claim it will brighten mental awareness and stimulate physical processes without the nervousness associated with caffeine.

Ma Huang contains several active ingredients, one which provides the basis for synthetic ephedrine. This herb stimulates the cerebral cortex and increases the heart rate. It opens up the bronchi and eases breathing. *Overuse of Ma Huang has recently been linked to cardiac problems.* **Fo-ti-tieng** is believed to have rejuvenating properties. It is reputed to enhance memory, decrease fatigue, and calm nerves. **Radix Astregulus** is favored in China as an overall tonic. It is said to increase energy and aid tissue regeneration.

CONDITIONING

Others

Ginkgo biloba is an herb than improves cerebral oxygenation, and therefore brain function and memory. **Coenzyme Q**$_{10}$ is a vitamin-like substance that also increases cerebral oxygen. Both are available commercially.

(Publisher's Note: You are advised to consult a physician before using any supplements or performance boosters)

The Most Powerful Nutrient of All

The most important nutrient for good health and peak performance is also the most common. It is *water*. Your body is made up of over 60 % water. Almost all of your bodily processes require the use of water. The more active you are, the more water you need.

The *thirst mechanism*, which lets you know when you require water, is not effective for peak performance. When you recognize *thirst*, it too late because you are *already* dehydrated. If you properly manage your need for water, you will never experience thirst because you will always have enough water in your system.

Experts recommend that you consume 6 to 8 cups of water every day. They also suggest that you drink a glass or two about 15 minutes before a competition. Drink water throughout the competition.

There are substances that sometimes appear to enhance performance, but in reality, and in the long term, will destroy the person using them. These substances are commonly referred to as *drugs and alcohol*.

THE PRO BOOK

Drugs

Here's the bottom line. If you are using drugs because you think they enhance your billiard performance, you are acting foolishly. Whatever impact you think you are receiving could be exceeded *on the natural* if you invest the proper effort developing yourself and your talents. The price you will pay for using cocaine, amphetamines, and other drugs, will be costly.

Alcohol

Booze has knocked quite a few players down. You can go into any *player's room* around the country and see washed-out old-timers who *used to play great*.

The United States government will not let you pilot an aircraft if you have had <u>any</u> alcohol in the last 8 hours. Most states will put you in jail if you attempt to drive a motor vehicle after about 5 or 6 drinks. Even a small amount of alcohol, three 12-ounce bottles of beer, can damage athletic performance. It is especially noted for *impairing hand-eye coordination, accuracy,* and *balance*. It can also cause temporary changes in vision. Alcohol is not the right ingredient for an inspirational pool experience.

Most people will pay a heavy price if they let alcohol take over their lives. Don't be one of them. Look at alcoholic drinks as an occasional luxury and treat them with respect.

THE MENTAL GAME

THE PRO BOOK

Note Page

* What would a breakthrough in your *mental game* look like?

Mental Training

"Man is what he believes."

—Anton Chekhov

Your best pool game is shaped by your natural talent and training, but it is empowered or weakened by your *mental condition*. In competition, the player with the most powerful *thoughts and beliefs* has a great advantage. The player with the greatest ability to *concentrate and focus* will be the most formidable. The player with the deepest understanding of *momentum and strategy* will most often win.

The mental abilities of a champion and a novice are dramatically different. Like any other area of human endeavor, we start with unique gifts and weaknesses, and we all have the ability to improve. A serious player continually strives to:

1. **Upgrade his mental conversation.**

2. **Expand his mastery of focus.**

3. **Learn more about strategy.**

The Unstoppable You

You are unstoppable. You are the original *unstoppable you*. This is not a statement said to *pump you up*. It is the truth. You are unstoppable because *no one* can stop you. Nothing that your opponent or anyone else can say or do in a billiard competition gives them power over you. All your opponent can do is offer something you can use to stop yourself. Only *you* can stop yourself.

If your opponent helps you do this, make sure to express your gratitude. Thank him for making you aware of something that you can now handle. You see, a lot of what is going on with each of us is below our conscious awareness. Some of the things that show up in competition are things you didn't even know existed before they were right in your face. Competition is a growth discipline, and it forces you to face yourself. Make the commitment to never hide from that confrontation with drugs, alcohol, or any other smoke screen. Be willing to accept whatever shows up for you. If you have the proper attitude, you are never a loser. You are always a winner if each opportunity brings you closer to a properly directed goal.

Mental Conversation

It is easy to see yourself as a physical entity; all you have to do is look in a mirror. It is much more difficult to see who you are as a mental entity. Think about it for a moment. Who are you as a mental entity? Are you what you know? What you believe? What you hope for? What you think?

Some of the greatest philosophers of all time have come to the conclusion that each human being, as a mental entity, is an on-going conversation made up of *thoughts and beliefs*. Perhaps you remember the phrase *"you are what you think."* You are the person, at any single moment, who is defined by the mental

MENTAL TRAINING

conversation you are having. If you are in the player's chair talking to yourself about how great your opponent is and how you don't have a chance, that is who will get up to shoot when the opportunity presents itself. If you are in the chair having a mental conversation about running a couple of racks as soon as *he* misses, you are an altogether different person.

The mental conversation you are having at any specific time is the product of the current stimulus and all the previous mental conversation you have ever had. If you want to change how you perform in a particular situation, you have to alter the mental conversation you have about that situation both before and while you are in it. In other words, you have to *change yourself mentally*.

Most of the words and images we use to talk to ourselves are *just there*. We don't know where they came from. Many times, they are so common to our mental experience that we don't even notice their presence. They are just part of who we consider ourselves to be. At rare times we talk to ourselves with words and images that are chosen on purpose. We pick them and play them on our mental screens with the intention of producing a specific result.

Mastery begins by taking responsibility for the conversation within our minds. In psychological fields much of this conversation is identified as *scripts and tapes*. These are the patterns that worked their way into our psyches before we were aware enough and mature enough to pick and choose for ourselves. Much of the course of personal development is involved with weeding out scripts and tapes that inhibit and obstruct and substituting ones that serve and empower.

Your mental conversation is the train tracks and you are the train. If you know where the train tracks are going, then you know where the train is going. If you want to *change* where the train is going, you have to lay down new tracks made up of positive and empowering statements, or *affirmations*. You have to work *ahead* of the train and be prepared to handle the mental obstacles you will encounter.

Disappearing Mental Obstacles

One of the laws of the universe is that *two things cannot occupy the same space at the same time.* If you fill your mind with positive and empowering thoughts, you will force other, unwanted thoughts out. Be prepared to have thoughts and patterns inconsistent with your new affirmations rear their ugly heads in defiance. They are fighting for their lives in your psyche and will try to convince you that they, and not your powerful new thoughts, are true.

Be strong. What you put your attention on will expand. It is a creative action. Whatever statements show up in your mind inconsistent with your affirmations are <u>NOT TRUE</u>. They are only mental obstacles that need to be dealt with to get to where you want to go. Do not resist these old voices. This is one of the biggest traps to avoid, because what you resist will persist. Welcome the inconsistent voices that are already within you. Invite them to step forward and let themselves be known.

You disappear mental obstacles by acknowledging their presence. If something is already in your mind, it has a certain power, but that doesn't make it true. What is true is that it is *present* in your mind. You begin to claim that power back when you recognize its presence and tell the truth about it. Let's look at an example with a player named Bill:

Bill was a very good player. He liked the game, played in a lot of tournaments, and really wanted to win. Sometimes he would play very well. He would win matches from good players and sometimes even get in the money, but he never won.
"I can win," he'd say to himself and friends. "I can win, I know I can." But in competition, when he got into a position to win, it was like he hit a brick wall. He couldn't make it happen.
"How come you never win?" a friend asked one day.
The question reverberated inside Bill. He braced himself, rallied his energies, and replied. "I can win," he said. "I haven't won yet, but I will."
"You've been saying that for years," the friend retorted.

MENTAL TRAINING

"Don't worry about it," Bill said resolutely. "I can win."

The conversation stayed on Bill's mind for several days. It was a very uncomfortable period for him. In his mind, It seemed like something was trying to *get* him. It was all he could do to fight it off. Finally, he surrendered.

"I can't win," a voice in his mind said. Bill was greatly saddened. It seemed as if his dreams were being shattered. For several hours he was enmeshed in the emotion of that reality. The next day, he called his friend. "I have to tell you something," he said.

"What's that?".

Bill struggled—it was so hard to face, so painful to admit, so difficult to put into words.

"Tell me," his friend encouraged.

"I can't win," he said. In the moment of speaking, it felt as if a hand reached out and physically moved him backwards a foot and a half. A wave of emotion passed through him.

Over the next few hours, Bill underwent an amazing metamorphosis. He felt light and giddy. He was in a place he had never been before. He realized that he had stepped through *"I can't win,"* and was on the other side of it. He stopped in at the local pool emporium the next night and watched as the top players in town played and socialized. He was experiencing bodily sensations totally new to him. The fingers on one hand were buzzing with a pins and needles sensation and his belly was vibrating with unfamiliar energy. When he finally got to the table, he played beautifully.

Affirmations

The Power Of Affirmations

The power associated with *affirmations* comes from taking control of your mental domain. When you choose affirmations, you choose the words and images that will make up the content of your mental conversation. You are taking a stand about who you will be in the future.

THE PRO BOOK

When you shoot pool, your performance is shaped by the mental conversation you take into the game. It is also shaped by the words you speak and the thoughts you entertain while playing. That in turn shapes tomorrow's mental conversation.

A List Of The Best

Remember those contests they used to have on TV where someone wins a spree in a supermarket? They shoot a starter pistol and the contestant runs like hell through the aisles with a shopping cart. Anything they can get in three minutes is theirs!

That's the way to look at this section of the *Pro Book*. This is the best mental food for pool players that can be found. Run down the aisles with your mental shopping cart and grab whatever looks best to you. Get a pen and check each statement that grabs you. Pick at least 15 or 20. Good shopping!

I am a winner and I always play to win.

I am calm and relaxed.

My best game comes when I need it.

The right knowledge comes when I need it.

I am self-assured.

I am confident and sure.

I am relaxed and invincible.

I am relaxed and at ease.

I release my power with finesse and control.

My body responds with ease and confidence.

My stroke is smooth and rhythmic.

MENTAL TRAINING

I've got all it takes to win.

I am great, I am the best.

I play like a champion and I always play to win.

The more I practice, the better I play.

I maintain concentration throughout the game.

I always have the winner's edge.

I am a born winner.

I am filled with power and energy.

I release my power with confidence and control.

My ability is unlimited.

I play with finesse and power.

The more I play, the better I play.

I have perfect control and concentration.

Nothing distracts me from playing my best.

I am ready and prepared.

I have everything it takes to win.

I always play at my natural pace.

I expect good things to happen.

I shoot one shot at a time.

I deserve to play well.

I deserve to win.

THE PRO BOOK

I attract success.

It is natural for me to win.

I am a winner.

I am comfortable with winning.

I am free to perform.

I am relaxed and powerful.

I enjoy a tough match.

The tougher the match, the better I play.

I am poised and self-assured.

I commit myself fully to each shot.

I stay down until the shot is over.

I have perfect touch and balance.

I shoot with confidence, one shot at a time.

I always play my best.

I assume my stance with ease and confidence.

My aim is consistent and dependable.

My stance is stable and precise.

My eyes are relaxed and focused.

I focus *exclusively* on what I want.

My entire mind is committed to my shot.

My entire body is committed to my shot.

MENTAL TRAINING

My strokes are precise and unrestricted.

I accept the responsibilities of a winner.

I take care of my body and it takes care of me.

I know what I want and I plan to get it.

I train smart, I train hard, and I train to win.

I surrender to my natural rhythm.

The more I study, the better I play.

I deliver when the opportunity shows.

I am comfortable in competition.

I make decisions with confidence.

I am a fearless and powerful competitor.

I am perfect health, perfect health I am.

Using Affirmations

You will maximize the effectiveness of your affirmations if you tie each one to a specific mental image. Create images that have an emotional impact for you. Emotion is one of the most powerful tools for establishing affirmations firmly into your mental identity.

Affirmations will have a rhythmic quality and a fullness to them if you form them in a *mirror image*. This works especially well with affirmations that start with "*I am.*" For instance: the statement "*I am relaxed and powerful,*" is a great and useful affirmation, but it is even more powerful when mirror balanced as *"I am relaxed and powerful, relaxed and powerful I am."*

It is also valuable to put key affirmations into first, second, and third person voices. Make sure you create the proper mental image for each voice. Visualize people talking whose opinion you value. Some examples are:

1. ***"My stroke is smooth and rhythmic."*** (You are speaking to yourself.)

2. ***"Bill's stroke is smooth and rhythmic,"*** or ***"His stroke is smooth and rhythmic."*** (Others are speaking about you.)

3. ***"Your stroke is smooth and rhythmic."*** (Someone is speaking to you.)

There are several different ways to use affirmations. Some people write them down and read them every day when they rise and every night when they retire. You can tape a copy to your bathroom mirror so it is the first thing you see in the morning. You can fold a copy and carry it in your pool case for a burst of support when you're in the player's chair.

It is powerful training to read your affirmations out loud at regular intervals. It also works to write them over and over like teachers have children do to correct behavior. Repetition is the key to maximizing the value of affirmations. One of the easiest ways to accomplish this is to make an audio tape.

Making a Tape

An *audio tape* of your affirmations can serve two different purposes. You can structure one side for subliminal learning and one for pre-competition motivation.

MENTAL TRAINING

Subliminal Messages

Subliminal learning has been around for a long time. It is when you place messages just below the level a person can pick up with his conscious senses. A famous example is the movie theater that took film of popcorn and spliced single frames into the film of the *coming attractions*. The frames showing the popcorn came and went so fast that people were not consciously aware of seeing them, yet popcorn sales climbed dramatically. In the field of learning and personal change, subliminal messages work because they bypass the conscious, censoring part of the mind.

The first step in making a subliminal tape is to choose a recording of your favorite instrumental music. Pick something light that you will enjoy listening to several times in succession. The next step is to record a reading of your affirmations. Begin by finding a place and time where you will not be interrupted. Sit quietly and do a few breathing exercises with your eyes closed. Get yourself centered and relaxed. Speak each affirmation in a clear and relaxed tone of voice. Read as if you are talking to a close friend and pause for two or three seconds between each statement. Keep your tempo and your pauses uniform and fill up an entire side of tape.

The final mix is easiest if you have access to professional, multiple track recording equipment, but it can be done with three different tape players. Place the music tape in one machine and your affirmation reading in another. Place the speakers of these machines equal distance from the microphone of the third machine and load that one with a blank tape. Start the music tape first and set your volume at a normal level. Start the affirmation tape, also at normal level, and then very slowly dial the volume down until the words are just barely lost in the music. When the entire side of tape is recorded, shut off the machines and label the new tape.

You can listen to this tape while you are driving or doing any other activity. If the music you picked is light enough, you can even use it while doing breathing, relaxation, and visualization exercises.

THE PRO BOOK

A Pre-Competition Tape

The purpose of this side of the tape is to get you into fighting spirit. It is to *pump you up;* to get you into the right frame of mind; and to wake up your mind and body.

The key to making this tape is choosing the music. You want to end up with something that *turns you on.* It is ideal if you can find one instrumental piece that begins in a relaxed fashion and builds to a more energizing tempo. If not, use two different but complementary pieces. You want to pump yourself up to the energy level *where* you play your best.

After you have chosen the music, prepare a recording of it about fifteen minutes long. Set it up to play in one of two tape players. Position the microphone of the second tape player equal distance between your voice and the speaker of the first machine. Start recording, start the music, and begin speaking your chosen affirmations in time with the music.

Speak as if you are encouraging your best friend, a great competitor, to go out and do his best. In the first part of the tape concentrate on reassuring statements such as *"I am well prepared... I am physically ready... I am mentally ready and prepared... etc."* In the second part use statements focusing on what you will to do, such as *"I always keep my head down... Nothing distracts me from winning my game...etc."* In the last few minutes of the tape, use affirmations that have an immediate impact such as *"I am ready!... I am better than I ever have been!... My mind is clear and ready!... etc."* Choose final suggestions that have worked for you in the past.

Label your final product and use it as close to the beginning of an event as possible. Update it as you learn more about what works best for you.

(Note: If you know how to do it, you can probably make similar recordings with electronic and digital devices.)

Concentration

"The Eternal secret...of every mortal achievement."

—Steven Zweig

Getting the Distinctions

The ability to concentrate is the major factor that will determine whether you can maintain the same level of play in competition that you can on a practice table by yourself. Good players understand *concentration* and often discuss the abilities and development of other players in this area. *Concentrating* is a verb just like running, walking, or talking. It is an action completely different than any other action. Once you can recognize the action *to concentrate*, it is easy to see who is doing it and who is not. Once you have the distinction yourself, you can command it.

The dictionary defines the verb *concentrate* as *drawing or directing toward a common center*. What you are drawing to a common center is your attention. Attention is defined as *concentration of one's mental powers upon an object*. The what, when, and how of directing your attention is determined by your *focus*. The definition of focus as a noun is *the point to which something converges*. As a verb it is *adjusting to make a clear image*.

THE PRO BOOK

When you concentrate, you converge your mental powers to a point and adjust that point to give a clear and appropriate image. Think of the beam of an adjustable flashlight in a dark room. Everything not illuminated is blocked out—unseen, out of the picture. The beam is adjusted to include the area of importance only. In pool, this varies as we go through each stage of the shot sequence. It starts fairly wide, but ends up, as would be expected in a sport which requires pinpoint accuracy, as a laser beam of light.

The Secrets Of Focus

When you are not focusing, your attention may wander extensively. There is no limit to where it can go. It is harnessed only by the focus that you impose on it. If you impose no focus, it will wander randomly, reacting to whatever input it encounters.

The *first secret* of focus is that it can only be in *one place at a time*. The *second secret* is that if you perform the *same actions* with the same focus *sequence*, you get the *same results*. The *third secret* is that focus *follows fun*. When you are high energy, relaxed, and having fun, you will have automatic concentration.

In these three secrets lies the difference between a master and a novice. A master knows the correct sequence and is able to perform each action with the right focus. A novice knows neither what to do nor when or how to do it.

The Shot Sequence

A typical shot sequence starts when you inspect the table and ends when the object ball is pocketed. To perform this sequence correctly, your focus needs to be on different areas at specific times. There are seven distinct areas of focus in a *standard shot sequence*.

CONCENTRATION

In Focus #1, you are reading the table. If you visualize attention as a beam of light, this light would be focused only on the table surface and the pool balls. If spectators, opponents, music, or anything else is in the picture, the focus is too wide and needs to be narrowed. Everything except the playing field should be in the dark.

The left side of the brain, the logical thinking part, is welcome in this focus. In fact its assistance in determining the best course of action is helpful as long as it does not try to overrule the instinct. *Trust your instinct first.* In this circle of light, you are having a conversation with yourself. You are asking and answering questions. You are determining the best course of action. Sometimes this stage of focus lasts only a second—you recognize the situation and know exactly what to do. Other times, you may need to consider several options.

Never focus on what you fear, or what you don't want. *Always focus on what you want!* Fear should always be acknowledged and never repressed. *Never, ever* act on top of it. It is your mind and body telling you that you are focused on something you *don't* want. Deal with fear in the open and handle it before leaving Focus #1. Once you commit to a plan of action, this stage is ended. It is time to narrow your focus both internally and externally.

The transition to the second focus includes a shift to the right side of the brain. In Focus #2 you narrow your beam of attention to a *three ball pattern*, visualizing where you need to place the cue ball for the second shot so you can get to the third ball. As soon as this is clearly visualized, move on.

In Focus #3, you narrow your focus to include only the cue ball and the object ball. You visualize the line, hit, and intended destination of both balls. As soon as this is clearly seen, get down on the shot and move into the fourth focus.

Focus #4 includes the line of the shot, the stroke, and the contact points on the object ball and cue ball. The finer your points of concentration, the finer your aim and execution. As soon as you are confident about the stroke, go to the fifth focus.

THE PRO BOOK

In Focus #5, your attention is reduced to just the point of contact on the object ball. The stroke is executed and at the moment of contact your focus is at its greatest concentration.

In Focus #6 your beam of attention widens slightly to include the entire object ball as you follow it to its destination. As soon as that is confirmed, shift your attention to the cue ball, Focus #7. If the cue ball is still moving, follow it to its final destination. Once that is confirmed, relax your focus and stand up. Move into either Focus #1 or Focus #2, whichever is appropriate, and begin another sequence.

One common problem with pool players is to concentrate correctly all the way through the aiming sequence and then to stop. They don't concentrate on the final stroke. This is referred to as *letting up on the stroke*. They stop concentrating to *watch* the result. Make sure you hold your concentration all the way to the end of the shot. The highest intensity of concentration should be at the final execution.

Roving Focus

Serious players spend years discovering where their focus should be during competition. If you have been pursuing this game for a number of years, it's a safe bet that you have discovered and tried hundreds of different things to focus on. You have learned to see powerful distinctions within the simple act of choosing, getting down on, and executing a billiard shot.

You will continue to improve and find things that work at different times. You will never, however, find one *single focus* that will work for you today and tomorrow and the day after that. The best you can hope for is to find something that holds your attention right now—and right now—and right now—and right now—and right now—and right now—and right now—and right now—and right now—and right now.

CONCENTRATION

Your best performance is a function of awareness and awareness only lives as a living, breathing thing in the *present*. If it's in the past, it is called a *memory*. If it's in the future, it is called a *dream*. Every moment is a new moment—a new challenge—and a new opportunity to be aware. Every moment can be the opening for your best game yet. Keep your focus on *what you are doing*, but allow it to *rove* from distinction to distinction as it wants. Remember that the third secret of focus is that *focus follows fun*. Keep your concentration efforts fresh and interesting and your mind will cooperate. Try to *force* it to stay with one specific and mundane distinction and it will rebel. It is far more productive to lead a mule with a carrot then it is to beat it with a stick.

THE PRO BOOK

<u>Note Page</u>

* Examine your game in terms of concentration and focus.

Rituals & Routines

"Nothing is more powerful than habit."

—Ovid

Rituals

Rituals are actions you use to center yourself. They are the keys to open doors, the tools to unlock potential, the starting pistol to signal to yourself where and in what frame of mind you need to be at any given moment. A ritual may be simple or complex and is often used as a triggering mechanism for entering a routine. A good example is tennis player Andre Agassi looking at his fingers as he straightens the weave of his racket. He does this every time he needs to recover from the last point and prepare to answer the next serve. He has a specific routine, or sequence of mental and physical actions, for preparing to answer the serve, and he starts it with this ritualistic gesture. The strings don't actually need to be straightened, but he uses the action to center his focus and start his routine. Rituals can be made up of anything that works for you. There are no essential ingredients.

There are three basic types of rituals. Preparatory rituals are used to gain familiarity. Transition rituals are used to ease the shift from one focus to another and recovery rituals are used to get back on track.

Preparatory Rituals

The *preparatory ritual* does exactly as its name implies. It prepares you to begin and it helps you feel comfortable with your surroundings. It makes the unfamiliar, such as a new competitor or a different room or table, feel like the same familiar venue where you trained. Preparatory rituals reduce pressure and prepare you to perform.

They can contain a single physical action or a series of actions. They may or may not be tied to specific thoughts. A good example is how you assemble your cue. In reality, it doesn't matter how you do it as long as you end up with a cue in your hand. But to keep yourself centered, it makes sense to do it the same way every time. Set the case down the same way every time. Pull the cue out of the case the same way. Use the same hand movements to screw it together. Put the joint protectors in the same place every time.

In the movie "Hoosiers," Gene Hackman takes a small town high school basketball team to the big city auditorium for the state playoffs. Most of them had never been to a big city before and all were feeling nervous and out of place. He had them measure the distance from the free throw line to the basket and the height of the basket. He showed them that it was the same playing field, a court they were very familiar with, even though it was surrounded by thousands of theater seats. He made the unfamiliar familiar. Do the same for yourself by developing good preparatory rituals.

Transitional Rituals

A *transitional ritual* is a communication to your nervous system that you are shifting gears. Think of it as a turn signal so that all parts of you are making the shift at the proper time. This ritual signals the transition from one routine to another

RITUALS & ROUTINES

and is a single physical action which may or may not be tied to specific thoughts.

At one of the best cue academies in Texas, they teach each student to put the chalk on the rail after they have committed to their shot and are ready to get down to execute it. This signals the mind and body to shift from a left brain, logical thought, to a right brain, instinctive mode. It signals the end of the shot selection routine and the start of the pre-shot routine.

Recovery Rituals

The *recovery ritual* is used to get back on track. It is used to counteract distractions from your opponent, the surroundings, or even yourself. Recovery rituals always include a specific mental statement tied to a specific physical action. You need a recovery ritual for each of the major execution routines. This can be the same ritual for all or several different ones.

For example: whenever your cue is in your hand, a very good recovery ritual can be linked to chalking it. Focus totally on the tip and chalk it with authoritative and purposeful strokes. Concentrate on the color of the new chalk being applied. Coordinate a powerful affirmation or two in time with your chalking movements. *"Nothing distracts me from winning my game... I am relaxed and concentrated."* Do not return to the game until you are centered.

Routines

Routines are used in all sports to enhance consistency. Even if you don't now know what the term refers to, you have seen them many, many times. A baseball player is doing a routine when he steps to the plate and taps home plate with the end of his bat, carefully grips his spikes into the dirt, tugs at his shirt sleeve, takes three practice swings, and then looks up at the pitcher. A basketball player at the free throw line is doing a routine when he bounces the ball a precise number of times, spins it in his hands, looks at it, looks at the hoop, and then shoots.

What is missing in these examples is what we cannot see. What is going on in the mind of each of these athletes? What are they saying to themselves? Why are they doing these routines? Why are they doing the exact sequence that they are? The easy answer to all of these questions is simple: they are *doing what works* to ensure their best performance. They have developed these routines, and many others, over a long period of trial and error.

Routines help you get into the specific details of what you are doing, and assist in focusing your attention on what is important. They help you ignore distractions and your own mental anxieties. Use them to create a harmony of *purpose, thought,* and *physical action.*

All routines contain *physical actions, mental statements,* and *specific focuses.* Serious pool players are advised to create the following essential routines: the *warm-up,* the *break,* the *table evaluation,* the *pre-shot,* and the *chair routines.* This chapter will examine only the two most important, the *table evaluation routine* and the *pre-shot routine.*

The Table Evaluation Routine

The *table evaluation routine* is the sequence you go through to determine your game strategy and specific shot selection. Except for eye movements and some walking around the table, this routine consists of mental activity. The best way to understand it is to think of it as a series of questions.

Every good salesman knows how to lead with questions. It is the key to control and success. When you are at the billiard table, you control the flow of your thinking process with

RITUALS & ROUTINES

questions. The order, content, and appropriateness of these questions will determine your success and the consistency of your results.

These questions may not be in the form of an actual question, but anytime you are looking for an answer you are responding to a question, even if it is unspoken.

For training purposes it is valuable to:

1. **Examine the questions you *are* asking yourself.**

2. **Discover where you should, but are not, asking questions.**

3. **Make sure you are asking the right questions at the right times.**

4. **Put these questions into a simple flow format that can lead you into a good, consistent performance.**

Every different game played on a billiard table has its own unique flow of questions. The rest of this chapter, however, will focus only on the game of *Nine Ball*. If there are other games that you want to create evaluation routines for, follow the same process to discover the proper content. Keep in mind that evaluation routines are *trained* in great detail, but are simplified and automatic in actual competition.

The *first situation* to examine is an open table with random balls on it. This is what you have after you break or when your opponent turns the table over to you. Anytime you move balls on an already examined table, you return to this scenario. The first thing to ask is:

I. **What is the nine-ball situation?**

You must answer this question before you can determine what course of action to take. There are four possible answers:

A. The nine-ball is makeable early (it can be pocketed on a combo or a carom.)

    1. If it is a *gimme*, go for it.

    2. If it is *probable* and I go for it, how can I protect myself?

    3. What should I focus on? (cue ball hit, position, speed, aim, etc.)

B. The nine-ball can be made, but I can't get to it.

    1. How can I protect myself?

    2. What should I focus on?

C. The nine-ball is tied up.

    1. Can I free it easily?

    2. If not, can I play safe and move a ball into position to free it?

    3. What is my best option?

    4. What should I focus on?

D. The nine-ball is open and makeable. Move to question II.

All of the above questions move you to action except **D** which leads to question **II**.

II. Is the rack runable?

There are three possible answers to this question.

RITUALS & ROUTINES

    A.   **Yes** (if all balls are spread and makeable, go to **III**)

    B.   **Maybe** (it would require moving balls or very exact position)

        1.   **What is the key situation?**

        2.   **What is the best way to handle it?**

        3.   **How can I protect myself if things go wrong?**

        4.   **Will I run this rack?** (If yes, go to **III**, if no, go to **C**)

    C.   **No** (this rack is either too difficult to attempt or I do not have a shot)

        1.   **Can I play safe and improve the layout?**

        2.   **Can I push favorably?**

        3.   **What is my best option?**

        4.   **What should I focus on?**

C leads to action and **A** leads to question **III**.

III. Where is my pattern?

This question forces you to choose a pattern of three or four balls. It forces you to look at the balls in a sequential order and will eliminate shooting balls out of order. Once you see your pattern, move to the first shot.

IV. What side of the second ball do I need to put the cue ball?

This question will determine the most crucial thing you need to know about executing your chosen pattern. Which side of the second ball do you need to put the cue ball to get to the third shot? Unless you move balls or get yourself into a jam, **III** and **IV** are the only questions you need to keep asking as you run the table. If you move balls, always go back to **I**.

Once you have trained yourself to ask and answer the basic questions in the proper order, a simplified version is all you need to remember. A good checklist for the four major questions to ask when coming to a new table is:

1. Nine-ball?
2. Runable?
3. Pattern?
4. Side?

If you get yourself into a jam, or you don't know what to do, ask these questions:

1. **What does it look like from around the table?** (walk around to get perspective)
2. **What are three options?**
3. **Which is best?** (go for simple)
4. **What should I focus on?**

The Pre-Shot Routine

The *pre-shot routine* is the foundation of consistency in pool performance. A good routine allows you to be decisive, trusting, confident, and focused on the shot. It takes you into your own private world where distractions cannot reach you.

RITUALS & ROUTINES

The purpose of a pre-shot routine is to get your body properly aligned and your mind calm, focused, and decisive.

Your pre-shot routine will evolve as you develop and will eventually mature into the perfect routine to facilitate *your* performance. Once it is mature, it will have the right sequence of actions, thoughts, and focus for you. It will have the right rhythm and tempo. It may take years for it to mature, but you <u>will</u> know it when it does.

The pre-shot routine, by definition, starts from the moment you choose your shot and ends when the shot is executed. There are two basic parts, the *preparation* and the *set*. These two phases are the same as the first two steps in the familiar phrase *on your mark, get set, go*.

The Preparation

This stage of the pre-shot routine starts as soon as you commit to your shot selection. The basic steps are:

1. <u>*Face*</u> the shot.

2. <u>*Visualize*</u> the shot.

3. <u>*Get down*</u> on the shot.

These three steps can be broken down into literally hundreds of different distinctions. How your personal version is worded and focused depends on your development as a player and how your body and mind work together. A personalized example *for training purposes* might be:

1. I stand directly behind the shot...

2. and align my eyes with the line of the shot.

3. I visualize the shot complete.

    a. I *see* the object ball go into the pocket...

THE PRO BOOK

    b.   ...and the cue ball go to its final resting point.

    c.   I *see* where to contact the cue ball to make this happen...

    d.   ...and make my adjustments.

4.   I keep my eyes and cue stick aligned with the line of the shot and get down.

The Set

The *set* phase of your pre-shot routine begins when your hand touches the cloth and ends when you complete the shot. The basic steps of the set phase are:

    1.   <u>*Settle*</u> into your stance.

    2.   <u>*Aim*</u> the shot.

    3.   <u>*Execute*</u> the shot.

How your personal version is worded and focused depends on your development as a player and how your body and mind work together. A personalized example *for training purposes* might be:

1.   While stroking, I settle into my stance and....

2.   adjust my sight picture as I...

3.   *freeze* my eyes into position and ...

4.   *freeze* my stroking hand in relationship to them.

5.   I focus on my cue ball contact point and make sure it is aligned with my eyes, hand, and sight picture.

6.   I confirm my balance and the stability of my stance.

RITUALS & ROUTINES

7. I look at the cue ball and prepare a full stroke.

8. I look at the object ball and deliver the final stroke.

9. I stay down and watch the ball go into the pocket.

Pre-Shot Guidelines

It has been said that a *pre-shot routine* should include a set number of practice strokes. The number of strokes, however, is not as important as having the last one leave you confident and trusting of your execution stroke.

After the set is complete and locked on target, do not delay unnecessarily. You will only invite mechanical thoughts to enter your mind. Once the set is complete and locked in, look at the cue ball, look at the object ball, and stroke.

When you are *practicing* your pre-shot routine it is good to accompany each step with a suitable mental statement. In actual play, however, it is better to *just do it* without mental comments. If you feel that you need to have a stroke thought, make sure it is one that is simple, rhythmic, and effortless.

Make your routine as *simple* as possible. The simpler it is and the less time it takes to go through it, the easier it will be to remember and perform under pressure.

Note Page

* Examine your table evaluation and pre-shot routines.

Game Styles

*"There is no need to fear the strong.
All one needs to know is the method of overcoming them.
There is a special jujitsu for every strong man.*

—Yevgeny Yevtushenko

Every player has a unique and individual style of play that evolves as he does. In the beginning, he imitates the form of others and tries different approaches and techniques. Eventually, however, his development will hinge on *discovering* his own style, that unique collection of nuances and strategies that *mirrors his personality* and makes him comfortable.

The three basic types of game style are the *offensive player*, the *defensive player*, and the *percentage player*. You may have experimented with all of these styles, but the key to success is to find your strength, gain an understanding of it, and stay with it even under pressure.

The Shotmaker

The offensive player, or the *shotmaker* as he is commonly called, is an attractive, pleasing, and exciting player to watch. He is always trying to get out, always trying to run the table. A shotmaker has a high level of confidence and is comfortable with

THE PRO BOOK

a high degree of risk. He is willing to *go for it* even when a miss could cost him the game. He instills fear and tentativeness in his opponent because he is so often successful. The shotmaker is a performer, and the table is his stage.

He rarely takes into consideration the strengths or weaknesses of his opponent. This type of player will opt to break out clusters even when good safeties are available and rarely turns the table over to his opponent except when he misses. Momentum and rhythm are important to this type of player and if he gets it he is very dangerous. He is like a shark, always going after what he wants. Watching a match between two shotmakers is a great crowd pleaser, but the disadvantage of this style is obvious. If you attempt a difficult shot and miss, you are in the chair.

The Defensive Player

The *defensive player* is cautious and calculated. He has a more conservative view of himself and is less willing to put himself in jeopardy. He will take a gamble, but only if he is highly favored to succeed. His strategy is to do what he can and then lock it up. This player is more aware of his opponent than the shotmaker, and will often take into consideration the strengths and weaknesses of his opponent. This player is more concerned with disrupting the momentum and rhythm of his opponent than he is with establishing his own. The defensive player is a spider and only comes out when the web is complete and the prey is entangled, helpless and waiting to be devoured. A game between two defensive players will often take several innings, even with world-class players. The disadvantage of this style is that many winning opportunities may be lost to excessive caution.

The Percentage Player

The *percentage player* is a combination of the other two. This style of play requires a disciplined and realistic view of oneself, one's opponent, and the reality of the table. All the skills that allow the shotmaker and the defensive player to win are needed to play a percentage game. It requires more thought and evaluation than the other two styles. This player chooses action on the probability of outcome. He will risk big time if the payoff is large and he will have the patience to wait when it is not. He understands momentum and will do what is necessary to seize it. He is aware of the opponent's strengths and weaknesses, but will only respond to them when he can do so by staying within his own skills. He is like a cougar, bold yet calculating. The disadvantage of this style is that the abundance of choices sometimes results in confusion, tentativeness, and poor results.

Playing Against a Different Style

If you are a *shotmaker playing a defensive player*, there are several things to take into consideration when you plan your game strategy. As a shotmaker, momentum and rhythm are more important to you than they are to your opponent. It is essential for you to seize the momentum and establish dominance as soon as possible. What you want is the opportunity to *get something going*. You want three or four balls sitting in the open that you can string together with authority and *let your stroke out*. An early lead is a huge advantage for a shotmaker playing a defensive player.

You must avoid the *web* of the defensive player. Do this by keeping the pressure on him. Take your highest risks when there are fewer balls on the table. If you turn the table over with a lot of balls on it, he has more opportunity to do what he does best. If you have an early lead and run into trouble, you can sometimes tempt a defensive player to play *outside his game* by offering a low percentage *shotmaker's* shot. If he is feeling the *pressure*, he might take it in a rush to narrow your lead.

The beginning of each game is also crucial to the *defensive player playing a shotmaker*. He must force the shotmaker into a *thinking* posture. The way to do this is to present him with

THE PRO BOOK

game situations that cause him to stop and assess. Give him situations where he doesn't instinctively know what to do or where his responses are all low percentage. You want to break his confidence. What you absolutely do not want to do is give him an open table with several makeable balls on it. If he is acting cocky, you can sometimes tempt him with a tough, but makeable shot, which is just out of his skill range. Be careful here, however, because if he makes it, he could be off on a rack running spree. On the other hand, if you break his confidence, he will have to run several balls to regain it. A good defensive player will annoy the shotmaker with repeated obstacles prohibiting the shotmaker from doing what he loves to do—running balls.

The *percentage player*, by definition, is often a more experienced player. He will react to his opponent less often, as his game is determined more by the table than by a particular personality trait. He is most vulnerable to the shotmaker, who can capitalize on aggressiveness to pull ahead and stay there. The percentage player will have an easier time with a defensive player. He knows and can deliver the correct responses to the defensive player's moves and can run balls at a high level, too.

The *defensive player's* best strategy for success when playing a percentage player is to stay with his own style. Offer the percentage player situations where the proper response could be any of several low percentage opportunities. If you can get him to experience indecision, he may play tentatively and give you a chance to score. If you get the chance to score, you must do so, because the percentage player's confidence, once shaken, comes back fast and easily.

Playing Against a Similar Style

When playing opponents with the *same game style*, the more identical the style, the more likely the superior player will triumph. A small difference in proficiency can result in lopsided scores. This is because the lesser player has no means by which to attack the superior player. The longer the format, the more predictable it is that the better player will end up on top. When playing a better player with a nearly similar style of game, always try to get a *short race format*. If you are the better player, try to get a long format.

Whether you are a shotmaker, defensive player, or percentage player, the first rule of thumb is to know and stay with your own style. Your style, if it has properly evolved, is an expression of who you are. It is how you play best. Win by staying *in your own game*. Even when you are the lesser player, you can win by staying at the top of your proficiency bracket and catching the better player napping.

THE PRO BOOK

Note Page

* Analyze several games from the past in terms of game styles.

Match Dynamics

"He who seizes the right moment, Is the right man."

—Goethe

There is a common phrase in billiard circles which has been published in many books and magazines. It goes something like this: *forget your opponent and just play the table.* Let's take a look at this concept.

In business, you take care of your own business, but you also take the competition into consideration, especially in the marketing arena. How can you capitalize on a niche that they have missed? How can you capture more of the market share?

In other sports, understanding your competitors and how to deal with them is an accepted field of study. Even high school football and basketball coaches analyze game films with their players to formulate strategy. In fact, pool may be the one and only competitive field where *experts* suggest that students ignore the competition.

Sports are classified either *static or dynamic.* A sport is static when you are alone on the playing field. Your opponent is not allowed to interfere with your ability or opportunity to perform. You are playing completely on your own. Golf and bowling are examples of a static sport. A dynamic sport, on the other hand, is when you and your opponent are directly engaged. You are allowed to physically interfere with each other's game. Tennis is an example of this type of sport. You must play what your opponent serves up.

Pool is both dynamic and static. No one can actively interfere with your inning, but you must accept the table that your opponent gives you. Your opponent, in turn, must accept the table that you turnover. You cannot directly interfere with his inning, but what you do during your inning can definitely affect his performance.

Different situations in pool present different pressures and affect performance uniquely. One situation is not the same as every other. If you are ranked 35th on the Pro Billiards Tour, you would be dealing with completely different mental and emotional pressures playing an unknown amateur in one match and the number one seed in the next. They are different games and you need to respond appropriately. You must know and be ready for the *expected,* otherwise you are reacting and *reacting,* in a competitive sport, is also known as *losing.*

When it is your inning and you are at the table, by all means keep your attention on your game. When you are preparing yourself for a tournament, match, or table turnover, however, evaluate your situation to formulate your strategy. In pool, both of the adages: *play the table,* and *know your competitor,* are true, applicable, and appropriate.

In the Box

Another phrase in competitive billiards is represented in the following examples: *"You might not think he can shoot, but wait until you get in the box with him,"* or *"I got in the box with James and he beat my brains out."*

MATCH DYNAMICS

This phrase refers to the imaginary boundaries in which competition takes place. These boundaries section off the playing field in physical, mental, and emotional dimensions. When you are competing you are *in the box* with your opponent and that gives rise to certain emotional pressures. In the box:

1. **You are <u>alone</u> with your opponent.**

2. **You will have the experience of knowing him as a player.**

3. **You will discover how you rate, as a player, compared to him.**

<u>Match Roles</u>

Pool is a *ranked sport*. There is a *pecking order* even in the smallest of localities. Positions can be recognized by league statistics, association points, calcuttas, reputation, or any other means. Even without a handicap rating system or a ranking point system, everybody knows where everybody belongs, and everybody knows who's coming up and who's falling behind. It's just like the top fifty list on your local radio station. If you ever want to find out how you rate with the other talent in your area, participate in a player's auction. You will find out exactly where you stand!

This ranking phenomenon results in specific pressures and roles that a player may face in a match. First of all, you may or may not know your opponent. If you *don't know* him, then either:

1. You are favored to win.

2. He is favored to win.

3. You are evenly matched.

If you *know* your opponent, then either:

1. You have played before and won.

2. You have played before and lost.

3. You have not played each other.

In which case:

1. You are favored to win.

2. He is favored to win.

3. You are evenly matched.

Don't Know Him / You're Favored

This is a tough match for you. You have something to lose, but little to gain. In the *box* with this player, you are *the king of the hill*. In terms of the pecking order, he is trying to pull you down, and you are trying to stop him. Your advantage as the favored player lacks first hand impact because it is only hearsay, it has not been proven. Furthermore, you don't know anything about your opponent; you are in the dark.

This is a common scenario for *upsets*. Unless this is a match for the cash, the unfavored player is in a low pressure situation. He has nothing to lose and will often play fearlessly. Your key to winning is to expect a tough match. Remember that the underdog usually plays with bold enthusiasm, but the favorite usually wins. You will win if you prepare right and accept the pressure of being the favorite.

In this match, the unfavored player will often jump ahead in the first few games, and then make unforced errors in the last half of the contest. You, the favored player, must be prepared to capitalize on these expected mistakes when they occur.

MATCH DYNAMICS

Immediately take your place as the *leader*, because nothing gives an underdog a bigger burst of confidence than the hesitation of the leader. Focus entirely on giving your best performance.

Don't Know Him / He Is Favored

When you don't know your opponent and he is favored, you are actually in a strong position to win. You are an *unknown factor* and people unconsciously fear the unknown. The difference between your position and his is that he has something to lose and you don't. There is less pressure on you because you are not expected to win. If you know he is favored, so does everyone else, and that puts him in a defensive position.

You can *have fun* in this situation, but don't let yourself get out of control. The biggest concern for you is that the lack of pressure will tempt you to swing out, play above your capabilities for the first part of the match, then crash and burn. Guard against this possibility by keeping a moderate level of pressure on yourself. Play as if *you* are the favorite. Expect your opponent to play well and expect a tough match.

Don't enter this contest with the mental position that he is the better player and your job is to prove otherwise. Assume the position that *you* are the better player and he will have to prove otherwise to keep his favored status. Keep your confidence intact by keeping your mental focus on your game.

Don't Know Him / Evenly Matched

When you don't know your opponent and you are evenly matched, there is no history and therefore no expectations. You have your goals and he has his, but nobody real knows how it will turn out. The unknown is a major factor to exploit.

Project confidence and authority right from the start. He has curiosity about you and wants the unknown resolved. Help

THE PRO BOOK

him decide by presenting strong body language. Sit up straight and confident when you are in the chair. No slouching!

Stick to a solid game plan and stay within your box of skills. Early mistakes on your part will give him a burst of confidence. In this match *the truth is being agreed upon as it unfolds.* The player who can keep his confidence intact is going to win. Keep a mental conversation of powerful, confidence-building affirmations going whenever you are not directly focused on your execution routines.

Played Before / You Won

Expect a strong match from your opponent in this scenario. He is familiar with you and how you play. You have established yourself above him in the pecking order, but not dramatically so, unless you have won several matches in a row. It takes winning at least two matches in a row to establish dominance in pool. If you only have one win on him, he is a dangerous foe. He is wounded, but not out.

It is normal for him to play his strongest in the beginning and middle of the contest. If you let him build his confidence during this time period, you may lose. Resist the normal temptation to *let up* in the beginning until he proves that you need to *bear down*. Give him a full load of respect right from the start. Take charge as soon as the match begins and project authority and confidence with your body language. Don't let him set the tempo.

Prepare yourself well and be at your best. This is not the time to skip your pre-competition tape, eat twinkies, or change equipment. Don't manufacture excuses to lose.

Played Before / He Won

If your opponent beat you the last time you played, he will have a tendency to *let up* in the beginning of this match. You need to be watching for this opportunity, capitalize on it, and establish a significant lead. If you can do this and set the tempo, you are likely to win.

Play your best and avoid taking unnecessary or unprotected risks. Your tendency in the beginning of this match is to *press* or try too hard. If you surrender to this tendency, you will make sloppy mistakes and confirm his lack of respect for you. Stay in the present and play your best game. An effective affirmation to focus on is ...*I shoot one shot at a time.*

You must bring genuine confidence to this match because it often turns into a *grinder*, where both of you start falling apart and playing poorly. These matches often go to the hill with neither player getting a significant lead at any one time. Be prepared to win *gritty* instead of *pretty*. You must deliver when the opportunity arises.

Never Played / You Are Favored

All of the scenarios where you know him, but have never played him have interesting dynamics. There is a lot of ego and emotional risk involved for both players. The favored player is *supposed* to win and will if he prepares properly.

When you are favored, your opponent knows you and has an established mental conversation about you. He has talked about you, watched you, and made judgments about your game. He has expectations and they determine the level of confidence he will bring to the match.

It is important for you to express strong body language and confidence. At the same time, keep a healthy level of respect for him. Don't let him disarm you with compliments or displays of admiration. Play your best and resist the tendency to *let up*. If you get behind, keep up a confident posture. He is supposed to make the mistakes which allow you to get back into your *rightful* leadership position.

THE PRO BOOK

Never Played / He Is Favored

The mental conversation you have had in the past about this player may be your *most formidable opponent.* If you put him on a pedestal or elevated him in your mind, you will have to dissolve those images before you have a real chance at winning. It is essential to enter this match with the attitude that you are the superior player regardless of previous results. Make him prove otherwise. Have confidence in your training and match preparation. Believe in it, and convince him, too!

You can set him up by appearing like you don't expect to be a serious challenge. An off-hand comment such as *"Don't beat me too bad."* can sometimes accentuate his natural tendency to let up. Watch for this and be prepared to slam him before he can get his best game out.

Never Played / Evenly Matched

This is a *tough match*. The difference in skill is small and the prize is large. Someone will be established higher in the pecking order, and somcone will be established lower. The loser will suffer and there is often more attention on *not losing*, than there is on winning.

This type of match often progresses in spurts. It can be exciting when you feed off of each other and play better and better or it can be agonizing when you both play terrible. Expect a conservative game from him and watch for that same tendency in yourself. The key to winning this match is to **<u>PREPARE.</u>** Have a clear and simple game plan and stick with it. Don't let the flow of the match determine your action or you will sink into hesitation and tentative play. Trust your game.

Momentum

"Energy is eternal delight."

—William Blake

Momentum is one of the most powerful forces in sports. If a competitor can learn to hang on to it when he has it, and take it away when his opponent has it, he will win consistently.

It is also a very elusive state. Although most experienced performers can recognize when it is present, they would be hard pressed to either explain or define it. So what is momentum?

Momentum as Energy

Momentum is associated with *energy* and managing momentum is similar to managing energy. To capitalize on the power of momentum, you need to be able to stay synchronized with a natural flow of energy. Just like a surfer riding the crest of an ocean wave, you need to be balanced and surrendered to the intrinsic power of the wave.

THE PRO BOOK

If there is only you and your opponent in a room somewhere playing a match, the energy available for momentum is limited to the energy the two of you brought into the room. There is no large wave of energy to crest, because the energy associated with momentum is the kind of energy created by the attention of people. The more people focusing their attention on a match, the more of this energy is available.

Riding a wave of energy is a matter of timing. People talk about *seizing* the momentum, but this is misleading. It moves you, you don't move it. When you are utilizing the energy of momentum, you are going for a ride. The more you *let go*, the farther you ride.

Momentum crests like a wave. You can surf it short or long, but not indefinitely. It ebbs and flows with a volition of its own. The more conscious you are of this flux, the more proficient you will be at managing momentum as energy. If you *try to be careful* or *think your way through, it will pass you by*.

Although spectators play a major role in this scenario, they have no control over this energy. They cannot give this power to you on a conscious and volitional basis. It is not the same as support, so any attention given to spectators is wasted effort. In fact, the less attention you have on yourself, your opponent, and others, the easier it is to surrender to the energy stream of momentum.

You can, however, concentrate the energy of spectators in a way which maximizes momentum. This is the same energy that rock stars and performers speak about when they say *"the energy of the crowd came through me."* Performance energy is maximized when there is an absence of conscious thought. The keys to generating this state are *rhythm* and *form*.

Think about the last time you really enjoyed a great musical, theatrical, or sports performance. At some point you blended with the performers and the activity. You were so entranced by the *rhythm and form* of the performance that you ceased to think independently.

MOMENTUM

As a pool player, you can still your mind and others when the rhythm and form of your play flows like that of a fine musical performance. The purity in people that transcends their individual minds will respond. This is the source of the energy associated with momentum. Release yourself to it.

Momentum and Confidence

Momentum is associated with *confidence* and *initiative*. It takes confidence to move ahead and take control—to step out in front and dare to be the leader. It requires confidence to stay in the moment and it requires confidence to *let go*.

The winner of a match tends to shoot with *more* confidence as the match proceeds. The loser tends to shoot with *less* confidence. The loser tends to shoot more tentatively and with more conscious thought as the match proceeds.

When you get ahead, start shooting with more confidence. This is confidence as a *state of being*, not as a thing to *do*. Hold to this state when you are ahead and allow it to expand. When you have the momentum, it is far better to error in the direction of over-confidence than it is to be tentative.

Confidence is:

1. **executing without conscious thought.**

2. **having natural, controlled eye movements.**

3. **having a relaxed stroking arm.**

4. **having sound, dependable fundamentals.**

5. *seeing* **the ball go** *in* **the pocket.**

Momentum and the NOW

Momentum only exists in the *present moment* and if you want to capitalize on it, *you* need to be there, too. The player who can grab the momentum is the player who stays in the present moment. The player who loses the momentum has slipped into the future or the past. A common pool room phrase, *to stand the heat*, refers to the ability to stay in the ever vulnerable present regardless of the pressures applied.

The two main things which move people out of the present moment are *fear* and *anger*. Experienced players know this and will *play you*. They will *push your buttons* and take you out of the present via fear or anger. Your best defense for the short term is to stay focused and communicate whenever necessary or appropriate. Do not withhold your self-expression. Accept your opponent and the playing conditions as they develop. Handle each item completely. Do not resist. If you experience anger or fear, make sure you have centered yourself in the present moment of <u>*now*</u> before you shoot again.

The best defense in the long term is to complete whatever emotional issues you have from your past that can be reactivated in competition. You don't have to go searching for them. If you compete often enough they will present themselves. In fact, head to head competition is a great course of therapy, because you will face yourself again and again. If you resolve the issues that present themselves, you will advance as a competitor. If you try to avoid them or deny them, you will be handicapped. You will be competing with less than all of yourself available. Many people in this position resort to drugs and alcohol to block them out. Resolve the issues that show up for you. Clean up the messes you have made in the past that effect your performance today.

MOMENTUM

Defining Match Momentum

In matches where momentum plays a pivotal role, there are a limited number of dynamic possibilities. If you learn to recognize these possibilities, you will learn to *recognize the flow* of momentum in a match. If you analyze games which contain these dynamics, you will further your ability to control the flow of momentum during competition.

To make this easier, let's define momentum in measurable terms so you are not operating on a *feeling only* basis. A good and workable way to define momentum is in terms of score. For this example, let's look at Nine Ball matches consisting of races of seven or more games. Consider the following definition.

Momentum is established when a player takes two games in a row and control of the table was not contested.

In other words, if a player maintains control of the table long enough to score two games in a row, momentum is established. This is obvious if he runs two racks in a row, and less obvious if there have been table turn-overs. The number of innings, however, is irrelevant. A player establishes momentum if he retains *winning control* of the table for a period of two consecutive games.

The Dynamics of Momentum

Think of different matches from your past that fit the above definition of momentum. Try to find a match from your past that fits each of the following situations.

1. You had it and *he* took it away.

2. You had it and kept it.

THE PRO BOOK

    3.   He had it and kept it.

    4.   He had it and *you* took it away.

Once you have examples from your own competitive experience, analyze each one with the following questions:

    1.   Who had the momentum?

    2.   How was it established?

    3.   How was it maintained?

    4.   Was there a momentum switch?

    5.   If so, what caused this switch?

Other powerful questions to ask yourself are:

    1.   How did I take the momentum?

    2.   How did I lose it?

    3.   How did I regain it?

Controlling Momentum

Do your own inquiry with the preceding questions and discover your own answers. This is the way to get the maximum result from this section. After you have made your own discoveries, go ahead and continue reading. If you discover anything valuable not already listed, add it.

MOMENTUM

None Established / How To Take It

1. Play *smart*. (within yourself)

2. Play to *control* the table.

3. *Avoid taking foolish risks.*

4. Seize opportunities to *establish leadership*.

5. Present a *confident* and *intimidating posture*.

6. <u>ACT</u>. *Do not react.*

7. Maintain personal *integrity*.

8. *Deliver* when an opportunity is presented.

9. Do the *unexpected*.

10. Focus *totally* on the table situation.

11. _____

12. _____

He Has It / How To Take It

1. You <u>MUST</u> be *aggressive*.

2. You must <u>ACT</u> *decisively*.

3. Concentrate on being *in the moment*.

4. Assert *control* over the *rhythm* of play.

5. Offer *distractions*. (if this has integrity for you)

6. *Deliver* when the opportunity is presented.

THE PRO BOOK

7. Make your opponent aware of your *presence*.

8. Seize opportunities to *assert leadership*.

9. Maintain a *confident* presentation.

10. Do the *unexpected*.

11. _____

12. _____

You Have It / How To Keep It

1. *Never argue* when ahead.

2. *Know the rules* and keep him in the chair!

3. *Keep shooting*! Don't take a break.

4. Enjoy it!

5. Keep it *simple*. (shot selection)

6. Stay *confident*.

7. Respond immediately to all inner cues. (physical and mental.)

8. Let any praise or complaint, from you and others, pass *right on by*.

9. Use your rituals to *stay focused*.

10. Keep your attention on the *table!*

11. _____

12. _____

MOMENTUM

You Have It / How To Lose It

1. Get distracted by your thoughts, your opponent, or others. **DO NOT DO THIS!**

2. Relax your concentration. **DO NOT DO THIS!**

3. Shy away from the *dirty job* of *finishing him off*. **DO NOT DO THIS!**

4. Make stupid mistakes. **DO NOT DO THIS!**

5. Start doing something different (change rhythm, etc.) **DO NOT DO THIS!**

6. Be over-cautious and hesitate on a critical shot. **DO NOT DO THIS!**

7. Shoot with less confidence as you proceed instead of with more. **DO NOT DO THIS!**

8. Interact with your opponent instead of continuing to shoot. **DO NOT DO THIS!**

9. Give in to anger or fear. **DO NOT DO THIS!**

10. Change your focus to an inappropriate target. **DO NOT DO THIS!**

11. _____
    DO NOT DO THIS!

12. _____
    DO NOT DO THIS!

Special Situations

There are special situations or events that can happen in a match and sometimes they determine the flow of momentum and even who wins. It is important to recognize these events when they happen and adjust your game focus if necessary.

He Makes A Critical Mistake

Take note when your opponent makes a stupid mistake such as missing an easy shot, shooting the wrong ball, or dramatically missing a kick. These are important indicators of his mental condition, especially if they happen at a critical point in the game or match. These type of errors show that his confidence is breaking.

Your objective at this time should be to *increase the pressure on him*. Stay inside your own game, but choose your course of action based on this objective. If the best way to do this is to run out and rack up another score, then do that. If the best way to do this is to hide the cue ball and make him kick, do that. It is a common mistake to attempt a difficult run-out after an opponent has made a stupid mistake. Do not increase the pressure on yourself when your opponent is shaky. Break him, not yourself.

He Makes A Great Play

When your opponent has just made a great run-out or played a masterful series of safeties, he has asserted himself. You must stand up and come right back at him. He has increased his confidence and you must take that edge away.

Whether you choose an offensive or a defensive strategy at this point, it must be aggressive. The worst thing you can do

MOMENTUM

at this point is to hesitate or play tentatively. Keep strong and confident inner conversation, a strong physical presence, and stay within your game.

You Make A Critical Mistake

When you make a mistake at a critical point in the game, your focus needs to be immediately shifted to *regrouping*. You cannot indulge in *any* negative mental conversation at this time. *You are on the edge of a potential downward spiral.* You must regroup your confidence in your game and your overall composure.

This is not the time to *press* or *rush* to make up for lost ground. It is also not the time to be reacting to your opponent's actions. Take a moment, and use your recovery routine to get yourself centered. Your goal is to *control your mental conversation*, *make a plan*, and *execute it*.

You Make A Great Play

How many times have you seen a player shoot an utterly fantastic shot only to follow it a few shots later, with a bonehead shot? It happens all the time.

When you are shooting really well, there is a tendency for your confidence in your game to spiral upward. This is wonderful and good, but if you let it take you too far, you spiral out of control. Your goal when playing well is to *enjoy it* and keep it within your limitations. Be aware of the tendency to press beyond those *real* limitations. Play one shot at a time and stay inside your game.

Note Page

* How will you handle special situations in the future?

THE

EMOTIONAL

GAME

THE PRO BOOK

<u>Note Page</u>

* What would a breakthrough in your *emotional game* look like?

Motivation

"Nothing great was ever achieved without enthusiasm."
—Ralph Waldo Emerson

The word motivation is derived from the Old French word *motif* which means *"causing to move."* It is the beginning of all human endeavor and the source of all accomplishment. It is the answer to the question *why do we do what we do?* In its most basic form motivation is energy, and the form of that energy shapes the quality of your performance.

Sometimes people are motivated by *fear*. They act to avoid certain consequences. At other times they are motivated by *outcome*. They act to receive something in the future. In both cases, the motivation comes from *outside* of the person and is directed from either the past or the future.

In the best of performances, motivation comes from *inside* the person and is directed by the present. It is facilitated and enhanced by an *attitude* of responsibility and courage. It is an act of self-expression and is motivated by enthusiasm, commitment, and passion.

Passion

One of the definitions in the dictionary for the word *passion* is *"boundless enthusiasm."* The word *enthusiasm* is described as coming from the Greek word *entheos,* which means *"the spirit of God within."*

What you feel passionate about is very personal. It relates to who you are as a person and to what you need. Passion is associated with joy and is always in the present moment. When your motivation comes from boundless, natural passion, you are an inspired performer.

A pool player who is motivated by passion *loves* to play. He plays with all his heart, because the *play itself* is the object of desire. He may have goals to win championships and money, but pursuing those goals is a natural extension of following his passion. Losses might sting for a while, but are quickly overshadowed by the excitement of another opportunity to practice or play. A pool player motivated by passion plays because he is inspired to do so.

If you don't know whether or not you are passionate about the game of pool, one way to get clear about it is to *act* the way you *want* to feel. In other words, *fake it until you make it.* Put fun in your game and see what happens. Get into your performance and enjoy it. Find your fulfillment in doing what you are doing and enjoy the process.

Passion moves in cycles so don't get too concerned if yours seems to have disappeared. Take a break and step back from what you are doing. Look at your game anew and see if you can rediscover your passion in a new way. If you can't, go and find something else to do.

MOTIVATION

Commitment

If you have the passion to play pool, you most likely have also been blessed with a natural talent and ability. What you will accomplish with your passion and how you will develop your talent is directly related to your level of commitment.

When you *commit* to something, you put yourself *at risk*. You put yourself on the line. You set yourself up to deliver a full effort, *because* you have so much at stake. The bigger the commitment, the greater the elation when you win, and the greater the disappointment when you fail. The best motivation of all is a combination of passion *and* commitment. The following quotation is well understood by great performers.

"Until one is committed there is hesitancy, the chance to draw back, always ineffectiveness. Concerning all acts of initiative (and creation), there is one elementary truth, the ignorance of which kills countless ideas and splendid plans: that the moment one definitely commits oneself, then providence moves, too.

All sorts of things occur to help one that would never otherwise have occurred. A whole stream of events issues from the decision, raising in one's favor all manner of unforeseen incidents and meetings and material assistance, which no man could have dreamt would have come his way.

I have learned a deep respect for one of Goethe's couplets."

Whatever you can do, or dream you can, begin it. Boldness has genius, power, and magic in it.

W. H. Murray
The Scottish Himalayan Expedition

THE PRO BOOK

Attitude

Attitude is defined in the dictionary as a *"state of mind or feeling."* It is considered by many sport professionals as one of the major variables which determine performance level. Negative people, you may have noticed, do not make it to the top. Only natural passion, realistic confidence, true commitment, and appropriate action on a consistent basis will make it to the top. You must have a proper attitude that allows you to *risk and persist.*

The first step in managing your attitude is to claim responsibility for it. *You* put together the attitude you have had in the past, and *you* will determine the shape and form of the attitude you will have in the future. Commit yourself to developing the attitude of a winner. Practice and demonstrate the following attributes and characteristics.

1. **Have _respect_ for yourself, the game, and others.**

2. **Have _confidence_ in your talent.**

3. **_Train_ in a professional manner.**

4. **Have _courage_ and _persistence._**

5. **_Love_ the journey more than the destination.**

Goals

"Hitch your wagon to a star."

—Ralph Waldo Emerson

The Nature of Reality

To perceive the creative nature of goals and visualizations, it is necessary to address the nature of *reality* and your place in it. At any given moment, you are being who you are being, you are doing what you are doing, and you are having what you are having. At any point in the future, any of this can be different. Why? *Because reality is constantly changing.* What is true today may not be true tomorrow, and what is not true today, may become reality tomorrow.

Goals *have the power* to alter reality. When you *visualize* a future possibility as a goal, it exists in the mental world. The more detailed you make it and the more emotional energy you put into it, the more definitively it exists. Whenever you *take action* on a goal, you bring it a little bit more into the physical world. If you take action on a consistent basis for long enough, you will eventually realize it. Once you *realize* it, it <u>is</u> reality.

Goals Can Start or Stop You

The *kind of goals* you set for yourself will have a great deal to do with the outcome of your efforts. It is a common sight to see a sport champion on TV saying, *"I finally reached the goal I have been working on for so long."* This represents the power of a properly constructed goal. Unfortunately, it is far more common for people to be hindered and even stopped by having unworkable goals. It's hard to hit a target if you don't have one, but is even more difficult to score if you have the *wrong* target.

The most important thing to remember about goals is that you are the author. You create them; they don't create you. A master brings a goal into existence to assist him in staying on a course he has chosen. He never allows a goal to be imposed on him from the outside, and he never defines himself in terms of his goals. If a goal becomes unworkable or no longer empowers him, a master destroys it with the same power he used to create it. Never subjugate yourself to your goals. They are only tools.

Guidelines for Successful Goals

Goals are most likely to empower you and keep you on course if they conform to the following guidelines:

1.   All goals need to be measurable.

You need to know when you have achieved them and when you have not. If you can't measure a goal by something physical, it is not a workable goal. Make sure each goal is understandable in terms of what, where, and when. It is measurable if someone who does not know you could tabulate the results, compare them with the goal, and determine how well you did. Feelings are not measurable.

GOALS

2. All goals need to be compatible.

If a goal conflicts with something else you are already committed to, it is not a workable goal. Goals must be able to work together or they will not serve you.

3. All goals need to be believable.

A goal is not a hope, wish, or fantasy. You must actually *believe* that it can be *realized*.

4. Goals are not predictable.

A workable goal has an element of risk to it. If the outcome is predictable, it is not a goal, but a projection. The possibility of failure must be inherent in a goal for it to be empowering. Make sure your goals stretch and develop you.

5. Goals need to be completed.

All goals need to be completed with a final accounting. It is great if someone else will act the role of an accountable party, but if not, you have to report to yourself. Either way, when the completion time of a goal comes around, the truth needs to be told. This is not an opportunity for shame, blame, guilt, or pride. It is a simple stating of the facts. For example: "I said I would win three tournaments by March 1st and I did." or "My goal was to win $300 by March 1st, and I only won $200."

Visualizing the Future

The first step in creating goals is to visualize the future. Find a quiet place where you can sit without being interrupted. Take this book, a pen or pencil, and any extra paper you may need. Get comfortable, shut your eyes, and mentally project yourself ten years into the future. Imagine how you want to *be,* what you want to be *doing*, and what you want to *have*.

THE PRO BOOK

Release yourself completely from all limitations of the past or present. Let your imagination go and visualize whatever you want. Accept whatever shows up on your mental screen. After a few moments, open your eyes and answer the following questions *as if* you are still in the future.

The Future Ten Years From Today

Who am I being? (relationships, roles, attitudes, feelings, etc.)

_____

_____

_____

_____

What am I doing? (working, playing, building, competing, etc.)

_____

_____

_____

_____

What do I have? (money, homes, cars, accomplishments, etc.)

_____

_____

_____

_____

GOALS

Shut your eyes again and project yourself into the future only *five years* from now. Ask yourself the same questions about who you want to be, what you want to be doing, and what you want to have. Keep this imagined scenario compatible with your ten year vision.

The Future Five Years From Today

Who am I being? (relationships, roles, attitudes, feelings, etc.)

_____

_____

_____

_____

What am I doing? (working, playing, building, competing, etc.)

_____

_____

_____

_____

What do I have? (money, homes, cars, accomplishments, etc.)

_____

_____

_____

_____

THE PRO BOOK

Repeat the process by projecting yourself *three years* into the future. Remember to release yourself totally from the constraints and limitations of the past and present. This vision only needs to be compatible with your five and ten year vision.

The Future Three Years From Today

Who am I being? (relationships, roles, attitudes, feelings, etc.)

_____
_____
_____
_____

What am I doing? (working, playing, building, competing, etc.)

_____
_____
_____
_____

What do I have? (money, homes, cars, accomplishments, etc.)

_____
_____
_____
_____

GOALS

The *short term* future is more closely related with the way things are *now*. To imagine it requires an acknowledgment of the limitations of today, but at the same time, a freedom from them. Create a short term future that bridges the gap between the present and the long term future.

The Future One Year From Today

Who am I being? (relationships, roles, attitudes, feelings, etc.)

_____

_____

_____

_____

What am I doing? (working, playing, building, competing, etc.)

_____

_____

_____

_____

What do I have? (money, homes, cars, accomplishments, etc.)

_____

_____

_____

_____

THE PRO BOOK

The closer you get to the present, the more an envisioned future tends to connect with the way things are now. It is a delicate dance to acknowledge what is true and still keep the door open to a miraculous future only *six months* away. Act as if the limitations of the present are only a myth.

The Future Six Months From Today

Who am I being? (relationships, roles, attitudes, feelings, etc.)

_____

_____

_____

_____

What am I doing? (working, playing, building, competing, etc.)

_____

_____

_____

_____

What do I have? (money, homes, cars, accomplishments, etc.)

_____

_____

_____

_____

GOALS

Envisioning a future only three months away will normally have a lot of the present mixed in it. This is all right as long as you do not deny your own creative power. Imagine a *challenging* three month future with just enough details of the present to make it believable.

The Future Three Months From Today

Who am I being? (relationships, roles, attitudes, feelings, etc.)

_____

_____

_____

_____

What am I doing? (working, playing, building, competing, etc.)

_____

_____

_____

_____

What do I have? (money, homes, cars, accomplishments, etc.)

_____

_____

_____

_____

Creating Powerful Goals

Now that you have envisioned the future, you can build from these mental pictures to create powerful goals for yourself. Start with your ten year visualization and design a single, concise statement that can serve as a target, *or goal*, to bring that visualized future into reality.

When you have completed designing your *major* ten year goal, design a single, concise statement that can serve as a target for your five year visualization. This goal should be a stepping stone to your ten year goal. When you have designed your *major* five year goal, do the same for your three year, one year, six month, and three month futures.

Make sure that each goal you create is in a definitive form and that it contains all of the ingredients of an empowering goal. It should have a measurable result and be compatible, believable, and challenging.

Use the goal setting forms on the following pages.

GOALS

Ten Year Goal

My ten year goal is _____

I will achieve this goal by _____

The resources I will need to utilize are _____

_____

_____

The organizations or people I will need to be involved with are

_____

_____

The obstacles I can expect to confront are _____

_____

_____

The things I will need to give up to accomplish this goal are ____

_____

_____

Is the final result of my goal measurable? _____

Is this goal compatible with my other commitments? _____

Do I honestly believe I can accomplish this goal? _____

Does this goal challenge and excite me? _____

(If you can't answer yes, go back and restructure your goal.)

THE PRO BOOK

Five Year Goal

My five year goal is _____

I will achieve this goal by _____

The resources I will need to utilize are _____

_____

_____

The organizations or people I will need to be involved with are

_____

_____

The obstacles I can expect to confront are _____

_____

_____

The things I will need to give up to accomplish this goal are _____

_____

_____

Is the final result of my goal measurable? _____

Is this goal compatible with my other commitments? _____

Do I honestly believe I can accomplish this goal? _____

Does this goal challenge and turn me on? _____

(If you can't answer yes, go back and restructure your goal.)

GOALS

Three Year Goal

My three year goal is _____

I will achieve this goal by _____

The resources I will need to utilize are _____

_____

_____

The organizations or people I will need to be involved with are

_____

_____

The obstacles I can expect to confront are _____

_____

_____

The things I will need to give up to accomplish this goal are ____

_____

_____

Is the final result of my goal measurable? _____

Is this goal compatible with my other commitments? _____

Do I honestly believe I can accomplish this goal? _____

Does this goal challenge and turn me on? _____

(If you can't answer yes, go back and restructure your goal.)

THE PRO BOOK

One Year Goal

My one year goal is _____

I will achieve this goal by _____

The resources I will need to utilize are _____
_____
_____

The organizations or people I will need to be involved with are
_____
_____

The obstacles I can expect to confront are _____
_____
_____

The things I will need to give up to accomplish this goal are ____
_____
_____

Is the final result of my goal measurable? _____

Is this goal compatible with my other commitments? _____

Do I honestly believe I can accomplish this goal? _____

Does this goal challenge and turn me on? _____

(If you can't answer yes, go back and restructure your goal.)

GOALS

Six Month Goal

My six month goal is _____

I will achieve this goal by _____

The resources I will need to utilize are _____

_____

_____

The organizations or people I will need to be involved with are

_____

_____

The obstacles I can expect to confront are _____

_____

_____

The things I will need to give up to accomplish this goal are ____

_____

_____

Is the final result of my goal measurable? _____

Is this goal compatible with my other commitments? _____

Do I honestly believe I can accomplish this goal? _____

Does this goal challenge and turn me on? _____

(If you can't answer yes, go back and restructure your goal.)

THE PRO BOOK

Three Month Goal

My three month goal is _____

I will achieve this goal by _____

The resources I will need to utilize are _____

_____

_____

The organizations or people I will need to be involved with are

_____

_____

The obstacles I can expect to confront are _____

_____

_____

The things I will need to give up to accomplish this goal are ____

_____

_____

Is the final result of my goal measurable? _____

Is this goal compatible with my other commitments? _____

Do I honestly believe I can accomplish this goal? _____

Does this goal challenge and turn me on? _____

(If you can't answer yes, go back and restructure your goal.)

GOALS

Event Goals

Event goals will help you control the outcome of specific competitive events. The two types of event goals are *result goals* and *performance goals*.

Result Goals

Result goals refer to the actual *outcome* of an event. They are what you want to have when the contest is over. The more specific you are when you create a result goal, the more potentially useful it can be. They need to have a measurable result and be compatible, believable, and challenging. It is best if you have only one result goal for an event, as having multiple targets can divide your attention and weaken your effectiveness.

Result goals are easily measurable when stated in terms of score or money. For example: "my goal is to go four rounds," or "my goal is to win $100." These are good goals because they are *totally objective*. There is no opportunity to delude yourself about the outcome, because you either achieve it or you don't. If you don't, you know exactly how close you came. Result goals should not be airy-fairy. For example a goal to "play hard," is not a useful goal because it is totally subjective.

When you create a result goal, get it on paper in the form of a clear and concise statement. Read it a few times before the performance, but don't take it into the performance with you. Once you create a result goal, your job is over. *Any attention on it during the event will only hinder you.*

Performance Goals

Performance goals are the only goals to carry into competition with you. They are based on what you are doing or being *during* a competition, rather than what you will have afterwards. They live in the present moment, not in the future.

Performance goals are totally within your control. No one, except yourself, has any power over whether you achieve them or not. This is not a brass ring goal where several people are striving for something only one person can have. Only you can attain your performance goal.

Like all goals, your performance goals need to have measurable results. You need to know whether you have attained them or how close you came. There is, however, a certain subjectiveness to performance goals and it is okay to have measurable results that are estimated after the fact.

For example: "my performance goal in this match is to *keep my head down* on every shot," or "my performance goal in this tournament is to *follow through* on every shot." Both of these results are measurable, but unless you have a friend watching and counting, you won't have a definitive report on how well you did. You will, however, be able to estimate it. For example: "my performance goal was to *keep my head down* on every shot and I was successful 90% of the time."

It is okay to take a performance goal into competition with you. You can write it on your hand or on a piece of paper you keep in your pocket. You can ask a friend to remind you periodically during the event. Remember your goal, but concentrate on your performance.

Key Points to Using Goals

1. **Once you create a goal, it is complete.**

2. **Take action.**

3. **Assess the results of your actions and alter your plan accordingly. Take action again.**

Peak Performance

"There are two kinds of talent, man-made talent and God-given talent. With man-made talent you have to work very hard. With God-given talent, you just touch it up once in a while."

—Pearl Bailey

Sometimes you just plain *shoot great*. Your thinking is crystal clear, your visualizations are vivid, and your execution is confident and authoritative. At other times, your thinking is confused, your mental images are muddy, and your execution is tentative and uncertain. Sometimes the difference in performance is so dramatic that an observer would think that you were two separate players. What causes this common and aggravating phenomenon?

Psychologists say that these fluctuations in performance are the result of being in different *states*. These states, in turn, are determined by various combinations of mental images, emotional energy, and biophysical chemicals. Your *best game state* is a *specific balance* of heart rate, muscle tension, focus, mental image, emotional energy, and other variables. When you are in your *best game state,* you are actually *physically* and *emotionally different* than when you are not.

THE PRO BOOK

Scouting Your Best Game

If you have been playing for several years, you have probably performed in many different *states*. Your game experiences may range from tedious and boring to effortless and exciting, and from gritty and sticky to open and easy. You can discover the characteristics of *your peak performance state* by analyzing the *best games* you have ever played.

Get a pen or pencil and find a place where you won't be disturbed. Take a moment to relax and center yourself, and then recall the *best match you have ever played*. Visualize it as fully as possible and remember as many details as you can. After you have done this, answer the following questions. There are no right answers, so don't try to edit or force a particular response. Just write down whatever shows up for you.

1. When and where did you play your very best?

   _____

2. Who were you playing? _____

3. Who else was present? _____

   _____

4. Did anything notable happen before the match?

   _____

   _____

5. What did you say to yourself before the match?

   _____

   _____

PEAK PERFORMANCE

6. What was the emotional tone of that conversation?
   _____

7. What did others say that had an impact on you?
   _____
   _____

8. Describe when you realized you were playing great.
   _____
   _____
   _____

9. How did you feel physically while playing great?
   _____
   _____
   _____

10. How did you feel emotionally while playing great?
    _____
    _____
    _____

11. What was your attitude while playing great?
    _____
    _____
    _____

THE PRO BOOK

12. What were you focused on while playing great?

   _____

   _____

13. What were you focused on when in the chair?

   _____

   _____

14. What is your most vivid memory of playing great?

   _____

   _____

The Elements of Peak Performance

There are characteristics common to all peak performances, and others that my be specific only to you. Review the following list of *peak performance elements* and compare them to the insights you gained from scouting your own best game. Add any unique insights to the end of the list. This is a great place to pick up material to update your mental training tapes. It is also valuable to include reading this list in your regular training routine. A peak performance state includes:

a high level of positive energy

unforced and effortless action

natural pace and rhythm

PEAK PERFORMANCE

being physically relaxed and highly focused

zero attention on technique or mechanics

attention on the physical details

attention focused in the moment

no attention on the outcome

being mentally calm and highly alert

positive and intimate mental conversation

no judgment or evaluation of performance

an optimum level of emotional arousal

a feeling of joy and satisfaction

commitment to a performance goal

Emotional Arousal

Your arousal level is essentially emotional even though it can express itself physically. How keyed-up you are when you are playing your very best is a wonderful thing to know. Everyone is different and you have to discover your own best arousal level and be able to set it during competition.

A great example of the dissimilarity between pool players in this area is demonstrated by Earl Strictland and Efren Reyes. Earl plays his best when he is wound up and highly charged. Efren, on the other hand, plays his best when he is very loose and relaxed.

Sports psychologists agree that individuals have different optimum arousal levels for the same task. Every sport, and each position within a sport, has different demands. Imagine a scale from 0 to 10.

0	—	**no emotion**
1-2	—	**slightly aroused**
3-4	—	**aroused**
5-6	—	**excited**
7-8	—	**charged up!**
9-10	—	**extremely excited!**

A football linebacker, for example, is *highly aroused*, maybe an 8 or 9. A golfer on the putting green is *much lower*, maybe a 2 or 3. If a linebacker played football as a 2 or 3, he would be out of a job. If a golfer putts as an 8 or 9, some golf clubs are going to end up in the lake.

The best arousal level for playing pool lies somewhere between these two examples. It's related to, but separate from,

PEAK PERFORMANCE

rhythm, pace, and physical relaxation. You can adjust your emotional arousal by altering the length of your breath exhalations, just like you do for physical relaxation. You can also adjust your arousal level with emotionally rich mental images. Experiment and find the range that works best for you with different opponents and conditions.

Energy

The energy of a performer can range from low to high and from negative to positive. Each of these polarities are identified with different attitudes and mental images. *Peak performance is always linked with* <u>*high positive energy*</u>.

Low negative energy is associated with irritability, boredom, lack of power, and lack of responsibility. When in this state, you don't have much energy and what you do have is not enjoyable. It is characterized by bickering and complaining. In competition, this player has tension, but not energy. He really does not want to play and will look for excuses to *get it over*.

Low positive energy, on the other hand, is associated with rest and recovery. You don't have much energy, but your experience of what you do have is pleasant. In *active* competition, this energy state will lack focus and drive. You are relaxed with neither tension nor energy.

High negative energy is often the result of putting your whole heart into a competition only to discover that your best is not good enough. It is associated with anger and emotional upsets. When you are in this state, you may have negative outbursts, either physical or verbal. You have a lot of energy, but it is definitely not enjoyable. Your mental conversation is punishing in nature and your performance can easily plunge downward in a vicious circle. Your focus is on either the past or the future.

THE PRO BOOK

High positive energy is the nectar of peak performance and is associated with *joy, power*, and *satisfaction*. You have a lot of energy and it is extremely enjoyable. It feels great! You are *totally engrossed* in your performance when in this state. Your mental conversation is positive and natural and your performance is effortless. Your focus is on the present.

Accessing Your Best Game

Using Images

Your energy state is determined largely by the emotional content of your mental images. When you change the content of those images, you *change* your energy state. Pool players interested in peak performance learn to identify the crucial states and develop the ability to move from one to another.

The ideal inner situation for your *best game* is a balanced emotional state that triggers a specific physical chemistry, resulting in *calmness, heightened arousal,* and *high positive energy.* The mental images that produce this condition are images of yourself at your best, being in control, and having an effortless and superb performance. One of your best ways to access the *high positive* energy state is through the mental images you created with your pre-competition psyche-up tape. If you made it and used it, you can concentrate on those images at any time and project yourself into a high positive state.

When you are tired and need to recover, you can access the *low positive state* by entertaining mental images of yourself as relaxed, calm, and unhurried. One of your best ways to access the *low positive* energy state is through the mental images you created with the breathing and relaxation exercises in Section I. If you worked with them sufficiently, you can concentrate on those images at any time and project yourself into a *low positive* state. See it clearly and you get it.

PEAK PERFORMANCE

Stay out of the *high negative* energy state by refusing to accommodate mental pictures of yourself being harmed or violated, or of getting even, getting revenge, getting angry, or attacking another. Stay out of the *low negative state* by avoiding images of yourself as bored, afraid, powerless, hopeless, or tired. If you fall into either negative state, recover by going first to the *low positive,* then to the *high positive.*

Managing Cycles

It is impossible to play continuously in a *high positive* energy state, because competition is stress and stress is a biological event. Like all biological events, it cannot be maintained forever. At some point you need to rest and recover.

Learn to recognize and manage your natural cycles of *work and rest.* Balancing these variables is as important to a competitive player as fuel is to an airplane pilot. A wise pilot always knows how much fuel he has and how fast he burns it. He plans his refueling stops before he takes off and he keeps an eye on the fuel gage while flying. He is very conscious of the need to balance output and recovery because if he fails to do so, he will *crash and burn.* If you fail to balance your stress and rest cycles, you too, will crash and burn.

You can keep your cycles steady by establishing basic routines in your game and in your life. Wake up at the same time each day and retire at the same time each night. Exercise and practice at regular times. Manage your personal rhythms and you will be better able to stay in the *positive energy states.*

Creating A Vision Statement

A very important visualization is called a *vision statement.* It is a paragraph designed to take you *directly* into a *peak performance state.* It is worded in the present progressive voice as if it is happening *right now* and when you read it or

THE PRO BOOK

mentally review it, it recreates the moment by moment thrill of playing your best pool.

A vision statement is the *see it* part of the phrase *see it, believe it, and achieve it.* The stronger your vision statement, the more likely you are to believe it and achieve it. Write a paragraph today that can serve as the foundation for your peak performance vision. Use juicy words that have personal meaning and comparisons that turn you on. Use a form similar to the following example:

"*Just like _____ , I'm looking confident and powerful at the table. I choose my shot with conviction and visualize it completely. I get right down, relax, and concentrate. I take my final stroke with full authority and watch the object ball, and then the cue ball, go exactly where I intended. Just like _____ , I do this over and over. I am filled with joy, power, peace, and satisfaction.*"

Create your vision statement in the space below and also write it on a 3" x 5" card. Carry it with you and read it on a regular, daily basis. Read it at special times such as before a match or when you need a boost. Update and embellish it from time to time and keep it fresh and effective. It should change and develop as you do.

My vision statement is:

_____

_____

_____

_____

_____

_____

PUTTING

IT

TOGETHER

THE PRO BOOK

Note Page

* How can you make it all work together?

Letting Go

*"Think? How the hell are you going
to think and hit at the same time?"*

—"Yogi" Berra

Letting go is one of the most beautiful of all human experiences. It is also one of the most difficult to allow to happen. It requires trust, confidence, and courage. To *let go,* the self-conscious part of you, the ego, needs to step aside and turn control over to your intuitive inner self. This can sometimes show up as a scary proposition. It may even seem to you, at some level, as if *you* disappear.

The natural result of *letting go* during a billiard match *is* the experience of being in *dead stroke*. Nothing exists for you except the table. You examine it and look at your options. You easily visualize the different patterns in full color. You choose your shot with trust and confidence and get right down. You execute *effortlessly and automatically.* In the entire process, there is no hesitation or dissension.

THE PRO BOOK

Using Your Brain

There has been a tremendous amount of research in recent years on the different parts of the brain. Scientists have found that the two hemispheres, or sides, of the brain work differently and perform separate functions. The reason there is no dissension in the experience of *dead stroke* is that the two hemispheres of the brain, the left brain and the right brain, are working together. Neither side is trying to dominate the other. Left brain functions are being handled by the left brain and right brain functions are being handled by the right brain.

The Left Brain

Most people in the modern day world are *left brain* dominant. They live most of the time from the perspective of the left hemisphere of the brain. This side of the brain is associated with thinking, language, and self-identity. It is conceptual in nature and is the home of understanding, reasoning, evaluation, and judgment. The left brain exists in the world of time.

When a pool player is operating from the left side of the brain, he shows up as the *thinker*. The *thinker* is the person who is conscious of himself and of his effort. He has a natural tendency to want to *control the action*. At his best, he is able to analyze multiple options and make plans. At his worse, he's like a good friend that talks too much. He knows exactly *how* it should be done and can tell you all about it. He is also the guy who beats you up when you miss! Think of the paradox: a billiard stroke encompasses the cooperation of millions of muscle cells, nerve endings, and synapses, yet the conscious thinking mind, which can only juggle about seven items at one time, will try to take control if you let him.

LETTING GO

The Right Brain

The *right side* of the brain is intuitive in nature. It is associated with emotion, feelings, visualizations, and imagination. It is the source of creativity and all well-performed physical activity. It exists in the world of shapes and patterns and is sometimes thought of as the *unconscious* part of the mind.

When a pool player is operating from the perspective of the right brain, he shows up as the *player*. The *player* is the great performer. He is capable of executing a billiard stroke and can duplicate it over and over and over again—perfect every time. He is the product of millions of years of evolution and hours and hours of practice. Your *player* can only be present when you are *not thinking*.

The Obstacles to Letting Go

For most pool players, their best performances show up by accident. They can't predict when they are going to play their best, because they don't know when they will. They can play great one day and terrible the next and not know what caused one and what caused the other. It's one of the agonizing and painful mysteries of the game.

When there is good *communication* and *harmony* between the two hemispheres of the brain, there is proper function. In other words, the left brain is free to control the left brain activities and the right brain is free to control the right brain activities. When communication and harmony between the hemispheres is disrupted, it is impossible to play your best.

There are two major conditions that inhibit open communication and prohibit the natural balance of left and right brain function. These two conditions are fear and ignorance.

THE PRO BOOK

Fear

Most people identify themselves with their left brain perspective. The ego that they have formed over the course of life is *who* they consider themselves to be. Their *survival* is directly associated with the existence and continuation of this identity. It is in his efforts to reduce the risk that a player will attempt to control his entire performance, even the right brain activities, with the left brain *thinker*. It takes courage to put the ego aside and let the unconscious *player* come to the forefront.

Minnesota Fats said that what made him such a tough money player was that he did not experience fear. He wasn't afraid of being busted and losing what he had. All of the great money players from his era had the same trait. Fats experienced no fear about being busted, because he did not see it as a loss; it did not threaten his identity.

A pool player trying to reduce his vulnerability by *controlling* his performance is like an actor trying to play a role by following a *method*. It doesn't work. An actor works when he actually loses himself—when he surrenders himself and *becomes* the character he is playing. A pool player works when he loses himself and *plays pool*.

Ignorance

You cannot let go fully unless you know what you are doing. To be able to go with the flow of your own game, you have to know it and trust it. If you haven't trained yourself to deliver a smooth and level stroke, for instance, you can't trust yourself to do so in competition. If you haven't trained yourself to recognize the correct ways to move the cue ball around the table, you won't trust yourself during a match. Trust and confidence are based on belief and belief is based on training and experience.

LETTING GO

If you are constantly being interrupted with situations where you don't know what to do, you will probably have trouble. When you are not clear of the action to take, you move the *thinker* up to the front office. It's appropriate to turn the situation over to him because analysis is what he does best. The problem comes when you call upon him too often. He begins to think he is in charge. He can undermine your efforts to *let go* if you give him too much space. This is what people mean when they talk about *paralysis by analysis*—you have overextended your welcome to the *thinker* in you. In competition, if you *think* for more than about 20 or 30 seconds at a time, you are flirting with danger.

Training vs. Performance

One of the most valuable places to have the *thinker* is in the training room. In this domain, you are training yourself to perform. Your purpose is to refine your technique and master *new* distinctions with conscious repetition. It is a great place for left brain analysis and organization.

For example, imagine that you played a game where you missed a certain rail shot because of an awkward stance. You thought you where stable, but you moved slightly during execution and missed. In practice, you may shoot this shot over and over until you can tell what was *off* and how to correct it. You focus your attention on just this element, and shoot until you have ingrained the distinction and are confident you can automatically do the same in the future. When you are focusing on mechanics and techniques in this manner, you are *thinking about* what you are doing and *observing how* you are doing it, rather than simply *doing* it. This is a left brain activity and should remain in the training room.

Performance is the time for doing, not for watching. Everything your conscious mind focused on in training, such as your pre-shot routine, stroke dynamics, and aiming technique, must now be surrendered to the *player*. If you try to focus on one or two variables like you did in training, it will steal awareness from other areas and give you a stilted performance. You will handicap yourself if you try to control technique during a performance. You must have enough trust in your mechanics to be able to consciously forget about them.

Players who practice a lot often have a common problem. They go into competition with their conscious minds focused on one or two key items that they have been working on in practice. They try to hold on to these items in an attempt to control their performance. Subsequently, their true ability is never reflected because they never gave themselves the freedom to perform. It's like a musician trying to control the music instead of allowing it to flow.

This is why a player will sometimes play his best when facing overwhelming competition. There is no struggle. He is not *supposed* to win, so he surrenders and *just plays*. He is not using the match to *practice*. He's not trying to win or to look good. He is simply playing the best he can with no attention on technique or outcome. He is allowing himself to perform. You will be able to do the same if you follow this simple principle:

Train for Consistency and Play to Win!

The 60% Rule

Whenever you are faced with an increase in pressure, you will revert to whatever you feel *most comfortable* with. If you spend 60% of your training time focused on technique and procedure, for instance, you will tend to adopt that focus when you are under pressure.

If you keep at least 60% of your execution training time focused on *practicing* your performance mode, that's what you will become most comfortable with. When the pressure is increased, you'll tend to keep the proper focus.

The Training Program

*"Training is everything.
The peach was once a bitter almond;
cauliflower is nothing but cabbage with a college education."*

—Mark Twain

A training program is an organized and systematic form of training. Training is defined in the dictionary as *becoming proficient with specialized instruction and practice*. Instruction is defined as *teaching, knowledge, and understanding*. Practice is defined as *repeated performance of an activity in order to learn or perfect a skill*. To put it all together, a good training program should include specialized and repeated activity to perfect your skill and allow you to gain knowledge and understanding. It should also enhance conditioning and maintain skills and conditioning already acquired. A sound program should be detailed and thorough, and train the body, mind, and emotions.

A training program is a structure that supports you to fulfill your performance goals. It is basically a calendar that outlines which training exercises will be included and when they will be performed. To create a personalized *training program* choose the areas to include by doing a realistic evaluation of your competitive game. Decide which skills need to be maintained and which need to be developed. The skills you like

THE PRO BOOK

to practice are often already your strongest areas and the areas you *don't want* to practice are probably ones you *should* include. Your training program can include any or all of the following:

- **reference shots**
- **reference safeties**
- **reference kicks**
- **reference kick safeties**
- **reference banks**
- **drills**
- **fundamental work**
- **routine refinement**
- **relaxation exercises**
- **breathing exercises**
- **physical exercise**
- **diet & nutrition**
- **vision statement work**
- **affirmation work**
- **energy state work**
- **strategy study**

or any other area of study, exercise, or practice

Make sure to include days off in your training program and remember to keep a certain level of flexibility. If you drop out a planned activity one day, just put it in again at some future time. Don't let your training program dominate you. You are creating the program to *serve you,* not the other way around.

Take a look at the following examples for ideas and then fill out the 30 day training program section. It doesn't matter whether you are training light or heavy. Organize whatever time you have decided to commit to your pool game. Good luck and good shootin'!

THE TRAINING PROGRAM

Training Program — Example #1

Execution	Conditioning
Position Shots: #1-8 & #9x - 16x	Stretches: AM & PM
Safeties:	Aerobic Exercise:
Kicks: # 1-6	Anerobic Exercise: BIKE/RUN - 20 MINUTES
Kick Safeties:	Breathing Exercises:
Drills: 2 SETS #1 5-BALL & 5 SETS #2	Relaxation Exercises: AM & PM
Banks:	Diet & Nutrition: NO SUGAR, NO FAT
Other: 15 MINUTES ON BREAK SHOT	Other:

Mental	Emotional
Affirmation Work: READ AM & PM	Attitude Work:
Routines:	Energy State Work:
Strategy:	Vision Statement: AM & PM
Other:	Other:

NOTES: DO DRILLS FIRST.

Training Goal: SCORE 75% ON 5-BALL

Day: MON. Date: 8/4/97 Table Time: 2 HRS.

THE PRO BOOK

Training Program — Example #2

Execution	Conditioning
Position Shots: #9-16 & #1x - 8x	Stretches:
Safeties: #1-8	Aerobic Exercise:
Kicks: #1-6	Anerobic Exercise: 30 MINUTES - ROPE / CALISTHENICS
Kick Safeties:	Breathing Exercises: AT LEAST ONCE
Drills: 2 SETS #1 - 4 BALL	Relaxation Exercises: AM & PM
Banks:	Diet & Nutrition: SEE NOTES.
Other:	Other:

Mental	Emotional
Affirmation Work: SUBLIMINAL TAPE - ONCE	Attitude Work:
Routines:	Energy State Work:
Strategy: READ SPECIAL SITUATIONS. P. 180	Vision Statement: AM & PM
Other:	Other:

NOTES: TOURNAMENT TOMORROW! NO MILK PRODUCTS OR FAT TODAY!

DO DRILL FIRST - LISTEN TO SUBL. TAPE WHILE DOING IT.

Training Goal: KEEP MENTAL CONVERSATION POS.

Day TUES.   Date 8/5/97   Table Time 3 HRS.

THE TRAINING PROGRAM

Training Program — Day #1

Execution	Conditioning
Position Shots:	Stretches:
Safeties:	Aerobic Exercise:
Kicks:	Anerobic Exercise:
Kick Safeties:	Breathing Exercises:
Drills:	Relaxation Exercises:
Banks:	Diet & Nutrition:
Other:	Other:

Mental	Emotional
Affirmation Work:	Attitude Work:
Routines:	Energy State Work:
Strategy:	Vision Statement:
Other:	Other:

NOTES:

Training Goal: _____

Day _____ Date _____ Table Time _____

THE PRO BOOK

Training Program — Day #2

Execution	Conditioning
Position Shots:	Stretches:
Safeties:	Aerobic Exercise:
Kicks:	Anerobic Exercise:
Kick Safeties:	Breathing Exercises:
Drills:	Relaxation Exercises:
Banks:	Diet & Nutrition:
Other:	Other:

Mental	Emotional
Affirmation Work:	Attitude Work:
Routines:	Energy State Work:
Strategy:	Vision Statement:
Other:	Other:

NOTES:
_____
_____
_____
_____

Training Goal: _____

Day _____ Date _____ Table Time _____

THE TRAINING PROGRAM

Training Program — Day #3

Execution	Conditioning
Position Shots:	Stretches:
Safeties:	Aerobic Exercise:
Kicks:	Anerobic Exercise:
Kick Safeties:	Breathing Exercises:
Drills:	Relaxation Exercises:
Banks:	Diet & Nutrition:
Other:	Other:

Mental	Emotional
Affirmation Work:	Attitude Work:
Routines:	Energy State Work:
Strategy:	Vision Statement:
Other:	Other:

NOTES:
_____
_____
_____
_____

Training Goal: _____

Day _____   Date _____   Table Time _____

THE PRO BOOK

Training Program — Day #4

Execution	Conditioning
Position Shots:	Stretches:
Safeties:	Aerobic Exercise:
Kicks:	Anerobic Exercise:
Kick Safeties:	Breathing Exercises:
Drills:	Relaxation Exercises:
Banks:	Diet & Nutrition:
Other:	Other:

Mental	Emotional
Affirmation Work:	Attitude Work:
Routines:	Energy State Work:
Strategy:	Vision Statement:
Other:	Other:

NOTES:
- -
- -
- -
- -

Training Goal: _____

Day _____   Date _____   Table Time _____

THE TRAINING PROGRAM

Training Program — Day #5

Execution	Conditioning
Position Shots:	Stretches:
Safeties:	Aerobic Exercise:
Kicks:	Anerobic Exercise:
Kick Safeties:	Breathing Exercises:
Drills:	Relaxation Exercises:
Banks:	Diet & Nutrition:
Other:	Other:

Mental	Emotional
Affirmation Work:	Attitude Work:
Routines:	Energy State Work:
Strategy:	Vision Statement:
Other:	Other:

NOTES:
_____
_____
_____
_____

Training Goal: _____

Day _____ Date _____ Table Time _____

THE PRO BOOK

Training Program — Day #6

Execution	Conditioning
Position Shots:	Stretches:
Safeties:	Aerobic Exercise:
Kicks:	Anerobic Exercise:
Kick Safeties:	Breathing Exercises:
Drills:	Relaxation Exercises:
Banks:	Diet & Nutrition:
Other:	Other:

Mental	Emotional
Affirmation Work:	Attitude Work:
Routines:	Energy State Work:
Strategy:	Vision Statement:
Other:	Other:

NOTES:
_____
_____
_____
_____

Training Goal: _____

Day _____   Date _____   Table Time _____

THE TRAINING PROGRAM

Training Program — Day #7

Execution	Conditioning
Position Shots:	Stretches:
Safeties:	Aerobic Exercise:
Kicks:	Anerobic Exercise:
Kick Safeties:	Breathing Exercises:
Drills:	Relaxation Exercises:
Banks:	Diet & Nutrition:
Other:	Other:

Mental	Emotional
Affirmation Work:	Attitude Work:
Routines:	Energy State Work:
Strategy:	Vision Statement:
Other:	Other:

NOTES: _____
_____
_____
_____

Training Goal: _____

Day _____ Date _____ Table Time _____

THE PRO BOOK

Training Program — Day #8

Execution	Conditioning
Position Shots:	Stretches:
Safeties:	Aerobic Exercise:
Kicks:	Anerobic Exercise:
Kick Safeties:	Breathing Exercises:
Drills:	Relaxation Exercises:
Banks:	Diet & Nutrition:
Other:	Other:

Mental	Emotional
Affirmation Work:	Attitude Work:
Routines:	Energy State Work:
Strategy:	Vision Statement:
Other:	Other:

NOTES: _____
_____
_____
_____

Training Goal: _____

Day _____ Date _____ Table Time _____

THE TRAINING PROGRAM

Training Program — Day #9

Execution	Conditioning
Position Shots:	Stretches:
Safeties:	Aerobic Exercise:
Kicks:	Anerobic Exercise:
Kick Safeties:	Breathing Exercises:
Drills:	Relaxation Exercises:
Banks:	Diet & Nutrition:
Other:	Other:

Mental	Emotional
Affirmation Work:	Attitude Work:
Routines:	Energy State Work:
Strategy:	Vision Statement:
Other:	Other:

NOTES:
_____
_____
_____
_____

Training Goal: _____

Day _____ Date _____ Table Time _____

237

THE PRO BOOK

Training Program — Day #10

Execution	Conditioning
Position Shots:	Stretches:
Safeties:	Aerobic Exercise:
Kicks:	Anerobic Exercise:
Kick Safeties:	Breathing Exercises:
Drills:	Relaxation Exercises:
Banks:	Diet & Nutrition:
Other:	Other:

Mental	Emotional
Affirmation Work:	Attitude Work:
Routines:	Energy State Work:
Strategy:	Vision Statement:
Other:	Other:

NOTES:
- -
- -
- -
- -

Training Goal: _____

Day _____   Date _____   Table Time _____

THE TRAINING PROGRAM

Training Program — Day #11

Execution	Conditioning
Position Shots:	Stretches:
Safeties:	Aerobic Exercise:
Kicks:	Anerobic Exercise:
Kick Safeties:	Breathing Exercises:
Drills:	Relaxation Exercises:
Banks:	Diet & Nutrition:
Other:	Other:

Mental	Emotional
Affirmation Work:	Attitude Work:
Routines:	Energy State Work:
Strategy:	Vision Statement:
Other:	Other:

NOTES:
_____
_____
_____
_____

Training Goal: _____

Day _____ Date _____ Table Time _____

THE PRO BOOK

Training Program — Day #12

Execution	Conditioning
Position Shots:	Stretches:
Safeties:	Aerobic Exercise:
Kicks:	Anerobic Exercise:
Kick Safeties:	Breathing Exercises:
Drills:	Relaxation Exercises:
Banks:	Diet & Nutrition:
Other:	Other:

Mental	Emotional
Affirmation Work:	Attitude Work:
Routines:	Energy State Work:
Strategy:	Vision Statement:
Other:	Other:

NOTES:
_____
_____
_____
_____

Training Goal: _____

Day _____ Date _____ Table Time _____

THE TRAINING PROGRAM

Training Program — Day #13

Execution	Conditioning
Position Shots:	Stretches:
Safeties:	Aerobic Exercise:
Kicks:	Anerobic Exercise:
Kick Safeties:	Breathing Exercises:
Drills:	Relaxation Exercises:
Banks:	Diet & Nutrition:
Other:	Other:

Mental	Emotional
Affirmation Work:	Attitude Work:
Routines:	Energy State Work:
Strategy:	Vision Statement:
Other:	Other:

NOTES: _____
_____
_____
_____

Training Goal: _____

Day _____ Date _____ Table Time _____

THE PRO BOOK

Training Program — Day #14

Execution	Conditioning
Position Shots:	Stretches:
Safeties:	Aerobic Exercise:
Kicks:	Anerobic Exercise:
Kick Safeties:	Breathing Exercises:
Drills:	Relaxation Exercises:
Banks:	Diet & Nutrition:
Other:	Other:

Mental	Emotional
Affirmation Work:	Attitude Work:
Routines:	Energy State Work:
Strategy:	Vision Statement:
Other:	Other:

NOTES:
_____
_____
_____
_____

Training Goal: _____

Day _____ Date _____ Table Time _____

THE TRAINING PROGRAM

Training Program — Day #15

Execution	Conditioning
Position Shots:	Stretches:
Safeties:	Aerobic Exercise:
Kicks:	Anerobic Exercise:
Kick Safeties:	Breathing Exercises:
Drills:	Relaxation Exercises:
Banks:	Diet & Nutrition:
Other:	Other:

Mental	Emotional
Affirmation Work:	Attitude Work:
Routines:	Energy State Work:
Strategy:	Vision Statement:
Other:	Other:

NOTES:
- -
- -
- -
- -

Training Goal: _____

Day _____ Date _____ Table Time _____

THE PRO BOOK

Training Program — Day #16

Execution	Conditioning
Position Shots:	Stretches:
Safeties:	Aerobic Exercise:
Kicks:	Anerobic Exercise:
Kick Safeties:	Breathing Exercises:
Drills:	Relaxation Exercises:
Banks:	Diet & Nutrition:
Other:	Other:

Mental	Emotional
Affirmation Work:	Attitude Work:
Routines:	Energy State Work:
Strategy:	Vision Statement:
Other:	Other:

NOTES:
- -
- -
- -
- -

Training Goal: _____

Day _____ Date _____ Table Time _____

THE TRAINING PROGRAM

Training Program — Day #17

Execution	Conditioning
Position Shots:	Stretches:
Safeties:	Aerobic Exercise:
Kicks:	Anerobic Exercise:
Kick Safeties:	Breathing Exercises:
Drills:	Relaxation Exercises:
Banks:	Diet & Nutrition:
Other:	Other:

Mental	Emotional
Affirmation Work:	Attitude Work:
Routines:	Energy State Work:
Strategy:	Vision Statement:
Other:	Other:

NOTES: _____
_____
_____
_____

Training Goal: _____

Day _____ Date _____ Table Time _____

THE PRO BOOK

Training Program — Day #18

Execution	Conditioning
Position Shots:	Stretches:
Safeties:	Aerobic Exercise:
Kicks:	Anerobic Exercise:
Kick Safeties:	Breathing Exercises:
Drills:	Relaxation Exercises:
Banks:	Diet & Nutrition:
Other:	Other:

Mental	Emotional
Affirmation Work:	Attitude Work:
Routines:	Energy State Work:
Strategy:	Vision Statement:
Other:	Other:

NOTES:
- -
- -
- -
- -

Training Goal: _____

Day _____   Date _____   Table Time _____

THE TRAINING PROGRAM

Training Program — Day #19

Execution	Conditioning
Position Shots:	Stretches:
Safeties:	Aerobic Exercise:
Kicks:	Anerobic Exercise:
Kick Safeties:	Breathing Exercises:
Drills:	Relaxation Exercises:
Banks:	Diet & Nutrition:
Other:	Other:

Mental	Emotional
Affirmation Work:	Attitude Work:
Routines:	Energy State Work:
Strategy:	Vision Statement:
Other:	Other:

NOTES: _____
_____
_____
_____

Training Goal: _____

Day _____   Date _____   Table Time _____

THE PRO BOOK

Training Program — Day #20

Execution	Conditioning
Position Shots:	Stretches:
Safeties:	Aerobic Exercise:
Kicks:	Anerobic Exercise:
Kick Safeties:	Breathing Exercises:
Drills:	Relaxation Exercises:
Banks:	Diet & Nutrition:
Other:	Other:

Mental	Emotional
Affirmation Work:	Attitude Work:
Routines:	Energy State Work:
Strategy:	Vision Statement:
Other:	Other:

NOTES:

Training Goal: _____

Day _____ Date _____ Table Time _____

THE TRAINING PROGRAM

Training Program — Day #21

Execution	Conditioning
Position Shots:	Stretches:
Safeties:	Aerobic Exercise:
Kicks:	Anerobic Exercise:
Kick Safeties:	Breathing Exercises:
Drills:	Relaxation Exercises:
Banks:	Diet & Nutrition:
Other:	Other:

Mental	Emotional
Affirmation Work:	Attitude Work:
Routines:	Energy State Work:
Strategy:	Vision Statement:
Other:	Other:

NOTES:
_____
_____
_____
_____

Training Goal: _____

Day _____ Date _____ Table Time _____

THE PRO BOOK

Training Program — Day #22

Execution	Conditioning
Position Shots:	Stretches:
Safeties:	Aerobic Exercise:
Kicks:	Anerobic Exercise:
Kick Safeties:	Breathing Exercises:
Drills:	Relaxation Exercises:
Banks:	Diet & Nutrition:
Other:	Other:

Mental	Emotional
Affirmation Work:	Attitude Work:
Routines:	Energy State Work:
Strategy:	Vision Statement:
Other:	Other:

NOTES:
- -
- -
- -
- -

Training Goal: _____

Day _____   Date _____   Table Time _____

THE TRAINING PROGRAM

Training Program — Day #23

Execution	Conditioning
Position Shots:	Stretches:
Safeties:	Aerobic Exercise:
Kicks:	Anerobic Exercise:
Kick Safeties:	Breathing Exercises:
Drills:	Relaxation Exercises:
Banks:	Diet & Nutrition:
Other:	Other:

Mental	Emotional
Affirmation Work:	Attitude Work:
Routines:	Energy State Work:
Strategy:	Vision Statement:
Other:	Other:

NOTES:
- -
- -
- -
- -

Training Goal: _____

Day _____ Date _____ Table Time _____

THE PRO BOOK

Training Program — Day #24

Execution	Conditioning
Position Shots:	Stretches:
Safeties:	Aerobic Exercise:
Kicks:	Anerobic Exercise:
Kick Safeties:	Breathing Exercises:
Drills:	Relaxation Exercises:
Banks:	Diet & Nutrition:
Other:	Other:

Mental	Emotional
Affirmation Work:	Attitude Work:
Routines:	Energy State Work:
Strategy:	Vision Statement:
Other:	Other:

NOTES:
- -
- -
- -
- -

Training Goal: _____

Day _____   Date _____   Table Time _____

THE TRAINING PROGRAM

Training Program — Day #25

Execution	Conditioning
Position Shots:	Stretches:
Safeties:	Aerobic Exercise:
Kicks:	Anerobic Exercise:
Kick Safeties:	Breathing Exercises:
Drills:	Relaxation Exercises:
Banks:	Diet & Nutrition:
Other:	Other:

Mental	Emotional
Affirmation Work:	Attitude Work:
Routines:	Energy State Work:
Strategy:	Vision Statement:
Other:	Other:

NOTES: _____
_____
_____
_____

Training Goal: _____

Day _____ Date _____ Table Time _____

THE PRO BOOK

Training Program — Day #26

Execution	Conditioning
Position Shots:	Stretches:
Safeties:	Aerobic Exercise:
Kicks:	Anerobic Exercise:
Kick Safeties:	Breathing Exercises:
Drills:	Relaxation Exercises:
Banks:	Diet & Nutrition:
Other:	Other:

Mental	Emotional
Affirmation Work:	Attitude Work:
Routines:	Energy State Work:
Strategy:	Vision Statement:
Other:	Other:

NOTES:
_____
_____
_____
_____

Training Goal: _____

Day _____ Date _____ Table Time _____

THE TRAINING PROGRAM

Training Program — Day #27

Execution	Conditioning
Position Shots:	Stretches:
Safeties:	Aerobic Exercise:
Kicks:	Anerobic Exercise:
Kick Safeties:	Breathing Exercises:
Drills:	Relaxation Exercises:
Banks:	Diet & Nutrition:
Other:	Other:

Mental	Emotional
Affirmation Work:	Attitude Work:
Routines:	Energy State Work:
Strategy:	Vision Statement:
Other:	Other:

NOTES:
- -
- -
- -
- -

Training Goal: _____

Day _____   Date _____   Table Time _____

THE PRO BOOK

Training Program — Day #28

Execution	Conditioning
Position Shots:	Stretches:
Safeties:	Aerobic Exercise:
Kicks:	Anerobic Exercise:
Kick Safeties:	Breathing Exercises:
Drills:	Relaxation Exercises:
Banks:	Diet & Nutrition:
Other:	Other:

Mental	Emotional
Affirmation Work:	Attitude Work:
Routines:	Energy State Work:
Strategy:	Vision Statement:
Other:	Other:

NOTES:
- -
- -
- -
- -

Training Goal: _____

Day _____ Date _____ Table Time _____

THE TRAINING PROGRAM

Training Program — Day #29

Execution	Conditioning
Position Shots:	Stretches:
Safeties:	Aerobic Exercise:
Kicks:	Anerobic Exercise:
Kick Safeties:	Breathing Exercises:
Drills:	Relaxation Exercises:
Banks:	Diet & Nutrition:
Other:	Other:

Mental	Emotional
Affirmation Work:	Attitude Work:
Routines:	Energy State Work:
Strategy:	Vision Statement:
Other:	Other:

NOTES: _____
_____
_____
_____

Training Goal: _____

Day _____ Date _____ Table Time _____

THE PRO BOOK

Training Program — Day #30

Execution	Conditioning
Position Shots:	Stretches:
Safeties:	Aerobic Exercise:
Kicks:	Anerobic Exercise:
Kick Safeties:	Breathing Exercises:
Drills:	Relaxation Exercises:
Banks:	Diet & Nutrition:
Other:	Other:

Mental	Emotional
Affirmation Work:	Attitude Work:
Routines:	Energy State Work:
Strategy:	Vision Statement:
Other:	Other:

NOTES:
- -
- -
- -
- -

Training Goal: _____

Day _____   Date _____   Table Time _____

Game Plans

*"The questions which one asks oneself
begin, at last, to illuminate the world, and
become one's key to the experience of others."*

—James Baldwin

As a serious sports competitor, you need to plan your action before you take it, and evaluate it soon afterwards. It is an essential part of being responsible for your performance and it plays a major role in the development of your ability. Even high school sports teams do this.

Many different variables can affect the outcome of a billiard competition. A forgotten or failed piece of equipment can handicap you unexpectedly. A single thought at the wrong moment can completely throw off your game and cost you the match. You can learn to control these variables by planning and evaluating your action in a disciplined and realistic fashion. If you can keep learning more about what contributes to your game and what detracts from it, you can continue to build yourself into a stronger performer.

The best way to maximize your efforts at self-examination is to have a structured program that you can plug into whenever necessary. The first step is to determine the crucial elements of competition preparation and review.

THE PRO BOOK

Match Planning

Planning your match begins the moment you commit to playing in it. In some cases this is days, weeks, or even months ahead of time; in other cases it is only a matter of a few minutes. For training purposes, it is better to avoid matches in the future that do not allow enough time for adequate preparation.

There are two different phases of a competitive event that require your attention ahead of time. They are the *Pre-Match Plan* and the *Competition Plan*.

The Pre-Match Plan

There are two major sections to a sound *pre-match plan*. The first section organizes your *early preparation* and the second organizes your *on-site preparation*.

Good *early preparation* works closely with your training program because it covers the time span from the moment you commit to a match until you arrive on site. The content of this plan should contain all the things that you need to *complete* before arriving at the match site. This includes such things as getting a new tip on your cue, preparing your clothes, and eating a good pre-game meal. It also includes coordinating your sleep, exercise, and training cycles so that you show up in prime condition.

Another valuable component of your early preparation is to list the items you need to have with you when you arrive on site. Examples are chalk, towels, talcum powder, energy bars, and your *vision statement* on a card. Once you have determined the content of your early preparation, arrange all of the items in a chronological sequence. This phase of your *pre-match planning* is completed when you *arrive at the match site*.

GAME PLANS

The on-site phase of a *pre-match plan* is basically a list of the activities you *intend* to do and the thoughts and images you *intend* to have from the moment you arrive on site until your match begins. It is best to break this list into three periods. The first period covers the important time from when you arrive until you begin your warm-up sequence. The outcome of many events are determined when contestants first enter the arena and greet each other. The second period covers your warm-up sequence and the third period covers the important time from then until the balls are racked.

Once you have determined the content of your plan, arrange it in chronological order. When you do this you are visualizing the flow of the event and creating the necessary pre-match routines for *getting familiar with your surroundings, warming up, waiting for your match, approaching the table,* and *preparing to start.*

The Competition Plan

A good *competition plan* helps to control the flow of a match and your own thoughts, images, and actions. It is best to create it the day before the event and to review it a couple of times before play actually begins. In this plan you establish your goals, formulate your strategy, and decide what you will focus on at different points in the match. You imagine the game situations that could develop that might have a critical impact on your performance. You decide on your preferred response and choose a ritual or cue word to direct you to that response during the pressure of competition.

When you create a *competition plan,* you are visualizing the entire match ahead of time and establishing key guideposts to direct you during the actual contest. You are determining which aspects of the match you can control and you are claiming that control. This puts you into a powerful position as a competitor.

Match Review

Doing a *match review* is as important to you as it is to a football team watching the film of yesterday's game. It is your chance to discover what worked, what went wrong, and how you can adjust in the future to maximize your competitive performance.

A *match review* is essentially a list of questions that focuses your attention on different aspects of your performance. These questions should cover all areas of training, conditioning, strategy, and execution. They should also refer back to your *preparation plans*. Take any insights that you discover in the evaluation process and adjust both your plans and your training program.

The Pro Book Game Plans

The Pro Book Game Plans is a set of standardized forms you can use to plan and evaluate your competitive performance. At the end of this section there are four sets of *plans,* one for each of four separate competitive events. Use them for either four consecutive events or space them out at regular periods, such as once a week or once a month.

Follow the instructions and fill out the *preparation plans* at least one day before your competitive event. Review them shortly before the contest. Do the *match review* no later than one day after the event.

GAME PLANS

Pre-Match Plan — Example   *for 8-6-97*

List the things you need to complete before arriving on site.
- DRESS CUE TIP - DAY BEFORE.
- PREP CLOTHES -   "   "
- LIGHT EXERCISE & STRETCHES - AM
- A GOOD PRE-GAME MEAL - 2 HRS. BEFORE.

List the items you need to take with you.
- VISION STATEMENT ON A 3x5 CARD.
- COPY OF COMP. PLAN.
- FRUIT & ENERGY BARS.
- HAND POWDER & A TOWEL.

List the things you intend to do and the thoughts and images you intend to have during each of the following segments:

Arrival on Site:
- LISTEN TO PRE-COMP. TAPE IN CAR.
- WALK IN W/CONFIDENCE & PURPOSE.
- BE FRIENDLY, BUT KEEP ENERGY CONSOLIDATED.
- THINK: "I AM EXCITED & READY TO PLAY!"
- GET A COFFEE & A PRACTICE TABLE.

Warming Up:
- SHOOT TO "GET LOOSE."
- FOCUS THOUGHTS ON VISION STATEMENT.
- SHOOT EASY DRAW & STOP SHOTS.
- "   A FEW SIMPLE BANKS.
- BREAK A FEW RACKS.

Waiting to Play:
- STAY RELAXED.
- GO OVER COMP. PLAN.
- LISTEN TO PRE-COMP. TAPE AGAIN IF POSSIBLE.

THE PRO BOOK

Competition Plan — Example (for 8-6-97)

What are your *result* and *performance* goals for this event?

1. TO WIN.
2. TO STAY MENTALLY POSITIVE.

What *situations* might have a *critical* impact on your performance? Write down your preferred response to each situation and choose a cue word or ritual to direct you to that response.

— <u>SHARKED</u> — CHALK TIP & FOCUS ON THE COLOR OF THE CHALK. THINK: "NOTHING DISTRACTS ME FROM PLAYING MY BEST. I SHOOT ONE SHOT AT A TIME."

What is your *general strategy* for this event?

— SHOOT EVERY SHOT W/ 100% CONFIDENCE. IF I DON'T HAVE IT ON A PARTICULAR SHOT, I DON'T SHOOT IT.

What will be your *main focus* in each of the following segments?

<u>Starting</u>:
— ON THE FIRST TWO LINES OF MY VISION STATEMENT.

<u>At the Table</u>:
"I SEE MY SHOT & I GET <u>RIGHT</u> DOWN."

<u>In the Chair</u>:
STAYING RELAXED & PROPERLY AROUSED. FOCUS ON BREATH & STAY AT A 5-6 LEVEL.

GAME PLANS

Match Review — Example

from 8-6-97

1. How do you feel about your performance in this event?
   - VERY GOOD!

2. What was your result goal? **TO WIN**
   To what degree (from 1-10) did you achieve it? **8 - SEMI-FINALS**

3. What was your performance goal? **TO STAY POSITIVE**
   To what degree (from 1-10) did you achieve it? **8**

4. In general, what worked well for you?
   - I WAS CALM & ON PURPOSE. I COULD SEE THE WHOLE MATCH INSTEAD OF REACTING TO THE SCORE OF THE MOMENT.

5. In general, what did not work well for you?
   - I RAN OUT OF STEAM NEAR THE END OF THE TOURNAMENT.

6. Rate the effectiveness of your prep work from 1 to 10:

Equipment	9	Diet	8	Exercise	8
Clothing	10	Sleep	10	Schedule	7

7. What can be improved in these areas?
   - HAVE TO GET A GOOD SHAFT CLEANER.
   - HAVE TO GET TO THE SITE EARLY ENOUGH TO GET A PRACTICE TABLE.

8. Rate the following areas from 1 to 10:

Physically Relaxed	10	Mentally Calm	9
Energy Level	8	Positive Self-Talk	9
Feeling Confident	9	Projected Confidence	7
Enjoyment	10	Motivation	8

THE PRO BOOK

9. Which mental / emotional areas need to be worked on?

— I NEED TO RECOVER QUICKER AFTER MAKING A MISTAKE. I CAUGHT MYSELF SLOUCHING IN THE CHAIR AFTER A MISS.

10. Rate your overall feeling of effectiveness in each segment:

    Before Event _10_   Waiting _7_   Match   _9_
    Warm-up   _7_   Start   _8_   In Chair _10_

11. Did your attention stay focused, or did it wander?

— MOSTLY FOCUSED. I GOT A LITTLE SCATTERED WHEN I GOT TO THE SITE LATE & COULD NOT GET A PRACTICE TABLE.

12. What was your mental conversation right before you started?

— I WAS TRYING TO GET MY CONFIDENCE UP & MY BODY LOOSE.

13. What was your mental conversation while in the chair?

— VERY POSITIVE. I WAS CALM & READY TO GET BACK ON THE TABLE.

14. When you were playing your best, where was your focus?

— ON EXECUTING W/ CONFIDENCE. "I SEE MY SHOT & I GET RIGHT DOWN!"

15. Where was your focus when you were not playing so well?

— IT WAS MIXED. I WAS SEEING BOTH WHAT I WANTED & WHAT I WAS AFRAID OF GETTING.

16. Was anything *unexpectedly* said or done that had an impact on your performance? If so, what?

C. SAID "GOOD-LUCK" TO ME AS I WAS ON MY WAY TO MY TOUGHEST MATCH. IT MADE ME FEEL STRONG.

17. Did you have a comeback in this event? _YES_ When?

W/ TONY. HE HAD ME DOWN 6-2.

GAME PLANS

18. What did you say or do to empower this comeback?

— I MADE SURE I WAS CENTERED AND GROUNDED. I FOCUSED ON MY BRIDGE HAND CONTACTING THE CLOTH.

19. How effective were you in the following skill areas? (1-10)

Breaking	8	Kick Safeties	8
Fundamentals	10	Banks	7
Position Play	9	Shot Selection	9
Safety Play	9	Rhythm / Pace	10
Kicks	7	Specialty Shots	6

20. In which skill areas do you attribute unforced errors?

— I MISSED AN IMPORTANT JUMP SHOT.
— " " AN EASY 2-RAIL KICK. I READ THE DIAMONDS WRONG!

21. In which skill areas were you not feeling confident?

— BANKS

22. In which areas should you focus future training?

— ON BOTH BANKS & KICKS.
— PUT MORE ATTENTION ON THE BREAK.

23. Where were you in this event in regards to your training / performance cycle? Did your level of play peak *during* the event or before or after? How should you adjust in the future?

— ASIDE FROM BEING LATE, I WAS RIGHT ON.

**Adjust your *training* and your next set of *game plan*s
to reflect any new insights discovered with this review.**

THE PRO BOOK

Pre-Match Plan — Event #1

List the things you need to complete before arriving on site.

List the items you need to take with you.

List the things you intend to do and the thoughts and images you intend to have during each of the following segments:

Arrival on Site:

Warming Up:

Waiting to Play:

GAME PLANS

Competition Plan — Event #1

What are your *result* and *performance* goals for this event?

What *situations* might have a *critical* impact on your performance? Write down your preferred response to each situation and choose a cue word or ritual to direct you to that response.

What is your *general strategy* for this event?

What will be your *main focus* in each of the following segments?

Starting:

At the Table:

In the Chair:

THE PRO BOOK

Match Review   Event #1

1. How do you feel about your performance in this event?

2. What was your result goal? _____
   To what degree (from 1-10) did you achieve it? _____

3. What was your performance goal? _____
   To what degree (from 1-10) did you achieve it? _____

4. In general, what worked well for you?

5. In general, what did not work well for you?

6. Rate the effectiveness of your prep work from 1 to 10:

   Equipment ___   Diet ___   Exercise ___

   Clothing ___   Sleep ___   Schedule ___

7. What can be improved in these areas?

8. Rate the following areas from 1 to 10:

   Physically Relaxed ___   Mentally Calm ___

   Energy Level ___   Positive Self-Talk ___

   Feeling Confident ___   Projected Confidence ___

   Enjoyment ___   Motivation ___

GAME PLANS

9. Which mental / emotional areas need to be worked on?

10. Rate your overall feeling of effectiveness in each segment:

    Before Event ___

                      Waiting ___   Match ___

        Warm-up ___   Start ___   In Chair ___

11. Did your attention stay focused, or did it wander?

12. What was your mental conversation right before you started?

13. What was your mental conversation while in the chair?

14. When you were playing your best, where was your focus?

15. Where was your focus when you were not playing so well?

16. Was anything *unexpectedly* said or done that had an impact on your performance? If so, what?

17. Did you have a comeback in this event? ___ When?

THE PRO BOOK

18. What did you say or do to empower this comeback?

19. How effective were you in the following skill areas? (1-10)

Breaking	___	Kick Safeties	___
Fundamentals	___	Banks	___
Position Play	___	Shot Selection	___
Safety Play	___	Rhythm / Pace	___
Kicks	___	Specialty Shots	___

20. In which skill areas do you attribute unforced errors?

21. In which skill areas were you not feeling confident?

22. In which areas should you focus future training?

23. Where were you in this event in regards to your training / performance cycle? Did your level of play peak *during* the event or before or after? How should you adjust in the future?

Adjust your *training* and your next set of *game plan*s to reflect any new insights discovered with this review.

GAME PLANS

Pre-Match Plan — Event #2

List the things you need to complete before arriving on site.

List the items you need to take with you.

List the things you intend to do and the thoughts and images you intend to have during each of the following segments:

Arrival on Site:

Warming Up:

Waiting to Play:

THE PRO BOOK

Competition Plan — Event #2

What are your *result* and *performance* goals for this event?

What *situations* might have a *critical* impact on your performance? Write down your preferred response to each situation and choose a cue word or ritual to direct you to that response.

What is your *general strategy* for this event?

What will be your *main focus* in each of the following segments?

Starting:

At the Table:

In the Chair:

GAME PLANS

Match Review — Event #2

1. How do you feel about your performance in this event?

2. What was your result goal? _____
   To what degree (from 1-10) did you achieve it? _____

3. What was your performance goal? _____
   To what degree (from 1-10) did you achieve it? _____

4. In general, what worked well for you?

5. In general, what did not work well for you?

6. Rate the effectiveness of your prep work from 1 to 10:

   Equipment ___   Diet ___   Exercise ___

   Clothing ___   Sleep ___   Schedule ___

7. What can be improved in these areas?

8. Rate the following areas from 1 to 10:

   Physically Relaxed ___   Mentally Calm ___

   Energy Level ___   Positive Self-Talk ___

   Feeling Confident ___   Projected Confidence ___

   Enjoyment ___   Motivation ___

THE PRO BOOK

9. Which mental / emotional areas need to be worked on?

10. Rate your overall feeling of effectiveness in each segment:

    Before Event ___   Waiting ___   Match ___

    Warm-up ___   Start ___   In Chair ___

11. Did your attention stay focused, or did it wander?

12. What was your mental conversation right before you started?

13. What was your mental conversation while in the chair?

14. When you were playing your best, where was your focus?

15. Where was your focus when you were not playing so well?

16. Was anything *unexpectedly* said or done that had an impact on your performance? If so, what?

17. Did you have a comeback in this event? _____ When?

GAME PLANS

18. What did you say or do to empower this comeback?

19. How effective were you in the following skill areas? (1-10)

Breaking	___	Kick Safeties	___
Fundamentals	___	Banks	___
Position Play	___	Shot Selection	___
Safety Play	___	Rhythm / Pace	___
Kicks	___	Specialty Shots	___

20. In which skill areas do you attribute unforced errors?

21. In which skill areas were you not feeling confident?

22. In which areas should you focus future training?

23. Where were you in this event in regards to your training / performance cycle? Did your level of play peak *during* the event or before or after? How should you adjust in the future?

**Adjust your *training* and your next set of *game plan*s
to reflect any new insights discovered with this review.**

THE PRO BOOK

Pre-Match Plan   Event #3

List the things you need to complete before arriving on site.

List the items you need to take with you.

List the things you intend to do and the thoughts and images you intend to have during each of the following segments:

Arrival on Site:

Warming Up:

Waiting to Play:

GAME PLANS

Competition Plan — Event #3

What are your *result* and *performance* goals for this event?

What *situations* might have a *critical* impact on your performance? Write down your preferred response to each situation and choose a cue word or ritual to direct you to that response.

What is your *general strategy* for this event?

What will be your *main focus* in each of the following segments?

Starting:

At the Table:

In the Chair:

THE PRO BOOK

Match Review   Event #3

1. How do you feel about your performance in this event?

2. What was your result goal? _____
   To what degree (from 1-10) did you achieve it? _____

3. What was your performance goal? _____
   To what degree (from 1-10) did you achieve it? _____

4. In general, what worked well for you?

5. In general, what did not work well for you?

6. Rate the effectiveness of your prep work from 1 to 10:

   Equipment   ___   Diet   ___   Exercise   ___

   Clothing   ___   Sleep   ___   Schedule   ___

7. What can be improved in these areas?

8. Rate the following areas from 1 to 10:

   Physically Relaxed   ___   Mentally Calm   ___

   Energy Level   ___   Positive Self-Talk   ___

   Feeling Confident   ___   Projected Confidence ___

   Enjoyment   ___   Motivation   ___

GAME PLANS

9. Which mental / emotional areas need to be worked on?

10. Rate your overall feeling of effectiveness in each segment:

    Before Event ___   Waiting ___   Match ___

    Warm-up ___   Start ___   In Chair ___

11. Did your attention stay focused, or did it wander?

12. What was your mental conversation right before you started?

13. What was your mental conversation while in the chair?

14. When you were playing your best, where was your focus?

15. Where was your focus when you were not playing so well?

16. Was anything *unexpectedly* said or done that had an impact on your performance? If so, what?

17. Did you have a comeback in this event? ___ When?

THE PRO BOOK

18. What did you say or do to empower this comeback?

19. How effective were you in the following skill areas? (1-10)

Breaking	___	Kick Safeties	___
Fundamentals	___	Banks	___
Position Play	___	Shot Selection	___
Safety Play	___	Rhythm / Pace	___
Kicks	___	Specialty Shots	___

20. In which skill areas do you attribute unforced errors?

21. In which skill areas were you not feeling confident?

22. In which areas should you focus future training?

23. Where were you in this event in regards to your training / performance cycle? Did your level of play peak *during* the event or before or after? How should you adjust in the future?

**Adjust your *training* and your next set of *game plan*s
to reflect any new insights discovered with this review.**

GAME PLANS

Pre-Match Plan   Event #4

List the things you need to complete before arriving on site.

List the items you need to take with you.

List the things you intend to do and the thoughts and images you intend to have during each of the following segments:

Arrival on Site:

Warming Up:

Waiting to Play:

THE PRO BOOK

Competition Plan   Event #4

What are your *result* and *performance* goals for this event?

What *situations* might have a *critical* impact on your performance? Write down your preferred response to each situation and choose a cue word or ritual to direct you to that response.

What is your *general strategy* for this event?

What will be your *main focus* in each of the following segments?

Starting:

At the Table:

In the Chair:

GAME PLANS

Match Review   Event #4

1. How do you feel about your performance in this event?

2. What was your result goal? _____
   To what degree (from 1-10) did you achieve it? _____

3. What was your performance goal? _____
   To what degree (from 1-10) did you achieve it? _____

4. In general, what worked well for you?

5. In general, what did not work well for you?

6. Rate the effectiveness of your prep work from 1 to 10:

   Equipment ___   Diet   ___   Exercise ___

   Clothing   ___   Sleep ___   Schedule ___

7. What can be improved in these areas?

8. Rate the following areas from 1 to 10:

   Physically Relaxed ___   Mentally Calm   ___

   Energy Level   ___   Positive Self-Talk   ___

   Feeling Confident   ___   Projected Confidence ___

   Enjoyment   ___   Motivation   ___

THE PRO BOOK

9. Which mental / emotional areas need to be worked on?

10. Rate your overall feeling of effectiveness in each segment:

    Before Event ___   Waiting ___   Match ___

    Warm-up ___   Start ___   In Chair ___

11. Did your attention stay focused, or did it wander?

12. What was your mental conversation right before you started?

13. What was your mental conversation while in the chair?

14. When you were playing your best, where was your focus?

15. Where was your focus when you were not playing so well?

16. Was anything *unexpectedly* said or done that had an impact on your performance? If so, what?

17. Did you have a comeback in this event? ___ When?

GAME PLANS

18. What did you say or do to empower this comeback?

19. How effective were you in the following skill areas? (1-10)

Breaking	___	Kick Safeties	___
Fundamentals	___	Banks	___
Position Play	___	Shot Selection	___
Safety Play	___	Rhythm / Pace	___
Kicks	___	Specialty Shots	___

20. In which skill areas do you attribute unforced errors?

21. In which skill areas were you not feeling confident?

22. In which areas should you focus future training?

23. Where were you in this event in regards to your training / performance cycle? Did your level of play peak *during* the event or before or after? How should you adjust in the future?

**Adjust your *training* and your next set of *game plan*s
to reflect any new insights discovered with this review.**

287

THE PRO BOOK

Note Page

A Final Note

Thank you for giving me the opportunity to share this book. It was knowing that *you* were out there that kept me focused and it was in my attempt to make the material clear for you, that I have benefited the most.

No matter what your goals are with pool, I hope you approach them in a professional manner. I hope you receive the maximum results and enjoyment from whatever investment you put into the game.

It has been said that the only thing better than discovering what you love is discovering the others that love it too. It has been my great pleasure to meet you through this book and I look forward to meeting you in person.

Bob Henning

Acknowledgements

I thank and acknowledge all of the individuals in the pool community who have contributed to my development as a player, coach and trainer. I am especially grateful to Jerry Breisath, Ray Martin, Bert Kinister, Grady Mathews, John McCue and all the great players I have met in competition.

I also thank the many people outside of pool who have contributed to my development as a coach and trainer and whose work has so profoundly effected the creation of *The Pro Book*. Chief among these are Werner Erhard, Chuck Kriese, Peter Ralston, and all the great presenters from the *Nighting-Gale Conant Company*.

Lastly, I thank the people and companies who have broke the mold and sharpened the *professional edge* of pocket billiards in the last few years. A few who deserve special mention are:

Accu-Stats Video Productions for bringing cameras and sophisticated video equipment onto the tournament floor. *Diamond Billiard Products* for building a pool table designed to the specifications of professional players. *Predator Cues* for building a robot to analyze the consistency of cue sticks. *Lou Sardo Products* for designing a rack that reduced racking inconsistencies and *Elephant Balls* for developing and marketing a line of training aids.

More Pool Titles from BEBOB!

THE PRO BOOK DVD SERIES

$134.95 (PBD)

OVER 85 INSTANT ACCESS CHAPTERS!

This complete system breaks shot-making, position play, safeties, kick safeties, kicks, and banks into the most strategic forms and teaches an accelerated method to attain mastery with each one.

The coaching of pool has evolved greatly in the last few years and this series is on the cutting edge.

Increase your training effectiveness.
Expand your problem-solving skills.
Improve your ability to execute.
Enhance your creativity.

PRO SAFETIES

Pro Safeties is a 208 page book that is the definitive work on safety play. The top page of each shot displays the graphic and how to cue the cue ball. The lower page explains the strategic aspects of the shot and the perils to avoid. There is also a section to record your ratios of success.

Although this is a collection of shots and not of game situations, each safety is depicted in a nine-ball situation as an added benefit. All you have to set up is the cue ball, the active ball and the blocker balls. Once you learn it, you can employ it in any pool game!

These are the TOP 100 safeties used by TOP professionals today. Each safety is completely explained, named and categorized! Secrets are revealed! Easy to use format! Fits most cue case pockets! Become a defense monster! Win from tough positions! Never leave an easy table again! **$34.95 (PSF)**

For more information go to: bebobpublishing.com

More Pool Titles from BEBOB!

THE ADVANCED PRO BOOK

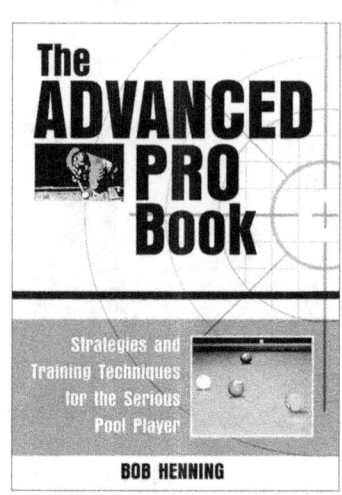

This wonderful book covers five major areas of strategy and training techniques for the serious player: **Honing Your Technique, Mastering the Shot Routine, Mastering Advanced Tools, Getting Your Game Out,** and **Match Strategy**.

Train to execute advanced shots, position play, defensive play, banks and kicks. **Learn** to get your best game out when you need it! Keep your focus under pressure! **Discover** advanced strategies for the front, mid, and end games. Learn to take control! **Hone** your technique to a master's edge by using your own natural coordination! **Increase** your consistency by incorporating personal alignment, stroke and rhythm. **Master** the shot routine, visualization, timing, and flow. **$49.95 (APB)**

Get The Advanced Pro Book and the DVD set for $169 and save $15!

THE ADVANCED PRO BOOK DVDS

The reference training shots and proven theories contained in *The Advanced Pro Book* are captured on this 4-disc DVD set. If you are an advanced pool player who is yearning to propel your game beyond its current limits, then *The Advanced Pro Book DVD Series* is exactly what you need!

Pro Shots takes an aggressive approach and contains confidence-building position shots and vital recovery tools to keep the pressure on your opponent. ***Pro Safeties*** teachs devastating safeties! Use them in front game situations to take control under pressure.

Advanced Kicking is mandatory training for competitive players! In an even match, the better kicker is always favored to win. ***Advanced Banking*** will help you see more opportunities to run out. Learn to use banks to play shape and to play safe. These are great tools to help you win! **$134.95 (APBD)**

For more information go to: bebobpublishing.com

More Pool Titles from BEBOB!

THE STROKE ZONE

This *Pool Player's Guide to Dead Stroke* will show you how to deal with pressure, remove the obstacles that get in the way and how to train to play in the zone. It unveils simple strategies you can use to influence how often you get in the zone and how long you stay there. Once you are aware of the actions needed, you'll be more able to trust your intuitive self, silence inner doubt, relinquish control and let it flow! Experience the exhilaration of functioning at a higher than normal state of awareness, shooting effortlessly and confidently time and time again! **$19.95 (SZ)**

FRENCH QUARTER DANNY

At age nine, Danny Toussaint is abandoned by his mother in New Orleans and a Cajun madam takes him in. In his teens, Danny is drawn to the thrill of gambling and hustling in local pool rooms. When he loses his 'country club' wife ten years later, he hopes to make it as a professional road player. Leaving Chenoa, an ambitious artist behind, he travels the country to pursue his dream. About to play in the game of his life at a pro event in Texas, Danny's plans are uninterrupted by Hurricane Katrina. **$19.95 (FQD)**

3 CUSHION BILLIARD SYSTEMS

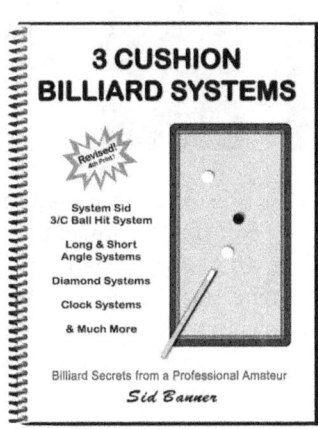

This book is a fully comprehensive three cushion billiard guide containing over 165 diagrams, historical pictures, an extensive billiard glossary and the rules. Nearly every billiard system in existence is covered, including: the Clock System, the Diamond System, the System Sid 3/C Ball Hit System, the Carom or Bank System, the Corner Plus System, the Cross Table System, the End Rail System, and the First Object Ball Hit Direction System. **$39.95 (3CS)**

For more information go to: bebobpublishing.com

More Pool Titles from BEBOB!

OVERCOMING CONTENDEROSIS

This 10-sesson audio CD set is a *"Hypnosis Success Program for Pool Players."* Created by Ryan Elliot, a sports and certified medical hypnotist, it has been used successfully by thousands of players. It is intended to help players deal with and eliminate the obstacles which prevent them from delivering their best game under pressure. All you have to do is plug into a CD player, get comfortable, and close your eyes. **$99 (OC)**

THE DEAD STROKE TAPES

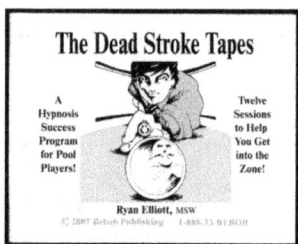

This 12-session CD set is intended to help competitive players recognize and increase their ability to get "the zone." Use this set to train your brain and nervous system to produce a "dead stroke" state on demand. When you see a great player fully focused in the flow of performance, he probably has this set! Includes a subliminal session and a pre-match psych-up. **$149 (DS)**

Get both Hypnosis Programs for $219 and save $29!

ROAD PLAYER

This book is a lifetime of stories from the vibrant memory of Danny Diliberto, one of pool's most colorful characters. A fascinating look into the immediate past of the game. From Las Vegas to Hollywood to the smallest towns on the most distant highways, this is the life of the roadman. A gambler's tale in his own words. **$19.95 (RP)**

CORNBREAD RED

This book takes the reader into the life of pool's legendary and colorful money player. It is action-packed, entertaining, and easy to read. An inside look at the Johnston City tournaments and the world-famous money room—the Rack. It has received rave reviews from pool publications and other reviewers! Great story! **$16.95 (CBR)**

**It's easy to order! Phone: 1-888-33-BEBOB
or go to: www.bebobpublishing.com**

www.ingramcontent.com/pod-product-compliance
Lightning Source LLC
Chambersburg PA
CBHW081801300426
44116CB00014B/2198